BEFORE BURNS

Christopher MacLachlan is Senior Lecturer in English at the University of St Andrews. He received his MA degree and his PhD from the University of Edinburgh. His areas of specialisation include eighteenth-century English and Scottish Literature, the Scottish Enlightenment and modern Scottish literature.

Before Burns

Eighteenth-Century Scottish Poetry

*

Edited and Introduced by

Christopher MacLachlan

*

CANONGATE
CLASSICS
106

First published as a Canongate Classic in 2002 by Canongate Books Ltd, 14 High Street, Edinburgh EH1 1TE

10 9 8 7 6 5 4 3 2 1

The publishers gratefully acknowledge general subsidy from the Scottish Arts Council towards the Canongate Classics series and a specific grant towards the publication of this volume.

Typeset in Monotype Plantin by
Hewer Text Ltd, Edinburgh
Printed and bound by Omnia Books Ltd, Glasgow

British Library Cataloguing-in-Publication Data
A catalogue record for this book is
available on request from the British Library

ISBN 1 84195 253 2
www.canongate.net

Contents

Introduction ix
Note on the Texts xix

THE POEMS 1

Anonymous
Blythsome Bridal 3
Maggie Lauder 6
Tarry Woo 8
O This is No my Ain House 10
Whistle O'er the Lave O't 11

Grizel Baillie (1665–1746)
Werena my Heart Light I Wad Die 12

Alexander Robertson of Struan (1668–1749)
Liberty Preserved, or Love Destroyed 14

William Hamilton of Gilbertfield (1670–1751)
The Last Dying Words of Bonnie Heck 15

Allan Ramsay (1685–1758)
An thou were my ain thing 18
The Lass of Peattie's Mill 19
Polwart on the Green 20
A Song: Lochaber No More 21
Up in the Air 22
The Marrow Ballad 23
Lucky Spence's Last Advice 25
Elegy on Lucky Wood in the Canongate, May 1717 30
Elegy on Maggy Johnston, who died Anno 1711 34
The Life and Acts of, or An Elegy on Patie Birnie 39
Elegy on John Cowper Kirk-Treasurer's Man 45

To the Right Honourable, The Town-Council of Edinburgh, the Address of Allan Ramsay 49
Epistle I [William Hamilton of Gilbertfield to Allan Ramsay] 51
Answer I [Allan Ramsay to William Hamilton of Gilbertfield] 54
Epistle II [Hamilton to Ramsay] 57
Answer II [Ramsay to Hamilton] 61
Epistle III [Hamilton to Ramsay] 64
Answer III [Ramsay to Hamilton] 67
Epistle to Robert Yarde of Devonshire, Esquire 71
Epistle to Mr John Gay 75
An Epistle Wrote from Mavisbank, March 1748, to a Friend in Edinburgh 79
An Ode to Mr Forbes 83
To R— H— B—, an Ode 85
The Vision 87
The Gentle Shepherd 100

Robert Crawford (1695–1733)
The Broom of Cowdenknowes 166
The Bush Aboon Traquair 168

Alexander Ross (1699–1784)
Married and Wooed an' A' 169
What Ails the Lasses at Me? 172
Billet by Jeany Gradden 174

William Hamilton of Bangour (1704–54)
The Braes of Yarrow 176
Inscription on a Dog 180

David Mallet (1705–65)
The Birks of Invermay 181

Alison Rutherford Cockburn (1712–94)
The Flowers of the Forest 182

Henry Erskine (1720–65)
Highland March 183

John Skinner (1721–1807)
Tullochgorum 185

Tobias Smollett (1721–71)
Ode to Leven-Water 188

William Wilkie (1721–72)
The Hare and the Partan 189

Jean Elliot (1727–1805)
The Flowers of the Forest 191

James Beattie (1735–1803)
To Mr Alexander Ross 192

Isobel Pagan (1741–1821)
Ca' the Yowes to the Knowes 196

Alexander, Duke of Gordon (1743–1827)
Cauld Kail in Aberdeen 198

Hector Macneill (1746–1818)
The Scottish Muse 200

Michael Bruce (1746–67)
Weaving Spiritualised 209
Ossian's Hymn to the Sun 210

Robert Fergusson (1750–74)
Auld Reikie, a poem 211
The Daft-Days 222
Hallow-Fair 225
Leith Races 229
The Rising of the Session 235
The King's Birth-Day in Edinburgh 238
Epilogue, spoken by Mr Wilson, at the Theatre Royal, in the Character of an Edinburgh Buck 242
Braid Claith 244
Caller Oysters 246
Mutual Complaint of Plainstanes and Causey, in their Mother-tongue 249
The Ghaists: A Kirk-yard Eclogue 254

Elegy, on the Death of Mr David Gregory, late Professor of Mathematics in the University of St Andrews 259
Elegy on John Hogg, late Porter to the University of St Andrews 261
An Eclogue, to the Memory of Dr William Wilkie, late Professor of Natural Philosophy in the University of St Andrews 265
To Dr Samuel Johnson: Food for a New Edition of his Dictionary 268
To the Principal and Professors of the University of St Andrews, on their superb treat to Dr Samuel Johnson 270
Elegy, on the Death of Scots Music 274
The Sow of Feeling 277
Ode to the Gowdspink 280
On Seeing a Butterfly in the Street 283
The Farmer's Ingle 286

Anne Lindsay (1750–1825)
Auld Robin Gray 291

John Tait (c. 1750–1817)
The Banks of the Dee 293

Elizabeth Hamilton (1758–1816)
My Ain Fireside 294

Joanna Baillie (1762–1851)
Wooed and Married and A' 295
Fy, Let Us A' to the Wedding 297

Notes 300
Glossary of Common Scots Words 331

Introduction

It is necessary to begin by explaining why this anthology of eighteenth-century Scottish verse contains nothing by the greatest Scottish poet of the period, if not of all time, Robert Burns. It surely does not need to be said that no slight is intended to the immortal memory. On the contrary, it is because of the dazzling brilliance of Burns's achievement and the brightness of his reputation that this collection omits him in order to bring to clearer view his contemporaries and immediate predecessors. Just as in a total eclipse of the sun the sky darkens so that lesser bodies whose light is usually lost in the solar glare become visible, so by a temporary and artificial occlusion of the star of Robert Burns may the lesser constellations of eighteenth-century Scottish poetry swim into our ken.

Not, to extend the simile a little more before dropping it, that all the other stars are so faint. Two at least, Allan Ramsay and Robert Fergusson, though their light fluctuates, are practically visible at all times, especially to those who know where to look. Too often, however, Ramsay and Fergusson have been located chiefly in relation to Burns, as his forerunners in what used to be called the vernacular revival of the eighteenth century. That phrase, with its implications of a teleology that condemns those before Burns to the role of humble harbingers, has dropped out of fashion. This anthology does not seek to revive it, since the notion that poetry grows towards moments of flowering in the work of a genius imposes a pattern on literary history which is more elegant and convenient than true or fair.

Nevertheless it is impossible to avoid some speculation about development and influence in introducing a collection of poetry spanning a century of verse. Poets as well as critics participate in the debate about literary history, and in the creation of its terms and periods. Allan Ramsay, for one, must be acknowledged as more than just a poet in his own right but also as a shaper of poetic history and tradition. Along with James Watson's *Choice Collection of Comic and Serious Scots Poems Both Ancient and Modern* (1706–11), Ramsay's collections of Scottish verse *The*

Tea-Table Miscellany (1723) and *The Ever Green* (1724), which between them include much of the most significant Scottish poetry of the previous two centuries, plus much contemporary work, including poems by Grizel Baillie, Robert Crawford, William Hamilton of Bangour and of course Ramsay himself, establish a sense of a Scottish tradition of verse. Later poets, even down to our own day, must attend to the tradition which Ramsay helped to create, and they must also contend with the idea of the Scottish poet he outlined, both in his own practice and in the way he presented that of others. By editing and publishing what he could of the work of the sixteenth-century makars, and by imitating earlier poetry, as in his additional cantos to *Christis Kirk on the Grene* and in 'The Vision', Ramsay not only reminded his contemporaries of the past but showed how it might be the foundation of a modern poetry. His verse is always in dialogue with that of his predecessors as well as with his own time. His example fashions the mould for the ambitious Scottish poet from his time to our own by the way he acknowledges and incorporates the traditions of late mediaeval and renaissance Scotland while adapting them to the culture, and often the everyday culture, of his day. Above all, he is aware of what he is doing. His self-consciousness about his use of verse-forms and themes, and about his position in a poetical tradition, past, present and future, means that later poets have also to see themselves as heirs of an inheritance, and responsible to those who follow them; even if they want to rebel they must explain and justify themselves. Ramsay set out to create a national tradition in Scottish poetry and largely succeeded in bringing about the consciousness of one, if not the thing itself.

His success would have been more limited had he not had worthy followers, notably Robert Fergusson. Lamentably brief though Fergusson's career was, he was quickly recognised as Ramsay's successor in Edinburgh and his poetry is full of the same kind of awareness of tradition and its vitality found in Ramsay's. He takes over the Christis Kirk stanza in 'Hallow-Fair' and 'Leith Races' and in turn makes it available to Burns, most notably in 'The Holy Fair'. He also takes over the six-line stanza Ramsay names 'Standart Habby' in his answer to William Hamilton of Gilbertfield's first epistle. Ramsay's name for the stanza alludes to its use by Robert Sempill of Beltrees (1590–1660) in his humorous elegy 'The Life and Death of Habbie Simson, the Piper of Kilbarchan'. Ramsay uses this stanza in his elegies for various low-life Edinburgh characters, and for 'Lucky

Spence's Last Advice', but also in epistles and an ode. Fergusson extends the range of the form further in poems of comment and observation like 'The Daft Days' and 'Braid Claith'. In his turn, of course, Burns would use the stanza so extensively, from 'To a Mouse' to 'Holy Willie's Prayer', that it became synonymous with him as 'the Burns stanza'. It is a perfect illustration of how an eighteenth-century poetic development relates to a venerable tradition.

The establishment of tradition through the century after Ramsay is, however, only one aspect of the marvellous interconnectedness of poetic life in eighteenth-century Scotland. Even a cursory glance will discover how poets and poems have links to others. Poets write verse to each other and about each other. They mention other poets and imitate other poems. Their lives bring them into contact with each other and each other's works, sometimes in surprising ways, but often in ways which make it clear how intimate and small was the world of Scottish letters in the eighteenth century. Some connections are obvious, such as that between Ramsay and William Hamilton of Gilbertfield, as evidenced by their exchange of verse letters. The tone of these is instructive, however. Both poets are courteous and complimentary, they take it for granted that to write Scots verse is a respectable accomplishment, they are humorous, even ribald, without embarrassment. Such easy-going literary conversation seems to set a pattern of behaviour for the Scottish republic of letters, at least in their century. Fellow-feeling and decent appreciation are the rule, seen for example in Fergusson's eclogue to William Wilkie, his mentor at St Andrews, or James Beattie's epistle to Alexander Ross. Though he lived most of his life in the isolation of Lochlee in the Grampians, Ross published his poetry through the good offices of Beattie, the Aberdeen professor, who brought him to the notice of a patron in the Duchess of Gordon, whose husband also made a contribution to the poetry of the century; she in turn was a friend of Burns. Such networks are typical of the period.

They were based on shared elements of culture, and none more common to all than the songs of Scotland. Songs seem to be everywhere in eighteenth-century Scottish poetry. They are collected, revised and imitated by all sorts of people, high and low. They provide a stock of allusions and images that can crop up in any sort of poem. Some are old enough for their origins to be forgotten and therefore have to be attributed to anonymous authors. These songs were clearly common currency, familiar to all, and regarded as available models for new songs and application to new occasions. Thus we find Alison Cockburn and Jean Elliot both making versions of 'The Flowers of the Forest', and Alexander Ross and Joanna Baillie working variations on the song 'Wooed and Married and A''. Ramsay and Baillie both take the old song known as 'The Blythsome Bridal' and in 'The Marrow Ballad' and 'Fy, Let Us A'' to the Wedding' respectively convert it into contemporary satire to quite different ends. This malleability of the song culture indicates its vitality. Poets at either end of the century could dip into the kitty and take what they wanted without affecting the original, which continued to be sung and offer itself for use by other poets, from his grace the Duke of Gordon to Tibby Pagan, the ale-house singer.

Arguably it was Scottish song which saved Allan Ramsay's most ambitious, even over-ambitious, project, his verse drama *The Gentle Shepherd*. Ramsay's struggles to see a theatre in Edinburgh in his lifetime proved abortive. He fell foul of religious opposition to the very idea of play-acting in public and was politically outmanoeuvred, retiring much hurt from the fray. His vision of a national literature crowned by a national drama, though clearly based on his understanding of the national literatures of France and England, was too advanced for Scotland by some years. Even after the middle of the century, when a theatre was opened in Edinburgh, John Home's tragedy *Douglas* (1756) would cause a controversy with the church, and a flourishing theatre eluded Scotland until much later. But if Ramsay's full programme was not realised his own pastoral drama survived and became a firm favourite with audiences, especially when he had added a number of songs to it, his own words fitted to popular tunes. What began as pastoral dialogues (roughly the two scenes of Act I) was expanded into a five-act comedy, observing the neo-classical rules of the unity of place, time and action, and then transformed into a ballad opera, well suited to amateur performance. The play became a grand example of the national pastime of song-singing, in which high and low entertained themselves at social gatherings. Once again Ramsay attached his work to a common stock of tradition.

The Gentle Shepherd, however, does not suit modern taste. Though for its time it seemed strikingly real, and some of its local colour and detail still has charm, it seems now as artificial in its plotting as any more conventional pastoral. Ramsay must have been pleased that his original pair of dialogues proved capable of expansion into a longer story, especially one involving a quasi-Jacobite restoration, thus allowing him to hint at the political fancies which coyly appear in some of his other poems (for example, 'The Vision'), but his complacent assumption that gentle birth will always make itself known, even when obscured by circumstances, is no longer to be admired. When the shepherd Patie is revealed as the son of Sir William Worthy, the crisis of the play becomes whether he will remain faithful to Peggy, his lowly sweetheart; that Ramsay solves the dilemma by also discovering high birth for Peggy is not attractive to modern audiences. The play comes close enough to questioning the social order to make it annoying that in the end it merely confirms the status of rank and position. All that is left to us now is to enjoy the details of country life, preserved mainly in the speeches of the lesser characters.

The neo-classical proprieties which Ramsay observes to the detriment of his play are evident enough in his other verse, but there they are surely tempered by local ties. Ramsay, like Pope, wished to seem an Augustan poet, capable of imitating Horace in a new dress. Being provincial is no bar to success in this aim and indeed the sense in Ramsay that urbanity is hard-won adds a spice to his verse that gives it strength. Roughness of speech and a relish for the disreputable side of city life make his aspiring to classical ideals of friendship and moderation seem real because they are not so assured of success. His poems of Edinburgh low-life, such as his elegies on Maggy Johnston and Lucky Wood, show a simple appreciation of the pleasures of the town that may not seem to fit with the classical references in his Horatian odes to R— H— B— and John Forbes, but the odes benefit from the reader's awareness that their neo-classicism is not preciousness. It comes rather from a deliberate choice of style and values which Ramsay strives to maintain in a world too easily drawn to coarse humour and basic instincts.

Such precariousness of achieved poise is evident in Robert Fergusson, too. Of course, it is coloured by awareness of Fergusson's unfortunate end, his decline into mental misery and death in a public asylum. It would be sentimental to read all that back into his poetry. Nevertheless much of that poetry is about the fragility of life and the delusions of hope and prosperity. Were it not for his public antagonism towards the Englishman one might apply to Fergusson the title of Samuel Johnson's greatest poem, 'The Vanity of Human Wishes'. So the Edinburgh poems, like 'The Daft Days', 'The King's Birth-Day in Edinburgh', 'Auld Reikie' and particularly 'Hallow-Fair', celebrate temporary felicity and remind the reader of the ominous alternatives. The City Guard lie in wait to punish the over-zealous reveller, and on the streets of the city one is as likely to meet a poor prostitute or a debtor as anyone more prosperous. In any case, a fine reputation may be bought with 'braid claith'. The mutual complaint of Plainstanes and Causey against the pressures of modern life is matched by the protests of the querulous Ghaists against threatened changes, and does not the poet identify with the gowdspink, caged for its song, and the errant butterfly in the streets, a fragment of colour fatally out of place?

Fergusson, of course, often writes with humour, mingling the good and the bad, and moralising so lightly that he hardly seems to judge at all. A broad tolerance for human foibles and an acceptance of the ups and downs of life emerges from his work. Although he ridicules the sentimental sympathy of the day in his parody 'The Sow of Feeling' of Henry Mackenzie's *The Man of Feeling* (1771), there is in Fergusson's picture of Edinburgh life something of T.S. Eliot's 'notion of some infinitely gentle/ Infinitely suffering thing' ('Preludes' IV) that lies behind images of city streets and their inhabitants.

Like Ramsay, Fergusson has touches of neo-classicism. Perhaps because of his university education, Fergusson can refer easily in passing to Latin deities and generally express a sense of continuity with a literary tradition reaching back to ancient Rome. His sense of the city as a place of danger and vivacity, and of himself as the poet who versifies this, takes up Augustan themes. He celebrates the annual festivals of Edinburgh as though they were civic rituals, and gives his contemporaries an historical context by his references to the past and his constant quiet awareness of the passage of years. Even his mocking elegies of David Gregory and John Hogg have historical perspective, with the reference to Euclid in one and the argument over Biblical cosmology in the other. There is nothing small or narrow about Fergusson's world.

This needs to be borne in mind when considering his poems against Samuel Johnson, and his hosts, the Principal and Professors at St Andrews. It is easy to think of Fergusson as some kind of David to Johnson's Goliath, or a midge teasing the hide of a mighty ruminant, but this is certainly not how the Scots poet presents himself. Rather he speaks as at least Johnson's equal, if not his superior in asserting the worth of his own country, its language and traditions, to an intrusive stranger. Fergusson's alternative menu for Johnson in St Andrews, stuffing the most aggressively Scottish dishes down his throat, is often read as a sign of insecurity, a tantrum of nationalist fear of English dominance, but the energy of the poem might equally come from self-confidence, a patriotism that does not need to hide its name.

Too much can be made of Fergusson's lampoon of Johnson's dictionary English as a sign of the parlous state of the Scots language. No doubt the poet saw that the standardisation of English the dictionary represented posed a threat to non-standard forms, and hence to Scots, but Fergusson, it must be remembered, was a poet in English as well as in Scots. So were most of the Scottish poets of the century. Much ink has been spilled on the language crisis of eighteenth-century Scotland, but the poets of the time might well have responded 'What crisis?' To judge by their works, they chose their language as they fancied, adapting it to different effect in different poems, and in different parts of them. Ramsay and Fergusson (and Burns) are like the rest in using English or Scots or a mixture of them whenever they like. The interrelation of their poetry with that of England is not a sign of weakness or lack of confidence. They range over the resources of the languages available to them with freedom and eagerness. This is not just a matter of vocabulary and rhymes but also of registers and tone. They know the value of imitating the Scots speaking voice in monologue and dialogue, but they also know how to exploit the elegance of Georgian English, as Smollett does in 'Leven Water', or its plangency, as in Michael Bruce's versification of Ossian's hymn. Hector Macneill uses Scots to describe the exotic flora of the Indies, while William Hamilton of Bangour gives a humble dog a plain English tongue. They seem to leave it to later critics to worry about these language choices while they get on with writing poetry.

If, then, we look before and beyond Burns we can find great riches of poetry in eighteenth-century Scotland, some in the same vein as his work, some quite different. The poems are arranged in this selection in the chronological order of the year of birth of the poets, with a small group of anonymous poems at the start. These anonymous poems are all quite early in date, probably in fact from the previous century, but some echo through the eighteenth and as a group they provide a starting point in theme and expression for later writing. Arranging the poems by known authors in a chronological order gives an approximate indication of what was being written at different times in the century, but this is not intended to suggest a clear progression or development. A chronological selection of English poetry would appear to provide the evidence for the shift from Augustan to Romantic in English literature of the period, but such a change is hardly apparent in Scottish verse in that time. It would be rash to assert that John Tait's mellifluous 'The Banks of the Dee' is in clear contrast with Robert Crawford's much earlier 'The Bush Aboon Traquair', or that Grizel Baillie's 'There ance was a may' is older in anything but date than Anne Lindsay's 'Auld Robin Gray'. Of course, later poets refer back to earlier ones. Both Beattie and Macneill name their predecessors and continue the work of tradition-making Ramsay initiates. But innovation and originality do not seem to be the aim of these poets, even when they write or rewrite freshly. Their verse is a medium for personal and sometime communal and national expression, not a device for experiment and revolution. Craftsmanship is more evident than change.

In the selections from Ramsay and Fergusson, the two largest sections in the anthology, the poems have been arranged in loosely thematic groupings. The Ramsay selection begins with some songs, following on from the many that begin the anthology. The most topical of the songs by Ramsay leads into poems about characters, which in turn lead to his verse epistles, and a pair of odes. Finally come the archaicising poem 'The Vision' and, at the end of the section, *The Gentle Shepherd*, in a version incorporating all the songs. The selection from Fergusson's work begins with his most ambitious poem on Edinburgh, 'Auld Reikie', followed by other Edinburgh poems, then poems connected with St Andrews, including those relating to Samuel Johnson, and finally a group of poems of more general concerns, culminating in the serious pastoral masterpiece, 'The Farmer's Ingle', which so influenced Burns's 'The Cotter's Saturday Night'. By arranging the poems of Ramsay and Fergusson in this way it is hoped the reader will find it easy to compare works similar in content or style and so form some idea of the range and consistency of the achievements of the two major poets of the anthology.

The choice of the other poems in the selection was influenced by two general intentions. The first was the desire to include poems such as the two versions of 'The Flowers of the Forest' and John Skinner's 'Tullochgorum', which one would expect to find in an anthology of eighteenth-century Scottish poetry, either because they are established favourites or because they have historical importance, through their influence on other poems or poets or prominent mention in other literary contexts. Some poems are included for both these reasons, though none is here without also being worth reading for itself.

That applies also to poems included on another broad principle, the aim to give a hearing to a wide range of representative poetic voices. In an anthology which has tried to keep itself to a readable length this project risks the charge of tokenism, but nevertheless it seemed worthwhile to include such things as Henry Erskine's 'Highland March' to represent the militaristic side of eighteenth-century Scotland and Michael Bruce's 'Weaving Spiritualised' to remind us of its religion. Elizabeth Hamilton's 'My Ain Fireside' brings us the Scot at home, while Hector Macneill's 'The Scottish Muse' gives us the Scot abroad. From poems such as these, reflecting quite specific facets of Scotland, the reader may go on to read the rest, exploring for echoes.

During this exploration much enjoyment is to be had. The poetry of eighteenth-century Scotland is full of vitality and rewards for the reader. Some of the language, especially the Scots, may present a little difficulty to the modern reader, which the glosses on the page and the endnotes on more complicated usages and allusions it is hoped will alleviate. Apart from that the poems are always most accessible, addressing themselves without complication or deviousness to the reader as equal. More often than not the poets seek to entertain. They display much humour, and good humour, with a zest for expression which is surely infectious. There is a great deal that is beautiful and much that is charming. These are not the virtues of modern poetry. Here there is little evidence of irony or doubt. Instead we find a wide range of subject, mostly drawn from ordinary life, a picture of society at many levels and a delight in a variety of poetical forms and styles. If asked for one stanza that typified all this, one could do worse than quote the penultimate verse of 'Tullochgorum':

May choicest blessings aye attend
Each honest, open-hearted friend,
And calm and quiet be his end,
And a' that's good watch o'er him;
May peace and plenty be his lot,
Peace and plenty, peace and plenty,
Peace and plenty be his lot,

And dainties a great store o' them;
May peace and plenty be his lot,
Unstained by any vicious spot,
And may he never want a groat,
That's fond o' Tullochgorum!

This is neither profound nor avant-garde, but it has other qualities, and if these are to your taste you will find more than enough to savour in this collection of Scottish poetry of the eighteenth century.

FURTHER READING

Crawford, Robert (ed.), *Robert Burns and Cultural Authority* (Edinburgh, 1997)
Crawford, Thomas, *Society and the Lyric: A Study of the Song Culture of Eighteenth-Century Scotland* (Edinburgh, 1979)
Daiches, David, *Robert Fergusson* (Edinburgh, 1982)
Fergusson, Robert, *Poems* (ed. Matthew P. McDiarmid, two vols, Edinburgh, 1954–6)
Herd, David, *Ancient and Modern Scottish Songs* (Edinburgh, 1776, reprinted 1973)
Hook, Andrew (ed.), *The History of Scottish Literature, Vol. 2, 1660–1800* (Aberdeen, 1987)
MacLaine, A.H., *Allan Ramsay* (Boston, 1985)
MacLaine, A.H., *Robert Fergusson* (New York, 1965)
MacQueen, John, *Progress and Poetry* (Edinburgh, 1982)
Pittock, Murray G.H., *Poetry and Jacobite Politics in Eighteenth-Century Britain and Ireland* (Cambridge, 1994)
Ramsay, Allan, *Works* (ed. Burns Martin, John W. Oliver, Alexander M. Kinghorn and Alexander Law, six vols, Edinburgh, 1944–74)
Simpson, Kenneth, *The Protean Scot: The Crisis of Identity in Eighteenth Century Scottish Literature* (Aberdeen, 1988)

Note on the Texts

The texts of the poems are taken from a number of sources. I am particularly grateful to the Scottish Text Society for their kind permission to use their edition of *The Works of Allan Ramsay* (edited by Burns Martin, John W. Oliver, Alexander M. Kinghorn and Alexander Law, six volumes, 1944–74) and *The Poems of Robert Fergusson* (edited by Matthew P. McDiarmid, two volumes, 1954–6). I have modernised the spelling of the English poems in the anthology quite freely, expanding contractions, removing capitals and altering such spellings as 'chear' and 'critick'. It seemed to me no service to the poets to make their work look quaintly old-fashioned to the modern reader. I have been less active in changing Scots spellings to more common forms, though occasionally I have altered a word into a more recognisable orthography. In both Scots and English poems I have amended and inserted punctuation to conform to modern practice and clarify meaning. Since punctuation and spelling were often left in the hands of the printer in the eighteenth century, what the poets actually wrote is difficult, if not impossible, to establish. They would expect to have their work presented to the reader in a form that would be most agreeable and acceptable. The texts of the poems here are presented in that spirit.

Much for the same reason I have glossed the language, principally, of course, the Scots, but here and there the English, too, to suggest modern English equivalents for the words used. I have also tried to explain names and allusions and points of local interest that may be obscure to readers. These glosses appear on the page where possible and where a longer explanation is required the reader is directed to notes at the end of the book. In longer poems I have sometimes glossed only the first occurrence of a word, especially if it is a relatively common one. There are a number of Scots words which are so widely used that to gloss each use would be repetitious. A list of these common words is therefore given after the notes at the end of the book. In glossing Scots words I have mostly used *The Concise Scots*

Dictionary (editor-in-chief Mairi Robinson, 1985), supplemented by *Chambers Scots Dictionary* (1911). I have also consulted the glossaries of various collections of poetry, especially Allan Ramsay's from the STS edition and that in David Herd's *Ancient and Modern Scottish Songs* (1776, reprinted by Scottish Academic Press, 1973).

The Poems

ANONYMOUS

Blythsome Bridal

Fy, let us a' to the bridal,
  For there will be lilting there,
For Jock's to be married to Maggie,
  The lass wi' the gowden hair.
And there will be lang kail and porridge, 5
  And bannocks of barley-meal,
And there will be good saut herring,
  To relish a cog of good ale.

And there will be Sawney the soutar,
  And Will wi' the meikle mou; 10
And there will be Tam the blutter,
  With Andrew the tinkler, I trow;
And there will be bowed-legged Robie,
  With thumbless Katie's goodman;
And there will be blue-cheeked Dowbie, 15
  And Lawrie the laird of the land.

And there will be sowlibber Patie,
  And plucky-faced Wat i' the mill,
Capper-nosed Francie, and Gibbie,
  That wons in the how o' the hill; 20
And there will be Alaster Sibbie,
  Wha in wi' black Bessy did mool,
With sniv'ling Lilly, and Tibby,
  The lass that stands oft on the stool.

And Madge that was buckled to Stennie, 25
  And coft him grey breeks to his arse,
Wha after was hangit for stealing –
  Great mercy it happened nae warse;

5 lang kail *uncut colewort*
8 cog *wooden bowl*
9 soutar *cobbler*
11 blutter *oaf*
17 sowlibber *swine-gelder*
18 plucky *pimply*
19 capper *copper*
20 wons *dwells* how *hollow*
22 mool *mix*
24 stool *see note*
26 coft *bought* breeks *breeches*

And there will be gleed Geordy Janners,
  And Kirsh wi' the lily-white leg, 30
Who gade to the south for manners,
  And banged up her wame in Mons Meg.

And there will be Juden Maclourie,
  And blinkin daft Barbara Macleg,
Wi' flea-lugged sharney-faced Lawrie, 35
  And shangy-mou'd halucket Meg;
And there will be happer-arsed Nansy,
  And fairy-faced Flowrie by name,
Muck Madie, and fat-hippet Grisy,
  The lass wi' the gowden wame. 40

And there will be girn-again Gibby,
  Wi' his glaiket wife Jenny Bell,
And measly-shinned Mungo Macapie,
  The lad that was skipper himsel;
There lads and lasses in pearlings, 45
  Will feast i' the heart of the ha',
On sybows, and rifarts, and carlings,
  That are baith sodden and raw.

And there will be fadges and brochen,
  With fouth of good gabbock of skate, 50
Powsowdie, and drammock, and crowdie,
  And caller nowt-feet in a plate;
And there will be partens and buckies,
  And whytens and spaldings enew,
And singit sheepheads, and a haggis, 55
  And scadlips to sup till ye spew.

29 gleed *squinting*
32 wame *womb* Mons Meg *see note*
35 lugged *eared* sharney *dirty*
36 shangy *scraggy, gaunt* halucket *noisy, crazy*
37 happer *hopper*
41 girn *grumble*
42 glaiket *stupid*
45 pearlings *lace*
47 sybows *spring onions* rifarts *radishes* carlings *peas*
48 sodden *boiled*
49 fadges *barley loaves* brochen *gruel*
50 fouth *plenty* gabbock *mouthful*
51 powsowdie *sheep's head broth* drammock *oatmeal and water* crowdie *soft cheese*
52 nowt *cattle*
53 partens *edible crabs* buckies *sea-snails*
54 whytens *whitings* spaldings *split dried haddocks* enew *enough*
55 singit *singed*
56 scadlips *broth*

And there will be lappered-milk kebbucks,
  And sowens, and farles, and baps,
With swats, and well-scraped paunches,
  And brandy in stoups and in caps; 60
And there will be meal-kail and castocks,
  And skink to sup till ye rive,
And roasts to roast on a brander
  Of flowks that were taken alive.

Scrapt haddocks, wilks, dulse, and tangles, 65
  And mill of good snishing to prie;
When weary with eating and drinking,
  We'll rise up and dance till we die.
Then fy, let us a' to the bridal,
  For there will be lilting there, 70
For Jock's to be married to Maggie,
  The lass wi' the gowden hair.

57 lappered *clotted, curdled* kebbucks *cheeses*
58 sowens *oats steeped in water and boiled* farles *fardels, quarters of oatcake* baps *bread rolls*
59 swats *small ale* paunches *tripe*
61 meal-kail *oatmeal and mashed cole* castocks *cabbage stalks*
62 skink *beef soup* rive *split*
63 brander *gridiron*
64 flowks *flounders*
65 wilks *periwinkles* dulse *edible seaweed* tangles *seaweed*
66 snishing *snuff* prie *taste, sample*

Maggie Lauder

Wha wadna be in love
  Wi' bonny Maggie Lauder?
A piper met her gaun to Fife,
  And speired what was't they ca'd her;
Right scornfully she answered him, 5
  'Begone, you hallanshaker,
Jog on your gate, you bladderskate,
  My name is Maggie Lauder.'

'Maggie,' quoth he, 'and by my bags,
  I'm fidging fain to see thee; 10
Sit down by me, my bonny bird,
  In troth I winna steer thee;
For I'm a piper to my trade,
  My name is Rob the Ranter,
The lasses loup as they were daft, 15
  When I blaw up my chanter.'

'Piper,' quoth Meg, 'hae you your bags,
  Or is your drone in order?
If you be Rob, I've heard of you,
  Live you upo' the border? 20
The lasses a', baith far and near,
  Have heard of Rob the Ranter;
I'll shake my foot wi' right goodwill,
  Gif you'll blaw up your chanter.'

Then to his bags he flew wi' speed, 25
  About the drone he twisted;
Meg up and walloped o'er the green,
  For brawly could she frisk it.
'Weel done,' quoth he. 'Play up,' quoth she.
  'Weel bobbed,' quoth Rob the Ranter, 30
' 'Tis worth my while to play indeed,
  When I hae sic a dancer.'

6 hallanshaker *beggar*
7 bladderskate *foolish talker*
10 fidging fain *itching eager*
12 steer *molest*
15 loup *leap*
27 walloped *danced*

'Weel hae ye played your part,' quoth Meg,
    'Your cheeks are like the crimson;
There's nane in Scotland plays sae weel, 35
    Since we lost Habby Simpson.
I've lived in Fife, baith maid and wife,
    These ten years and a quarter;
Gin you should come to Anster fair,
    Speir ye for Maggie Lauder.' 40

36 Habby Simpson *see note* 39 Anster *see note*

Tarry Woo

Tarry woo, tarry woo,
Tarry woo is ill to spin;
Card it well, card it well,
Card it well ere ye begin.
When 'tis carded, rowed and spun, 5
Then the work is haflens done;
But when woven, drest and clean,
It may be cleading for a queen.

Sing, my bonny harmless sheep,
That feed upon the mountains steep, 10
Bleating sweetly as ye go,
Through the winter's frost and snow;
Hart and hynd and fallow deer,
No be half so useful are;
Frae kings to him that hads the plow, 15
Are all obliged to tarry woo.

Up, ye shepherds, dance and skip,
O'er the hills and valleys trip,
Sing up the praise of tarry woo,
Sing the flocks that bear it too: 20
Harmless creatures without blame,
That clead the back and cram the wame,
Keep us warm and hearty fou;
Leese me on the tarry woo.

How happy is a shepherd's life, 25
Far frae courts and free of strife,
While the gimmers bleat and bae,
And the lambkins answer 'mae'!
No such music to his ear;
Of thief or fox he has no fear; 30
Sturdy kent and colly too,
Well defend the tarry woo.

1 woo *wool*
5 rowed *rolled*
6 haflens *half*
8 cleading *clothing*
22 clead *clothe* wame *stomach*
24 leese me on *blessings on*
27 gimmers *year-old ewes*
31 kent *long staff* colly *sheep dog*

He lives content, and envies none;
Not even a monarch on his throne,
Though he the royal sceptre sways, 35
Has not sweeter holidays.
Who'd be a king, can ony tell,
When a shepherd sings sae well,
Sings sae well, and pays his due,
With honest heart and tarry woo? 40

O This is No my Ain House

O this is no my ain house,
I ken by the biggin o't;
For bow-kail thrave at my door-cheek,
And thistles on the riggin o't.

A carle came wi' lack o' grace, 5
Wi' unco gear and unco face;
And sin' he claimed my daddie's place,
I downa bide the triggin o't.

Wi' routh o' kin and routh o' reek,
My daddie's door it wadna steek; 10
But bread and cheese were his door-cheek,
And girdle cakes the riggin o't.

My daddie bag his housie weel,
By dint o' head and dint o' heel,
By dint o' arm and dint o' steel. 15
And muckle weary priggin o't.

Then was it dink, or was it douce,
For ony cringing foreign goose
To claucht my daddie's wee bit house,
And spoil the hamely triggin o't? 20

Say, was it foul, or was it fair,
To come a hunder mile and mair,
For to ding out my daddie's heir,
And dash him wi' the whiggin o't?

2 biggin *building*
3 bow-kail *cabbage*
4 riggin *roof*
5 carle *fellow*
7 sin' *since*
8 downa *cannot*
9 routh *plenty*
10 steek *shut*
12 girdle *hot-plate*
13 bag *built*
16 priggin *haggling*
17 dink *nice* douce *kind*
19 claucht *seize*
20 triggin *neatness*
23 ding *beat*
24 whiggin *see note*

Whistle O'er the Lave O't

My mither sent me to the well,
She had better gane hersell,
I got the thing I dare nae tell,
   Whistle o'er the lave o't.

My mither sent me to the sea, 5
For to gather mussels three;
A sailor lad fell in wi' me,
   Whistle o'er the lave o't.

1 mither *mother*
2 gane *gone*
4 lave *rest*

GRIZEL BAILLIE (1665–1746)

Werena my Heart Light I Wad Die

There ance was a may, and she looed na men,
She biggit her bonny bower down in yon glen;
But now she cries dool, and a well-a-day,
Come down the green gate, and come here away.

When bonny young Johnny came o'er the sea, 5
He said he saw naething sae lovely as me;
He hecht me baith rings and mony bra things,
And werena my heart light I wad die.

He had a wee titty that looed na me,
Because I was twice as bonny as she; 10
She raised sic a pother 'twixt him and his mother,
That werena my heart light I wad die.

The day it was set, and the bridal to be,
The wife took a dwam, and lay down to die;
She mained and she grained out of dolour and pain, 15
Till he vowed he never wad see me again.

His kin was for ane of a higher degree,
Said 'What had he to do with the like of me?'
Albeit I was bonny, I was na for Johnny,
And werena my heart light I wad die. 20

They said I had neither cow nor calf,
Nor dribbles of drink rins through the draff,
Nor pickles of meal rins through the mill-eye,
And werena my heart light I wad die.

1 may *maiden*
2 biggit *built*
3 dool *alas*
7 hecht *promised*
9 titty *sister*
13 dwam *faint*
22 draff *dregs*
23 pickles *small amounts* mill-eye *opening through which meal comes from the mill-stones*

His titty she was baith wylie and slee; 25
She spied me as I came o'er the lee,
And then she ran in and made a loud din,
Believe your ain een, an ye trow na me.

His bonnet stood ay fu' round on his brow,
His auld ane looks ay as well as some's new, 30
But now he lets't wear ony gate it will hing,
And casts himself dowie upo' the corn-bing.

And now he gaes drooping about the dykes,
And a' he dow do is to hund the tykes;
The live-lang night he ne'er steeks his eye, 35
And werena my heart light I wad die.

Were I but young for thee, as I hae been,
We should hae been galloping down on yon green,
And linking it on the lily-white lee;
And, wow, gin I were but young for thee. 40

25 slee *sly*
32 dowie *doleful, sad* bing *heap, pile*
33 dykes *ditches*
34 dow *can* hund *hound* tykes *dogs*
35 steeks *shuts*
39 linking *run*

ALEXANDER ROBERTSON OF STRUAN (1668–1749)

Liberty Preserved, or Love Destroyed

At length the bondage I have broke
  Which gave me so much pain.
I've slipped my heart out of the yoke,
  Never to drudge again;
And, conscious of my long disgrace, 5
Have thrown my chain at Cupid's face.

If ever he attempt again
  My freedom to enslave,
I'll court the godhead of champagne
  Which makes the coward brave, 10
And, when that deity has healed my soul,
I'll drown the little bastard in my bowl.

6 Cupid *god of love, son of Mars and Venus (who was married to Vulcan)*

12 bowl *drinking vessel*

WILLIAM HAMILTON OF GILBERTFIELD (1670–1751)

The Last Dying Words of Bonnie Heck

A Famous Greyhound in the Shire of Fife

'Alas, alas,' quo' bonnie Heck,
'On former days when I reflect!
I was a dog much in respect
  For doughty deed;
But now I must hing by the neck 5
  Without remeed.

'Oh fy, sirs, for black, burning shame,
Ye'll bring a blunder on your name!
Pray tell me wherein I'm to blame?
  Is't in effect 10
Because I'm cripple, auld, and lame?'
  Quo' bonnie Heck.

'What great feats I have done mysel'
Within clink of Kilrenny bell,
When I was souple, young, and fell, 15
  But fear or dread,
John Ness and Paterson can tell,
  Whose hearts may bleed.

They'll witness that I was the vier
Of all the dogs within the shire; 20
I'd run all day and never tire;
  But now my neck,
It must be stretched for my hire!'
  Quo' bonnie Heck.

'How nimbly could I turn the hare, 25
Then serve myself; that was right fair!
For still it was my constant care

6 remeed *remedy, redress*
14 Kilrenny *see note*
15 souple *supple* fell *fierce*
19 vier *rival*

The van to lead.
Now what could sery Heck do mair?
Syne kill her dead. 30

At the Kings-muir and Kelly-law,
Where good stout hares gang fast awa',
So cleverly I did it claw,
With pith and speed;
I bure the bell before them a' 35
As clear's a bead.

I ran alike on a' kind grounds,
Yea, in the midst of Ardry whins
I gript the maukins by the buns
Or by the neck; 40
Where naething could slay them but guns,
Save bonnie Heck.

I wily, witty was, and gash,
With my auld felny packy pash;
Nae man might ance buy me for cash 45
In some respect;
Are they not then confounded rash,
That hang poor Heck?

I was a bardy tyke, and bauld;
Though my beard's grey I'm not so auld. 50
Can any man to me unfauld
What is the feid
To stane me ere I be well cauld?
A cruel deed!

Now honesty was aye my drift, 55
An innocent and harmless shift,
A kail-pot lid gently to lift
Or aumrie sneck;

29 sery *poor old*
31 Kings-muir and Kelly-law *see note*
35 bure the bell *took the prize*
38 Ardry *see note* whins *gorse*
39 maukins *hares* buns *tail*
43 gash *shrewd*
44 felny packy pash *wicked crafty head*
49 bardy *fierce* bauld *bold*
52 feid *feud, enmity*
58 aumrie sneck *cupboard latch*

Shame fa' the chafts dare call that thift!'
  Quo' bonnie Heck. 60

'So well's I could play *hocus-pocus*
And of the servants mak' *jodocus*
And this I did in every *locus*
  Through their neglect;
And was not this a merry *jocus*?' 65
  Quo' bonnie Heck.

'But now, good sirs, this day is lost
The best dog in the East-Neuk coast;
For never ane durst brag nor boast
  Me, for their neck. 70
But now I must yield up the ghost,'
  Quo' bonnie Heck,

'And put a period to my talking.
For I'm unto my exit making:
Sirs, ye may a' gae to the hawking, 75
  And there reflect
Ye'll ne'er get sic a dog for maukin
  As bonnie Heck.

But if my puppies ance were ready,
Which I gat on a bonnie lady, 80
They'll be baith clever, keen, and beddy,
  And ne'er neglect
To clink it like their ancient daddy,
  The famous Heck.'

59 chafts *jaws, mouth* thift *theft*
61 *hocus-pocus tricks*
62 *jodocus jest*
63 *locus place*
65 *jocus joke*
68 East-Neuk *see note*
80 gat *got, begot*
81 beddy *biddable*
83 clink *act smart*

ALLAN RAMSAY (1685–1758)

An thou were my ain thing

An thou were my ain thing,
I would love thee, I would love thee;
An thou were my ain thing,
How dearly would I love thee.

Like bees that suck the morning dew 5
Frae flowers of sweetest scent and hew,
Sae wad I dwell upo' thy mou,
And gar the Gods envy me.

Sae lang's I had the use of light,
I'd on thy beauties feast my sight, 10
Syne in saft whispers through the night,
I'd tell how much I loo'd thee.

How fair and ruddy is my Jean!
She moves a goddess o'er the green:
Were I a king, thou should be queen, 15
Nane but my sell aboon thee.

I'd grasp thee to this breast of mine,
Whilst thou, like ivy, or the vine,
Around my stronger limbs should twine,
Formed hardy to defend thee. 20

Time's on the wing, and will not stay,
In shining youth let's make our hay,
Since love admits of no delay,
Oh, let na scorn undo thee.

While love does at his altar stand, 25
Hae there's my heart, gi'e me thy hand,
And with ilk smile thou shalt command
The will of him wha loves thee.

1 an *if* ain *own*
7 wad *would* mou *mouth*
9 lang's *long as*
12 loo'd *loved*
16 sell *self*
27 ilk *each*

The Lass of Peattie's Mill

The Lass of Peattie's Mill,
So bonny, blyth and gay,
In spite of all my skill,
She stole my heart away. 5
When tedding of the hay
Bare-headed on the green,
Love 'midst her locks did play,
And wantoned in her een.

Her arms white, round and smooth,
Breasts rising in their dawn, 10
To age it would give youth,
To press 'em with his hand.
Through all my spirits ran
An ecstasy of bliss,
When I such sweetness fand 15
Wrapt in a balmy kiss.

Without the help of art,
Like flowers which grace the wild,
She did her sweets impart,
When e'er she spoke or smiled. 20
Her looks they were so mild,
Free from affected pride,
She me to love beguiled;
I wished her for my bride.

Oh, had I all that wealth 25
Hopeton's high mountains fill,
Insured long life and health,
And pleasure at my will;
I'd promise and fulfil,
That none but bonny she, 30
The Lass of Peattie's Mill
Should share the same wi' me.

4 tedding *spreading*
15 fand *found*
26 Hopeton's high mountains *see note*

Polwart on the Green

At Polwart on the green
If you'll meet me the morn,
Where lasses do conveen
To dance about the thorn;
A kindly welcome you shall meet 5
Frae her wha likes to view
A lover and a lad complete,
The lad and lover you.

Let dorty dames say na,
As lang as e'er they please, 10
Seem caulder than the sna',
While inwardly they bleeze;
But I will frankly shaw my mind,
And yield my heart to thee;
Be ever to the captive kind, 15
That langs na to be free.

At Polwart on the green,
Among the new-mawn hay,
With sangs and dancing keen
We'll pass the heartsome day, 20
At night if beds be o'er thrang laid,
And thou be twined of thine,
Thou shalt be welcome, my dear lad,
To take a part of mine.

2 the morn *tomorrow*
9 dorty *haughty*
11 sna' *snow*
12 bleeze *blaze*
18 mawn *mown*
20 heartsome *cheerful*
21 thrang *crowded*
22 twined *deprived*

A Song: Lochaber No More

Farewell to Lochaber, and farewell, my Jean,
Where heartsome with thee I've mony day been;
For Lochaber no more, Lochaber no more.
We'll maybe return to Lochaber no more.
These tears that I shed, they are a' for my dear, 5
And no for the dangers attending on weir,
Though bore on rough seas to a far bloody shore,
Maybe to return to Lochaber no more.

Though hurricanes rise, and rise ev'ry wind,
They'll ne'er make a tempest like that in my mind: 10
Though loudest of thunder on louder waves roar,
That's nathing like leaving my love on the shore.
To leave thee behind me, my heart is sair pained.
By ease that's inglorious no fame can be gained;
And beauty and love's the reward of the brave, 15
And I must deserve it before I can crave.

Then glory, my Jeany, maun plead my excuse;
Since honour commands me, how can I refuse?
Without it I ne'er can have merit for thee,
And without thy favour I'd better not be. 20
I gae then, my lass, to win honour and fame;
And if I should luck to come gloriously hame,
I'll bring a heart to thee with love running o'er,
And then I'll leave thee and Lochaber no more.

2 heartsome *cheerful* 6 weir *war*

Up in the Air

Now the sun's gane out o' sight,
Beet the ingle, and snuff the light:
In glens the fairies skip and dance,
And witches wallop o'er to France,
Up in the air
On my bonny grey mare. 5
And I see her yet, and I see her yet,
Up in the air, etc.

The wind's drifting hail and sna'
O'er frozen hags like a foot ba', 10
Nae starns keek through the azure slit,
'Tis cauld and mirk as ony pit,
The man i' the moon
Is carowsing aboon,
D'ye see, d'ye see, d'ye see him yet. 15
The man i' the moon, etc.

Take your glass to clear your een,
'Tis the elixir hales the spleen,
Baith wit and mirth it will inspire,
And gently puffs the lover's fire, 20
Up in the air,
It drives away care,
Ha'e wi' ye, ha'e wi' ye, and ha'e wi' ye lads yet,
Up in the air, etc.

Steek the doors, keep out the frost, 25
Come Willy gi'es about yer tost,
Til't lads, and lilt it out,
And let us ha'e a blythsom bout,
Up wi't there, there,
Dinna cheat, but drink fair, 30
Huzza, huzza, and huzza lads yet,
Up wi't there, there, etc.

2 beet *add fuel to*
4 wallop *gallop*
9 sna' *snow*
10 hags *boggy pits*
11 starns keek *stars peep*
12 mirk *dark*
18 hales *heals*
25 steek *shut*
27 til't *to it*

The Marrow Ballad

On Seeing a Strolling Congregation Going to a Field Meeting, May 9th, 1738.

To the Tune of 'Fy, let us a' to the Bridal'

O fy, let us a' to the meeting,
  For there will be canting there,
Where some will be laughing, some greeting,
  At the preaching of Erskine and Mair;
Then rouze ye up, Robie and Willy, 5
  The lassies are raiking awa,
In petty-coats white as the lilly,
  And biggonets prinned on fou braw.

And there will be blinkan-eyed Bessy,
  Blyth Baby, and sweet lippet Megg, 10
And mony a rosie-cheeked lassie,
  With coats kiltet to their mid-leg;
To gar them gang clever and lightly,
  We'll carry their hose and their shoon,
Syne kiss them and clap them fou tightly, 15
  As soon as the sermon is done.

The sun will be sunk in the west,
  Before they have finished the wark,
Then behind a whin bush we can rest –
  There's meikle good done in the dark; 20
There Tammy to Tibby may creep,
  Slee Sandy may mool in with Kate;
While other dowf sauls are asleep,
  We'll handle deep matters of state.

And should we deserve the black stools, 25
  For getting a gamphrell with wean,

3 greeting *weeping*
4 Erskine and Mair *see note*
6 raiking *roving*
8 biggonets *linen caps* prinned *pinned*
14 shoon *shoes*
15 clap *fondle*
18 wark *work*
19 whin *furze or gorse*
22 mool *mix*
23 dowf sauls *stupid souls*
25 black stools *stools of repentance*
26 gamphrell *fool* wean *child*

We'll answer we're no siccan fools,
  To obey them that have the oaths tane;
When the lave's to the parish kirk gawn
  On Sundays, we'll rest us at hame, 30
An' running to hills now and than
  Makes it nowther a sin nor a shame.

Then up with the Brethren true blew,
  Wha lead us to siccan delight,
And can prove it, although they be few, 35
  That there's naebody else wha is right;
And doun with all government laws,
  That are made by the Bishops of Baal,
And the thieves wha climb oer the kirk waw,
  And come not in by a right call. 40

27 siccan *such kind of*
28 tane *taken see note*
29 lave *rest*
32 nowther *neither*
38 Bishops of Baal *see note*
40 right call *see note*

Lucky Spence's Last Advice[1]

Three times the carline grained and rifted,
Then frae the cod her pow she lifted,
In bawdy policy well gifted,
  When she now faun,
That death na langer wad be shifted, 5
  She thus began:

My loving lasses, I maun leave ye,
But dinna wi' yer greeting grieve me,
Nor wi' your draunts and droning deave me,
  But bring's a gill; 10
For faith, my bairns, ye may believe me,
  'Tis 'gainst my will.

O Black-Eyed Bess and Mim-Mou'd[2] Meg,
O'er good to work or yet to beg;
Lay sunkots up for a sair leg, 15
  For whan ye fail,
Yer face will not be worth a feg,
  Nor yet yer tail.

Whan e'er ye meet a fool that's fow,
That ye're a maiden gar him trow, 20
Seem nice, but stick to him like glew;
  And whan set down,
Drive at the jango till he spew,
  Syne he'll sleep soun.

1 rifted *belched*
2 cod *pillow* pow *head*
4 faun *found*
8 greeting *weeping*
9 draunt *whine* deave *deafen*
13 mim *prim*
15 sunkots *provisions*
17 feg *fig*
23 jango *liquor*
24 soun *sound*

[1] Lucky Spence, a famous bawd who flourished for several years about the beginning of the eighteenth century; she had her lodgings near Holyrood House. She made many a benefit night to herself by putting a trade in the hands of young lasses that had a little pertness, strong pasions, abundance of laziness, and no fore-thought.

[2] Mim-Mou'd. Expresses an affected modesty, by a preciseness about the mouth.

When he's asleep, then dive and catch 25
His ready cash, his rings or watch;
And gin he likes to light his match[1]
  At your spunk-box,
Ne'er stand to let the fumbling wretch
  E'en take the pox. 30

Cleek a' ye can be hook or crook,
Ryp ilky poutch frae nook to nook;
Be sure to truff his pocket-book,
  Saxty pounds Scots
Is nae deaf nits:[2] in little bouk 35
  Lie great bank-notes.

To get a mends of whinging fools,[3]
That's frighted for repenting-stools,
Wha often, whan their metal cools,
  Turn sweer to pay, 40
Gar the kirk-boxie hale the dools[4]
  Anither day.

But dawt red coats, and let them scoup,
Free for the fou of cutty stoup;[5]
To gee them up, ye need na hope 45
  E'er to do well:

28 spunk-box *tinder-box*
31 cleek *hook*
32 ryp *search*
33 truff *steal*
34 Saxty pounds Scots *see note*
35 nits *nuts* bouk *bulk*
40 sweer *reluctant*
41 hale the dools *take the prize*
43 dawt red coats *caress soldiers*
  scoup *move fast*
44 cutty *short*
45 gee *stir*

---

[1] Light his match. I could give a large annotation on this sentence but do not incline to explain everything lest I disoblige future critics by leaving nothing for them to do.

[2] Is nae deaf nits, or empty nuts; this is a negative manner of saying a thing is substantial.

[3] To get a mends = to be revenged; of whinging fools, fellows who wear the wrong side of their faces outmost, pretenders to sanctity, who love to be snuggling in a corner.

[4] Gar the kirk-boxie . . . dools. Delate them to the kirk-treasurer. 'Hale the dools' is a phrase used at football where the party that gains the goal or dool is said to hail it or win the game, and so draws the stake.

[5] Cutty Stoup. Little pot, i.e., a gill of brandy.

They'll rive yer brats and kick your doup,
  And play the deel.

There's ae sair cross attends the craft,
That curst correction-house, where aft 50
Vild Hangy's taz[1] yer riggings saft
  Makes black and blae,
Enough to pit a body daft;
  But what'll ye say?[2]

Nane gathers gear withouten care, 55
Ilk pleasure has of pain a skare;
Suppose then they should tirl ye bare,
  And gar ye fike,
E'en learn to thole; 'tis very fair
  Ye're nibour like. 60

Forby, my looves, count upo' losses,
Yer milk-white teeth and cheeks like roses,
Whan jet-black hair and brigs of noses,
  Faw down wi' dads
To keep your hearts up 'neath sic crosses, 65
  Set up for bawds.

Wi' well crished loofs I hae been canty,
Whan e'er the lads wad fain ha'e faun t'ye;
To try the auld game 'Taunty Raunty',
  Like coofers keen, 70
They took advice of me your aunty,
  If ye were clean.

47 rive *tear* brats *rags* doup *bottom*
48 deel *devil*
51 vild Hangy's taz *vile hangman's belt* riggings *backs*
52 blae *blue*
53 pit *put*
56 skare *share*
57 tirl *strip*
58 fike *twitch*
59 thole *endure*
60 nibour *neighbour*
61 forby *besides* looves *loves*
62 brigs *bridges*
64 dads *thuds*
67 crished loofs *greased palms*
68 faun *fallen*
70 coofers *fools*

[1] Hangy's taz. If they perform not the task assigned them they are whipt by the hangman.

[2] But what'll ye say? The emphasis of this phrase, like many others, cannot be understood but by a native.

Then up I took my siller ca'
And whistled ben[1] whiles ane, whiles twa;
Rouned in his lug,[2] that there was a 75
  Poor country Kate,
As halesom as the well of Spaw,
  But unka blate.

Sae whan e'er company came in,
And were upo' a merry pin, 80
I slade away wi' little din,
  And muckle mense,
Left conscience judge,[3] it was a' ane
  To Lucky Spence.

My bennison come on good doers, 85
Who spend their cash on bawds and whores;
May they ne'er want the wale of cures
  For a sair snout:
Foul fa' the quacks wha that fire smoors,[4]
  And puts nae out. 90

My malison light ilka day
On them that drink, and dinna pay,
But tak a snack and rin away;
  May't be their hap
Never to want a gonorrhæa, 95
  Or rotten clap.

73 siller ca' *silver whistle*
74 ben *to the inner room* whiles *sometimes*
77 halesom *wholesome* Spaw *Spa in Belgium*
78 unka blate *strangely bashful*
80 pin *mood*
81 slade *slid*
82 mense *discretion*
87 wale *choice*
89 smoors *smothers*
93 snack *bite, moment*

[1] And whistled ben. 'But' and 'ben' signify different ends or rooms of a house; to gang but and ben is to go from one end of the house to the other.

[2] Rouned in his lug. Whispered in his ear.

[3] Left conscience judge. It was her usual way of vindicating herself to tell ye, when company came to her house, could she be so uncivil as to turn them out? If they did any bad thing, said she, between God and their conscience be't.

[4] Fire smoors. Such quacks as bind up the external symptoms of the pox and drive it inward to the strongholds, whence it is not easily expelled.

Lass gi'e us in anither gill,
A mutchken, jo, let's tak our fill;
Let death syne registrate his bill
  Whan I want sense, 100
I'll slip away with better will,
  Quo' Lucky Spence.

98 jo *sweetheart*

Elegy on Lucky Wood in the Canongate, May 1717[1]

O Cannigate, poor elritch hole,
What loss, what crosses does thou thole!
London and death[2] gars thee look drole,
  And hing thy head;
Wow, but thou has e'en a cauld coal   5
  To blaw indeed.

Hear me ye hills, and every glen,
Ilk craig, ilk cleugh, and hollow den,
And echo shrill, that a' may ken
  The waefou thud,   10
Be rackless death, wha came unsenn[3]
  To Lucky Wood.

She's dead, o'er true, she's dead and gane,
Left us and Willie[4] burd alane,
To bleer and greet, to sob and mane,   15
  And rugg our hair,
Because we'll ne'r see her again
  For evermair.

1 Cannigate *see note* elritch *hideous*
2 thole *endure*
3 drole *half-witted*
8 craig *cliff* cleugh *ravine* den *valley*
10 thud *sound*
11 rackless *careless* unsenn *unsent for*
14 burd alane *quite alone*
15 bleer *blind with tears* greet *weep*
16 rugg *tear*

[1] Lucky Wood kept an ale-house in the Canongate, was much respected for hospitality, honesty, and the neatness both of her person and house.
[2] London and death. The place of her residence being the greatest sufferer by the loss of our Members of Parliament, which London now enjoys, many of them having their houses there, being the suburb of Edinburgh nearest the King's palace; this with the death of Lucky Wood are [*sic*] sufficient to make the place ruinous.
[3] Came unsenn: or 'unsent for'. There's nothing extraodinary in this, it being his common custom, except in some few instances of late since the falling of the Bubbles.
[4] Willie. Her husband William Wood.

She gae'd as fait as a new prin,
And kept her housie snod and been; 20
Her peuther glanced upo' your een
  Like siller plate;
She was a donsie wife and clean,
  Without debate.

It did ane good to see her stools, 25
Her boord, fire-side, and facing tools;[1]
Rax, chandlers, tangs, and fire-shools,
  Basket wi' bread.
Poor Facers[2] now may chew pea-hools,
  Since Lucky's dead. 30

She ne'er gae in a lawin fause,
Nor stoups a froath aboon the hause,
Nor kept dowed tip within her waws,
  But reaming swats;
She never ran sour jute, because 35
  It gee's the batts.[3]

She had the gate sae well to please,
With gratis beef, dry fish, or cheese;
Which kept our purses ay at ease,
  And health in tift, 40

19 fait *neat* prin *pin*
20 snod *trim* been *well-stocked*
21 peuther *pewter*
23 donsie *tidy*
26 boord *table*
27 rax *racks* chandlers *candlesticks* tangs *tongs* fire-shools *fire-shovels*
29 pea-hools *pea-pods*
31 lawin fause *tavern reckoning false*
32 froath *froth* hause *neck*
33 dowed tip *flat twopenny ale* waws *walls*
34 reaming swats *foaming small ale*
35 jute *sour ale, dregs*
36 batts *colic*
40 tift *order*

[1] Facing tools. Stoups (or pots) and cups, so called from the Facers (see line 29).
[2] Poor Facers. The Facers were a club of fair drinkers who inclined rather to spend a shilling on ale than twopence for meat; they had their name from a rule they observed of obliging themselves to throw all they left in the cup in their own faces: wherefore to save their face and clothes they prudently sucked the liquor clean out.
[3] She ne'er gae in, etc. All this verse is a fine picture of an honest ale-seller – a rarity.

And lent her fresh nine gallon trees
  A hearty lift.

She ga'e us aft hail legs o' lamb,
And did nae hain her mutton ham;
Then ay at Yule, when e'er we came, 45
  A bra' goose pye,
And was na that good belly baum?
  Nane dare deny.

The writer lads fow well may mind her,
Furthy was she, her luck designed her 50
Their common mither, sure nane kinder
  Ever brake bread;
She has na left her make behind her,
  But now she's dead.

To the sma' hours we aft sat still, 55
Nicked round our toasts and snishing mill;
Good cakes we wanted ne'r at will,
  The best of bread,
Which often cost us mony a gill
  To Aikenhead.[1] 60

Could our saut tears like Clyde down rin,
And had we cheeks like Corra's Lin,[2]
That a' the warld might hear the din
  Rair frae ilk head;
She was the wale of a' her kin, 65
  But now she's dead.

41 trees *wooden barrels*
44 hain *skimp*
47 baum *balm*
49 writer *lawyer*
50 furthy *forward*
51 mither *mother*
53 make *match*
56 nicked *drink heartily* snishing *snuff*
64 rair *roar*
65 wale *choice*

[1] To Aikenhead. The Nether-bow porter, to whom Lucky's customers were often obliged for opening the port for them when they stayed out till the small hours after midnight.

[2] Like Corra's Lin. A very high precipice nigh Lanark over which the river of Clyde falls making a great noise, which is heard some miles off.

O Lucky Wood, 'tis hard to bear
The loss; but oh, we maun forbear:
Yet sall thy memory be dear
  While blooms a tree, 70
And after ages bairns will spear
  'Bout thee and me.

EPITAPH

  Beneath this sod
  Lies Lucky Wood,
Whom a' men might put faith in; 75
  Wha was na sweer,
  While she winned here,
To cram our wames for naithing.

69 sall *shall*
76 sweer *reluctant*
77 winned *dwelt*

Elegy on Maggy Johnston, who died Anno 1711[1]

Auld Reeky[2] mourn in sable hue,
Let fouth of tears dreep like May dew,
To braw tippony[3] bid adieu,
  Which we with greed
Bended as fast as she could brew, 5
  But ah, she's dead!

To tell the truth now Maggy dang,[4]
Of customers she had a bang;
For lairds and souters a' did gang
  To drink bedeen, 10
The barn and yard was aft sae thrang,
  We took the green.

And there by dizens we lay down,
Syne sweetly ca'd the healths arown,
To bonny lasses black or brown, 15
  As we loo'd best;
In bumpers we dull cares did drown,
  And took our rest.

2 fouth *plenty* dreep *drip*
3 tippony *twopenny ale*
5 bended *drank*
8 bang *crowd*
9 lairds *lords* souters *cobblers*
10 bedeen *quickly*
11 thrang *busy*
13 dizens *dozens*
14 ca'd *passed* arown *around*

---

[1] Maggy Johnston lived about a mile southward of Edinburgh, kept a little farm, and had a particular art of brewing a small sort of ale agreeable to the taste, very white, clear and intoxicating, which made people who loved to have a good pennyworth for their money be her frequent customers. And many others of every station, sometimes for diversion, thought it no affront to be seen in her barn or yard.

[2] Auld Reeky. A name the country people give Edinburgh from the cloud of smoke or reek that is always impending over it.

[3] To braw tippony. She sold the Scots pint, which is near two quarts English, for twopence.

[4] Maggy dang. 'He dings, or dang', is a phrase which means 'to excel or get the better'.

When in our poutch we fand some clinks,
And took a turn o'er Bruntsfield-Links,[1] 20
Aften in Maggy's at Hy-jinks,[2]
We guzled scuds,
Till we could scarce, wi hale-out drinks,
Cast aff our duds.

We drank and drew, and filled again, 25
Oh wow, but we were blyth and fain!
When ony had their count mistain,
Oh, it was nice,
To hear us a' cry, 'Pike yer bain[3]
And spell yer dice.' 30

Fou closs we used to drink and rant,
Until we did baith glowre and gaunt,

19 poutch *pouch* fand *found* clinks *money*
22 scuds *foaming ale*
23 hale-out *down in one*
24 duds *clothes*
26 fain *eager*
27 mistain *mistaken*
30 spell *play*
31 closs *close*
32 gaunt *yawn*

[1] Bruntsfield Links. Fields between Edinburgh and Maggy's where the citizens' commonly play at the gowff.

[2] Hy-jinks. A drunken game, or new project to drink and be rich; thus, the quaff or cup is filled to the brim, then one of the company takes a pair of dice and after crying 'Hy-jinks' he throws them out. The number he casts up points out the person [who] must drink, he who threw beginning at himself number one and so round till the number of the person[s] agree with that of the dice (which may fall upon himself if the number be within twelve); then he sets the dice to him, or bids him take them. He on whom they fall is obliged to drink or pay a small forfeiture in money, then throws, and so on; but if he forget to cry 'Hy-jinks' he pays a forfeiture into the bank. Now he on whom it falls to drink, if there be anything in bank worth drawing, gets it all if he drinks. Then with a great deal of caution he empties his cup, sweeps up the money, and orders the cup to be filled again, and then throws; for if he err in the articles, he loses the privilege of drawing the money. The articles are: (1) drink; (2) draw; (3) fill; (4) cry 'Hy-jinks'; (5) count just; (6) choose your doublet man, *viz.*, when two equal numbers of the dice is thrown, the person whom you choose must pay a double of the common forfeiture, and so must you when the dice is in his hand. A rare project this, and no bubble I can assure you; for a covetous fellow may save money and get himself as drunk as he can desire in less than an hour's time.

[3] Pike yer bain. Is a cant phrase; when one leaves a little in the cup, he is advised to pike his bone, i.e., drink it clean out.

And pish and spew, and yesk and maunt,
  Right swash I true;
Then of auld stories we did cant 35
  Whan we were fou.

Whan we were wearied at the gowff,
Then Maggy Johnston's was our howff;
Now a' our gamesters may sit dowff,
  Wi' hearts like lead, 40
Death wi' his rung raxed her a yowff,[1]
  And sae she died.

Maun we be forced thy skill to tine?
For which we will right sair repine;
Or hast thou left to bairns of thine 45
  The pauky knack
Of brewing ale amaist like wine?
  That gared us crack.

Sae brawly did a pease-scon toast
Biz i' the queff, and flie the frost;[2] 50
There we gat fou wi' little cost,
  And muckle speed,
Now wae worth death, our sport's a' lost,
  Since Maggy's dead.

Ae simmer night[3] I was sae fou, 55
Amang the riggs I geed to spew;

33 yesk *hiccup* maunt *stutter*
34 swash *fuddled*
37 gowff *golf*
38 howff *favourite pub*
39 dowff *gloomy*
41 rung *cudgel* raxed *reached*
  yowff *blow*
48 crack *boast*
50 biz *buzz* queff *drinking cup*
  flie *scare off*
56 riggs *fields*

---

[1] Raxed her a youff. Reached her a blow.
[2] Flie the frost. Or fright the frost or coldness out of it.
[3] Ae simmer night, etc. The two following stanzas are a true narrative.

> On that slid place where I 'maist brake my bains,
> To be a warning I set up twa stains,
> That nane may venture there as I have done,
> Unless wi' frosted nails he clink his shoon.

Syne down on a green bawk, I trow
  I took a nap,
And soucht a' night balillilow
  As sound's a tap. 60

And whan the dawn begoud to glow,
I hirsled up my dizzy pow,
Frae 'mang the corn like wirricow,
  Wi' bains sae sair,
And ken' nae mair than if a ew 65
  How I came there.

Some said it was the pith of broom
That she stowed in her masking-loom,
Which in our heads raised sic a foom,
  Or some wild seed, 70
Which aft the chaping stoup did toom,
  But filled our head.

But now since 'tis sae that we must
Not in the best ale put our trust,
But whan we're auld return to dust, 75
  Without remead,
Why should we tak it in disgust
  That Maggy's dead?

Of warldly comforts she was rife,
And lived a lang and hearty life, 80
Right free of care, or toil, or strife,
  Till she was stale,
And kenned to be a canny wife
  At brewing ale.

Then farewell Maggy douce and fell, 85
Of brewers a' thou boor the bell;

57 bawk *ridge*
59 soucht *sought* balillilow *lullaby*
60 tap *top*
61 begoud *began*
62 hirsled *rustled* pow *head*
63 wirricow *scarecrow*
64 bains *bones*
68 stowed *stuffed* masking-loom *mash-vat*
69 foom *fume*
71 chaping *chopin, a measure of drink*
76 remead *remedy*
79 rife *well supplied*
85 douce *prudent* fell *capable*
86 boor the bell *took the prize*

Let a' thy gossies yelp and yell,
  And without feed,
Guess whether ye're in heaven or hell,
  They're sure ye're dead. 90

EPITAPH
O Rare Maggy Johnston.

87 gossies *gossips, friends* 88 feed *dispute*

The Life and Acts of, or An Elegy on Patie Birnie

The famous fidler of Kinghorn;
Who gart the lieges gawff and girn ay,
Aft till the cock proclaimed the morn:
Though baith his weeds and mirth were pirny,[1]
He roosed these things were langest worn,
The brown ale barrel was his kirn ay,
And faithfully he toomed his horn.

And then besides his valliant acts,
At bridals he wan mony placks.
Hab. Simpson.

In sonnet slee the man I sing,
His rare engine in rhyme shall ring,
Wha slaid the stick out o'er the string
With sic an art;
Wha sang sae sweetly to the spring, 5
And raised the heart.

Kinghorn may rue the ruefou day
That lighted Patie to his clay,
Wha gart the hearty billies stay
And spend their cash, 10
To see his snowt, to hear him play,
And gab sae gash.

When strangers landed,[2] wow, sae thrang
Fuffin and peghing he wad gang

Intro gawff *laugh* girn *grin* pirny *uneven* roosed *praised* kirn *churn* placks *small coins*
1 slee *sly*
2 engine *ingenuity*
3 slaid *slid*
5 spring *tune*
9 billies *fellows*
11 snowt *snout, face*
12 gash *clever*
13 thrang *busily*
14 fuffin *blowing* peghing *panting*

[1] Weeds and mirth were pirny. When a piece of stuff is wrought unequally, part coarse and part fine, of yarn of different colours, we call it pirny, from the pirn or little hollow reed which holds the yarn in the shuttle.

[2] When strangers landed. It was his custom to watch when strangers went into a public house and attend them, pretending they had sent for him and that he could not get away sooner from other company.

And crave their pardon that sae lang 15
He'd been a coming;
Syne his bread-winner out he'd bang,
And fa' to bumming.

Your honour's father[1] dead and gane,
For him he first wad make his mane, 20
But soon his face could make ye fain[2]
When he did sough,
'O wiltu, wiltu do't again!'[3]
And graned and leugh.

This sang he made[4] frae his ain head, 25
And eke 'The auld man's mare she's dead,
Though peets and tures and a's to lead,'
Oh fy upon her!
A bonny auld thing this indeed,
An't like yer honour. 30

After ilk tune he took a sowp,
And banned wi' birr the corky cowp,[5]
That to the Papists' country scowp,
To lear 'Ha ha's',
Frae chiels that sing hap, stap, and lowp, 35
Wantin the ba's.

17 bang *hurry*
18 bumming *buzzing*
22 sough *sigh*
24 leugh *laughed*
27 peets *peats* turs *turfs* lead *bring home*
31 sowp *drink*
32 banned *cursed* birr *energy* corky cowp *feather-brained crowd*
33 Papists' country *Italy* scowp *run*
34 chiels *fellows* hap, stap and lowp *hop, step and jump*
36 wantin the ba's *castrato*

[1] Your honour's father. It was his first compliment to one (though he had never perhaps seen him, nor any of his predecessors) that well he kend his honour's father, and been merry with him, and an excellent good-fellow he was.

[2] Soon . . . fain. Shewing a very particular comicalness in his looks and gestures, laughing and groaning at the same time, he plays, sings, and breaks in with some queer tale twice or thrice e'er he get through the tune. His beard is no small addition to the diversion.

[3] O wiltu. The name of a tune he played on all occasions.

[4] This . . . made. He boasted of being poet as well as musician.

[5] Banned . . . cowp, etc. Cursed strongly the light-headed fellows who run to Italy to learn soft music.

That beardless capons are na men,
We by their fozie springs might ken;
But ours he said could vigour len'
  To men o' weir, 40
And gar them stout to battle sten'
  Withoutten fear.

How first he practised, ye shall hear,
The harn-pan of an umquhile mare,
He strung, and strak sounds saft and clear, 45
  Out o' the pow,
Which fired his saul, and gart his ear
  With gladness glow.

Sae some auld-gabet poets tell,
Jove's nimble son and leckie snell 50
Made the first fiddle of a shell,[1]
  On which Apollo,
With meikle pleasure played himsel
  Baith jig and solo.

O Jonny Stocks[2] what comes o' thee? 55
I'm sure thou'lt break thy heart and die;
Thy Birnie gane, thou'lt never be
  Nor blyth nor able
To shake thy short houghs merrily
  Upon a table. 60

How pleasant was't to see thee diddle,
And dance sae finely to his fiddle,

38 fozie springs *soft tunes*
40 weir *war*
41 sten' *march*
44 harn-pan *brain-pan* umquhile *deceased*
45 strak *stroked*
46 pow *head*
47 saul *soul*
50 Jove *Jupiter, father of the gods* leckie snell *lackey keen*
52 Apollo *god of music*
59 houghs *thighs*
61 diddle *dance*

[1] Tuque testudo, resonare septem
  Callida nervis.
    Horace.

[2] Jonny Stocks. A man of low stature but very broad, a loving friend of his, who used to dance to his music.

With nose forgainst a lass's middle,
  And briskly brag,
With cutty steps to ding their striddle, 65
  And gar them fag.

He catched a crishy webster loun
At runkling o' his deary's gown,
And wi' a rung came o'er his crown,
  For being there; 70
But starker thrums got Patie down,
  And knoost him sair.

Wae worth the dog, he maist had felled him,
Revengfu' Pate aft greened to geld him,
He awed a mends, and that he telled him, 75
  And banned to do't,
He took the tid, and fairly selled him
  For a recruit.

Pate was a carle of canny sense,
And wanted ne'er a right bein spence,[1] 80
And laid up dollars in defence
  'Gainst eild and gout,
Well judging gear in future tense
  Could stand for wit.

Yet prudent fowk may take the pet; 85
Anes thrawart porter[2] wadna let

65 cutty *short* ding *beat* striddle *striding*
66 fag *tire*
67 crishy webster *greasy weaver*
68 runkling *rumpling*
69 rung *cudgel*
71 thrums *ill-humour*
72 knoost *bruised*
74 greened *yearned*
75 awed a mends *owed revenge*
76 banned *swore*
77 tid *opportunity*
79 carle *fellow*
80 bein spence *well-stocked larder*
82 eild *age*
85 take the pet *take offence*
86 thrawart *obstructive*

---

[1] Bein spence. Good store of provision, the spence being a little apartment for meal, flesh, etc.

[2] Anes thrawart porter, etc. This happened in the Duke of Rothes's time; his grace was giving an entertainment and Patrick being denied entry by the servants he either from a cunning view of the lucky consequence or in a passion did what's described.

Him in while latter-meat was het,
  He gawed fou sair,
Flang in his fiddle o'er the yet,
  Whilk ne'er did mair. 90

But profit may arise frae loss,
Sae Pate gat comfort by his cross:
Soon as he wan within the closs,
  He dously drew in
Mair gear frae ilka gentle goss 95
  Than bought a new ane.

When lying bedfast sick and sair,
To parish priest he promised fair,
He ne'er wad drink fou ony mair:
  But hale and tight, 100
He proved the auld-man to a hair,
  Strute ilka night.

The haly dad with care essays
To wile him frae his wanton ways,
And telled him of his promise twice: 105
  Pate answered cliver,
'Wha tents what people raving says
  When in a fever?'

At Bothwell-Brig[1] he gade to fight,
But being wise as he was wight, 110
He thought it shawed a saul but slight,
  Dauftly to stand,
And let gun-powder wrang his sight,
  Or fidle-hand.

87 het *hot*
88 gawed *was irritated*
89 flang *flung* yet *gate*
93 closs *yard*
94 dously *prudently*
95 gear *money* goss *friend*
102 strute *crammed*
103 haly *holy*
107 tents *heeds*
109 brig *bridge*
110 wight *clever*
111 slight *cunning*
112 dauftly *stupidly*

[1] Bothwell-Brig. Upon Clyde, where the famous battle was fought, anno 1679, for the determination of some kittle points. But I dare not assert that it was religion carried my hero to the field.

Right pawkily he left the plain, 115
Nor o'er his shoulder looked again,
But scoured o'er moss and moor amain,
  To Rieky straight,
And tald how mony Whigs were slain
  Before they faught. 120

Sae I've lamented Patie's end;
But least your grief o'er far extend,
Come dight your cheeks, ye'r brows unbend,
  And lift yer head,
For to a' Britain be it kend 125
  He is not dead.

January 25, 1721.

117 scoured *rushed* moss *bog* 123 dight *wipe*
119 tald *told* Whigs *rebels*

Elegy on John Cowper Kirk-Treasurer's Man, Anno 1714[1]

I wairn ye a' to greet and drone,
John Cowper's dead, ohon, ohon!
To fill his post, alake there's none,
That with sic speed
Could sar sculdudry[2] out like John, 5
But now he's dead.

He was right nacky in his way,
And eydent baith be night and day,
He wi' the lads his part could play,
When right sair fleed, 10
He gart them good bill-siller[3] pay,
But now he's dead.

1 wairn *warn* greet weep
2 ohon *alas*
5 sar *savour, smell* sculdudry *fornication*
7 nacky *skilful*
8 eydent *diligent*
10 fleed *afraid*

---

[1] 'Tis necessary for the illustration of this elegy to strangers to let them a little into the history of the kirk-treasurer and his man; the treasurer is chosen every year, a citizen respected for riches and honesty; he is vested with an absolute power to seize and imprison the girls that are too impatient to have on their green gown before it be hemmed; them he strictly examines, but no liberty to be granted till a fair account be given of those persons they have obliged. It must be so: a list is frequently given sometimes of a dozen or thereby of married or unmarried unfair traders whom they secretly assisted in running their goods. These his lordship makes pay to some purpose according to their ability, for the use of the poor: if the lads be obstreporous, the kirk-session, and worst of all, the stool of repentance is threatened, a punishment which few of any spirit can bear.

The treasurer being changed every year never comes to be perfectly acquainted with the affair; but their general servant continuing for a long time is more expert at discovering such persons and the places of their resort, which makes him capable to do himself and customers both a good or an ill turn. John Cowper maintained this post with activity and good success for several years.

[2] Sa'r sculdudry. In allusion to a scent dog, 'sa'r' from 'savour' or 'smell', 'sculdudry' a name commonly given to whoring.

[3] Bill-silver. Bull silver.

'She saw the cow well serv'd, and took a groat.'
Gay

Of whore-hunting he gat his fill,
And made be't mony pint and gill:
Of his braw post he thought nae ill, 15
  Nor did nae need,
Now they may mak a kirk and mill
  O't, since he's dead.

Although he was nae man of weir,
Yet mony a ane, wi quaking fear, 20
Durst scarce afore his face appear,
  But hide their head;
The wylie carl he gathered gear,
  And yet he's dead.

Ay now to some part far awa, 25
Alas he's gane and left it a'!
May be to some sad whilliwhaw[1]
  O' fremit blood,
'Tis an ill wind that dis na blaw
  Some body good. 30

Fy upon Death, he was to blame
To whirl poor John to his lang hame:
But though his arse be cauld, yet fame,
  Wi' tout of trumpet,
Shall tell how Cowper's awfou name 35
  Could flie a strumpet.

He kend the bawds and louns fou well,
And where they used to rant and reel,
He paukily on them could steal,
  And spoil their sport; 40
Aft did they wish the muckle De'il
  Might tak him for't.

17 make a kirk and mill *make the best*
19 weir *war*
23 gear *possessions*
27 whilliwhaw *flatterer*
28 fremit *foreign*
29 dis *does*
35 awfou *awful*
36 flie *frighten*
37 louns *rogues*
38 rant *romp*
39 paukily *craftily*

[1] Whilliwha o' fremit blood. Whilliwha is a kind of insinuating deceitful fellow; fremit blood, not a kin, because he had then no legitimate heirs of his own body.

But ne'er a ane of them he spared,
E'en though there was a drunken laird
To draw his sword, and make a faird[1] 45
 In their defence,
John quietly put them in the Guard
 To learn mair sense.

There maun they ly till sober grown,
The lad neist day his fault maun own; 50
And to keep a' things hush and lown,
 He minds the poor,[2]
Syne after a' his ready's flown,
 He damns the whore.

And she, poor jade, withoutten din, 55
Is sent to Leith-Wynd fit[3] to spin,
With heavy heart and cleathing thin,
 And hungry wame,
And ilky month a well paid skin,
 To mak her tame. 60

But now they may scour up and down,
And safely gang their wakes arown,
Spreading the clap throw a' the town,
 But fear or dread;
For that great kow to bawd and lown, 65
 John Cowper's dead.

Shame faw yer chandler chafts,[4] o Death;
For stapping of John Cowper's breath;

44 laird *lord*
45 faird *bustle*
47 Guard *see note*
51 lown *calm*
52 minds *remembers*
56 fit *foot*
58 wame *stomach*
61 scour *rush*
62 wakes *wanderings*
65 kow *goblin*
67 chandler *candlestick* chafts *cheeks*

---

[1] Make a faird. A bustle like a bully.
[2] He minds the poor. Pays hush money to the treasurer.
[3] Leith-Wynd fit. The house of correction at the foot of Leith-Wynd, such as Bridewell in London.
[4] Chandler chafts. Lean or meagre cheeked, when the bones appear like the sides or corners of a candlestick, which in Scots we call a chandler.

The loss of him is public skaith:
  I dare well say, 70
To quat the grip he was right laith
  This mony a day.

POSTSCRIPT

Of umquhile John to lie or bann,
Shaws but ill will, and looks right shan,
But some tell odd tales of the man, 75
  For fifty head
Can gi'e their aith they've seen him gawn[1]
  Since he was dead.

Keek but up through the Stinking Stile,[2]
On Sunday morning a wee while, 80
At the kirk door out frae an isle,
  It will appear;
But tak good tent ye dinna file
  Yer breeks for fear.

For well we wat it is his ghaist, 85
Wow, wad some fouk that can do't best[3]
Speak till't, and hear what it confest;
  'Tis a good deed
To send a wand'ring saul to rest
  Amang the dead. 90

69 skaith *harm*
71 quat *quit* laith *loath*
73 umquhile *former* bann *curse*
74 shan *shabby*
77 aith *oath*
79 keek *look*
81 isle *aisle*
83 tent *care* file *defile*
84 breeks *breeches*
85 wat *know* ghaist *ghost*
89 saul *soul*

[1] Seen him gawn. The common people, when they tell their tales of ghosts appearing, they say he has been seen 'gawn' or stalking.
[2] Stinking Stile. Opposite to this place is the door of the church which he attends, being a beadle.
[3] Wow . . . do't best. 'Tis another vulgar notion that a ghost will not be laid to rest till some priest speak to it and get account what disturbs it.

To the Right Honourable, The Town-Council of Edinburgh, the Address of Allan Ramsay

Your poet humbly means and shaws,
That contrair to just rights and laws
  I've suffered muckle wrang
By Lucky Reid,[1] and ballad singers,
Wha thumbed with their coarse dirty fingers 5
  Sweet Edie's funeral-sang.
They spoiled my sense and staw my cash,
  My muses pride murgullied,
And printing it like their vile trash,
  The honest lieges whillied. 10
    Thus undone, to London[2]
    It gade to my disgrace,
    Sae pimpin and limpin
    In rags wi' bluthered face.

Yet gleg-eyed friends through the disguise 15
Received it as a dainty prize
  For a' it was sae hav'ren,
Gart Lintot take it to his press,
And clead it in a braw new dress,
  Syne took it to the tavern. 20
But though it was made clean and braw,
  Sae sair it had been knoited,

2 contrair *contrary*
3 wrang *wrong*
6 Edie *Joseph Addison* sang *song*
7 staw *stole*
8 murgullied *besmirched*
10 whillied *cheated*
13 pimpin *mean*
14 bluthered *tear-stained*
15 gleg *keen*
17 hav'ren *nonsensical*
18 Lintot *London publisher*
19 clead *clad*
22 knoited *beaten*

---

[1] Lucky Reid. A printer's relict, who with the hawkers reprinted my pastoral on Mr Addison, without my knowledge on ugly paper, full of errors.

[2] To London. One of their uncorrect copies was reprinted at London by Bernard Lintot in Folio first before he printed it a second time from a correct copy of my own, with the honourable Mr Burchet's English version of it.

It blathered buff[1] before them a',
And aftentimes turned doited.
It grieved me and reaved me 25
Of kindly sleep and rest,
By carlings and gorlings
To be sae sair opprest.

Wherefore to you ne'er kend to guide ill,
But wisely had the good town's bridle, 30
My case I plainly tell,
And, as your ain,[2] plead I may have
Your word of weight,[3] when now I crave
To guide my gear my sell.
Then clean and fair the type shall be, 35
The paper like the snaw,
Nor shall our town think shame wi' me,
When we gang far awa.
What's wanted if granted
Beneath your honoured wing, 40
Baith hantily and cantily
Your supplicant shall sing.[4]

23 blathered *chattered* buff *nonsense*
24 doited *crazy*
25 reaved *robbed*
27 carlings *old women* gorlings *youngsters*
34 gear *property* sell *self*
36 snaw *snow*
41 hantily *handsomely* cantily *cheerfully*

---

[1] Blathered buff. Spoke nonsense, from words being wanting and many wrong spelled and changed, such as 'gras' for 'gars', 'praise' for 'phrase', etc.
[2] As your ain. A free citizen.
[3] Your word of weight. To interpose their just authority in my favour, and grant me an act to ward off these little pirates, which I gratefully acknowledge the receipt of.
[4] Shall sing. There being abundance of their petitioners who daily oblige themselves to pray.

Epistle I [William Hamilton of Gilbertfield to Allan Ramsay]

Gilbertfield June 26th, 1719.

O famed and celebrated Allan!
Renowned Ramsay, canty callan,
There's nowther Highlandman nor Lawlan,
  In poetrie,
But may as soon ding down Tamtallan 5
  As match wi' thee.

For ten times ten, and that's a hunder,
I ha'e been made to gaze and wonder,
When frae Parnassus thou didst thunder,
  Wi' wit and skill, 10
Wherefore I'll soberly knock under,
  And quat my quill.

Of poetry the hail quintessence
Thou hast sucked up, left nae excrescence
To petty poets, or sic messens, 15
  Though round thy stool,
They may pick crumbs, and lear some lessons
  At Ramsay's school.

Though Ben and Dryden of renown
Were yet alive in London Town, 20
Like kings contending for a crown,
  'Twad be a pingle,
Whilk o' you three wad gar words sound
  And best to jingle.

Transformed may I be to a rat, 25
Wer't in my pow'r but I'd create
Thee upo' sight the Laureat
  Of this our age,

2 canty *cheerful* callan *fellow*
3 nowther *neither* Lawlan *Lowlander*
5 ding *beat* Tamtallan *Tantallon Castle*
12 quat *quit*
15 messens *mongrels*
19 Ben and Dryden *see note*
22 pingle *quarrel*

Since thou may'st fairly claim to that
 As thy just wage. 30

Let modern poets bear the blame
Gin they respect not Ramsay's name,
Wha soon can gar them greet for shame,
 To their great loss;
And send them a' right sneaking hame 35
 Be weeping-cross.

Wha bourds wi' thee had need be warry,
And lear wi' skill thy thrust to parry,
When thou consults thy dictionary
 Of ancient words, 40
Which come from thy poetic quarry,
 As sharp as swords.

Now though I should baith reel and rottle,
And be as light as Aristotle,
At Ed'nburgh we sall ha'e a bottle 45
 Of reaming claret,
Gin that my haff-pay siller shottle
 Can safely spare it.

At crambo then we'll rack our brain,
Drown ilk dull care and aiking pain, 50
Whilk aften does our spirits drain
 Of true content;
Wow, wow, but we's be wonder fain,
 When thus acquaint.

Wi' wine we'll gargarize our craig, 55
Then enter in a lasting league,
Free of ill aspect or intrigue,
 And gin you please it,
Like princes when met at the Hague,
 We'll solemnize it. 60

37 bourds *jests* warry *wary*
43 rottle *rattle*
46 reaming *foaming*
47 shottle *small drawer*
49 crambo *rhyme*
50 aiking *aching*
53 fain *fond*
55 gargarize *gargle* craig *throat*
59 the Hague *see note*

Accept of this and look upon it
With favour, though poor I have done it;
Sae I conclude and end my sonnet,
  Who am most fully,
While I do wear a hat or bonnet, 65
  Yours – wanton Willy.

POSTSCRIPT
By this my postscript I incline
To let you ken my hail design
Of sic a lang imperfect line,
  Lyes in this sentence: 70
To cultivate my dull ingine
  By your acquaintance.

Your answer therefore I expect,
And to your friend you may direct,
At Gilbertfield do not neglect 75
  When ye have leisure,
Which I'll embrace with great respect
  And perfect pleasure.

71 ingine *wit*

Answer I [Allan Ramsay to William Hamilton of Gilbertfield]

Edinburgh, July 10th, 1719.

Sonse fa me, witty, wanton Willy,
Gin blyth I was na as a filly;
Not a fow pint, nor short hought gilly,
  Or wine that's better,
Could please sae meikle, my dear Billy, 5
  As thy kind letter.

Before a lord and eik a knight,
In Gossy Don's be candle light,
There first I saw't, and ca'd it right,
  And the maist feck 10
Wha's seen't sinsyne, they ca'd as tight
  As that on Heck.

Ha, heh! thought I, I canna say
But I may cock my nose the day,
When Hamilton the bauld and gay 15
  Lends me a heezy,
In verse that slides sae smooth away,
  Well telled and easy.

Sae roosed by ane of well kend mettle,
Nae sma did my ambition pettle 20
My cankered critics it will nettle,
  And e'en sae be't:
This month I'm sure I winna fettle,
  Sae proud I'm wi't.

1 sonse *prosperity*
3 fow *full* hought gilly *see note*
7 eik *also*
8 Gossy Don's *Edinburgh pub*
  be *by*
10 feck *part*
11 sinsyne *since then*
12 Heck *see note*
16 heezy *lift*
19 roosed *praised*
20 pettle *seem flattered*
23 fettle *get to work*

When I begoud first to cun verse, 25
And could your Ardry Whins[1] rehearse,
Where Bonny Heck ran fast and fierce,
  It warmed my breast;
Then emulation did me pierce,
  Whilk since ne'er ceast. 30

May I be licket wi' a bittle,
Gin of your numbers I think little;
Ye're never rugget, shan, nor kittle,
  But blyth and gabby,
And hit the spirit to a tittle, 35
  Of Standart Habby.[2]

Ye'll quat your quill! That were ill-willy,
Ye's sing some mair yet, nill ye will ye,
O'er meikle haining wad but spill ye,
  And gar ye sour, 40
Then up and war them a' yet, Willy,
  'Tis in your power.

To knit up dollers in a clout,
And then to eard them round about,
Syne to tell up, they downa lout 45
  To lift the gear;
The malison lights on that rout,
  Is plain and clear.

The chiels of London, Cam, and Ox,
Ha'e raised up great poetic stocks 50

25 begoud *began* cun *learn*
31 licket *struck* bittle *mallet*
33 rugget *strained* shan *shabby* kittle *puzzling*
34 gabby *chatty*
36 Standart Habby *see note*
37 quat *quit*
39 haining *abstaining* spill *spoil*
41 war *excel*
43 clout *cloth*
44 eard *earth, bury*
45 tell *count* downa lout *cannot stoop*
46 gear *property*
47 malison *curse* rout *gang*
49 chiels *lads* Cam, and Ox *Cambridge and Oxford*

---

[1] Ardry Whins. The last words of *Bonny Heck*, of which he was author.
[2] Standart Habby. The elegy on Habby Simpson, Piper of Kilbarchan, a finished piece of its kind.

Of Rapes, of Buckets, Sarks and Locks,
While we neglect
To shaw their betters. This provokes
Me to reflect

On the leared days of Gawn Dunkell,[1] 55
Our country then a tale could tell,
Europe had nane mair snack and snell
At verse or prose;
Our kings[2] were poets too themsell,
Bauld and jocose. 60

To Ed'nburgh, sir, when e'er ye come,
I'll wait upon ye, there's my thumb,
Were't frae the Gill-bells to the Drum,
And take a bout,
And faith I hope we'll no sit dumb, 65
Nor yet cast out.

51 Of Rapes, of Buckets, Sarks and Locks *see note*
55 leared *learned* Gawn Dunkell *see note*
57 snack *active* snell *sharp*
66 cast out *quarrel*

[1] Gawn Dunkell. Gawn Douglas, brother to the Earl of Angus, Bishop of Dunkell, who besides several original poems hath left a most exact translation of Vergil's *Æneis*.
[2] James the First and Fifth.

Epistle II [Hamilton to Ramsay]

Gilbertfield, July 24th, 1719.

Dear Ramsay,

When I received thy kind epistle,
It made me dance, and sing, and whistle;
O sic a fyke, and sic a fistle
  I had about it!
That e'er was knight of the Scots thistle 5
  Sae fain, I doubted.

The bonny lines therein thou sent me,
How to the nines they did content me;
Though, sir, sae high to compliment me,
  Ye might deferred, 10
For had ye but haff well a kent me,
  Some less wad ser'd.

With joyfou heart beyond expression,
They're safely now in my possession:
Oh gin I were a winter-session 15
  Near by thy lodging,
I'd closs attend thy new profession,
  Without e'er budging.

In even down earnest, there's but few
To vie with Ramsay dare avow, 20
In verse, for to gi'e thee thy due,
  And without fleetching,
Thou's better at that trade, I trow,
  Than some's at preaching.

For my part, till I'm better leart, 25
To troke with thee I'd best forbear't;
For an' the fouk of Edn'burgh hear't,
  They'll ca' me daft,

3 fyke *twitch* fistle *fidget*
5 knight of the Scots thistle *see note*
6 fain *pleased*
12 ser'd *served*
17 closs *closely*
22 fleetching *flattery*
25 leart *learned, taught*
26 troke *barter, deal*

I'm unco' irie and dirt-feart
  I make wrang waft. 30

Thy verses nice as ever nicket,
Made me as canty as a cricket;
I ergh to reply, lest I stick it,
  Syne like a coof
I look, or ane whose poutch is picket 35
  As bare's my loof.

Heh, winsom, how thy saft sweet style,
And bonny auld words gar me smile;
Thou's travelled sure mony a mile
  Wi' charge and cost, 40
To learn them thus keep rank and file,
  And ken their post.

For I maun tell thee, honest Allie
(I use the freedom so to call thee),
I think them a' sae bra and wallie, 45
  And in sic order,
I wad nae care to be thy valet,
  Or thy recorder.

Has thou with Rosycrucians wandert?
Or through some doncie desert dandert, 50
That with thy magic, town and landart,
  For ought I see,
Maun a' come truckle to thy standart
  Of poetrie?

Do not mistake me, dearest heart, 55
As if I charged thee with black art;
'Tis thy good genius still alart,
  That does inspire
Thee with ilk thing that's quick and smart,
  To thy desire. 60

29 irie *eerie* feart *fearful*
30 waft *weaving*
31 nicket *clicked*
32 canty *cheerful*
33 ergh *hesitate*
34 coof *fool*
36 loof *palm of the hand*
45 wallie *fine*
49 Rosycrucians *see note*
50 doncie *dull* dandert *sauntered*
51 landart *country*
57 alart *alert*

E'en mony a bonny knacky tale,
Bra to set o'er a pint of ale:
For fifty guineas I'll find bail,
  Against a boddle,
That I wad quat ilk day a mail, 65
  For sic a noddle.

And on condition I were as gabby,
As either thee, or honest Habby,
That I lined a' thy claes wi' tabby,
  Or velvet plush, 70
And then thou'd be sae far frae shabby,
  Thou'd look right sprush.

What though young empty airy sparks
May have their critical remarks
On thir my blyth diverting warks, 75
  'Tis sma presumption
To say they're but unlearned clarks,
  And want the gumption.

Let coxcomb critics get a tether
To tie up a' their lang loose lether; 80
If they and I chance to forgether,
  The tane may rue it,
For an' they winna had their blether,
  They's get a flewet.

To learn them for to peep and pry 85
In secret drolls 'twixt thee and I,
Pray dip thy pen in wrath, and cry,
  And ca' them skellums;
I'm sure thou needs set little by
  To bide their bellums. 90

61 knacky *skilful*
64 boddle *small coin*
65 quat *quit* mail *rented farm*
66 noddle *head*
67 gabby *eloquent*
68 Habby *see note*
69 claes *clothes* tabby *silk taffeta*
72 sprush *smart*
80 lether *skin*
82 tane *the one of two*
83 blether *chatter*
84 flewet *slap*
88 skellums *scoundrels*
90 bellums *blows*

Wi' writing I'm so bleirt and doited,
That when I raise, in troth I stoited;
I thought I should turn capernoited,
  For wi' a gird,
Upon my bum I fairly cloited 95
  On the cald eard.

Which did oblige a little dumple
Upon my doup, close by my rumple:
But had ye seen how I did trumple,
  Ye'd split your side, 100
Wi' mony a long and weary wimple,
  Like trough of Clyde.

91 bleirt *bleary* doited *crazy*
92 raise *rose up* stoited *staggered*
93 capernoited *crazy*
94 gird *blow*
95 cloited *fell heavily*
96 eard *earth*
97 dumple *impression*
98 doup *bottom* rumple *rump*
99 trumple *go into spasms*
101 wimple *twist*
102 Clyde *a river*

Answer II [Ramsay to Hamilton]

Edinburgh, August 4th, 1719.

Dear Hamilton ye'll turn me dyver,
My muse sae bonny ye descrive her,
Ye blaw her sae, I'm feared ye rive her,
  For wi' a whid,
Gin ony higher up ye drive her, 5
  She'll rin red-wood.[1]

Said I, 'Whisht,' quoth the vougy jade,
'William's a wise judicious lad,
Has havins mair than e'er ye had,
  Ill bred bog-stalker;[2] 10
But me ye ne'er sae crouse had crawed,
  Ye poor scull-thacker.[3]

'It sets you well indeed to gadge![4]
E'er I t'Appollo did ye cadge,
And got ye on his honour's badge, 15
  Ungratefou beast,
A Glasgow capon and a fadge[5]
  Ye thought a feast.

1 dyver *debtor*
2 descrive *describe*
3 blaw *praise* rive *split*
4 whid *gust*
6 red-wood *stark mad*
7 whisht *silence* vougy jade *conceited girl*
9 havins *good manners*
11 crouse *confident* crawed *crowed*
13 gadge *talk grandly*
14 Apollo *god of poetry* cadge *peddle*
17 fadge *barley loaf*

---

[1] Rin red-wood. Run distracted.

[2] Ill . . . me, etc. The muse, not unreasonably angry, puts me here in mind of the favours she has done by bringing me from stalking over bogs or wild marishes to lift my head a little brisker among the polite world, which could never been acquired by the low movements of a mechanick.

[3] Scull-thacker, i.e., thatcher of skulls.

[4] It . . . gadge. Ironically she says it becomes me mighty well to talk haughtily and afront my benefactoress by alledging so meanly that it were possible to praise her out of her solidity.

[5] A Glasgow capon, etc. A herring. A fadge. A coarse kind of leavened bread, used by the common people.

'Swith to Castalius' fountain-brink,
Dad down a grouf,[1] and take a drink, 20
Syne whisk out paper, pen and ink,
And do my bidding;
Be thankfou, else I'se gar ye stink
Yet on a midding.'

My mistress dear, your servant humble, 25
Said I, I should be laith to drumble
Your passions, or e'er gar ye grumble,
'Tis ne'er be me
Shall scandalize, or say ye bummil
Ye'r Poetrie. 30

Frae what I've telled, my friend may learn
How sadly I ha'e been forfairn,
I'd better been a yont side Kairn-
amount,[2] I trow;
I've kissed the taz[3] like a good bairn, 35
Now, sir to you.

Heal be your heart, gay couthy carle,
Lang may ye help to toom a barrel;
Be thy crown ay unclowred in quarrel,
When thou inclines 40
To knoit thrawn gabbed sumphs that snarl
At our frank lines.

Ilk good chiel says, ye're well worth gowd,
And blythness on ye's well bestowed,
'Mang witty Scots ye'r name's be rowed, 45
Ne'er fame to tine;

19 swith *quickly* Castalius *fount of inspiration*
20 dad *fall* grouf *prone*
24 midding *midden*
26 laith *loath* drumble *muddy*
29 bummil *speak badly*
32 forfairn *abused*
33 yont *further*
35 taz *leather belt used for school punishment*
37 heal *sound* couthy carle *agreeable fellow*
38 toom *empty*
39 unclowred *unbeaten*
41 knoit *beat* thrawn gabbed sumphs *stubborn mouthed blockheads*
43 chiel *fellow*
45 rowed *listed*

---

[1] Dad down a grouf. Fall flat on your belly.
[2] Kairn-amount. A noted hill in the north of Scotland.
[3] I've . . . taz. Kissed the rod. Owned my fault like a good child.

The crooked clinkers shall be cowed,[1]
  But ye shall shine.

Set out the burnt side of your shin,[2]
For pride in poets is nae sin, 50
Glory's the prize for which they rin,
  And fame's their jo;
And wha blaws best the horn shall win:
  And wharefore no?

Quisquis vocabit nos vain-glorious, 55
Shaw scanter skill, than malos mores,
Multi et magni men before us
  Did stamp and swagger,
Probatum est, exemplum Horace,
  Was a bauld bragger. 60

Then let the doofarts fashed wi' spleen,
Cast up the wrang side of their een,
Pegh, fry and girn wi' spite and teen,
  And fa a flyting,
Laugh, for the lively lads will screen 65
  Us frae back-biting.

If that the gypsies dinna spung us,
And foreign whiskers ha'e na dung us;
Gin I can snifter through mundungus,
  Wi' boots and belt on,[3] 70
I hope to see you at St. Mungo's
  Atween and Beltan.

47 clinkers *rhymers*
52 jo *sweetheart*
55 quisquis vocabit nos *whoever will call us*
56 malos mores *bad manners*
57 multi et magni *many and great*
59 probatum est, exemplum Horace *this is proved by the example of Horace see note*
61 doofarts *stupid people* fashed *troubled*
63 pegh *gasp* fry *fret* girn *snarl* teen *rage*
64 flyting *scolding*
67 spung *rob*
68 dung *beaten*
69 snifter *sniff* mundungus *bad tobacco*
72 atween *between now* Beltan *first of May*

[1] The crooked clinkers, etc. The scribling rhimers, with their lame versification. Shall be cowed, i.e., shorn off.
[2] Set out . . . shin. As if one would say, walk stately with your toes out. An expression used when we would bid a person (merrily) look brisk.
[3] St Mungo's. The High Church of Glasgow.

Epistle III [Hamilton to Ramsay]

Gilbertfield, August 24th, 1719

Accept my third and last essay
Of rural rhyme, I humbly pray,
Bright Ramsay, and although it may
  Seem doilt and donsie,
Yet thrice of all things, I heard say, 5
  Was ay thought sonsie,

Wherefore I scarce could sleep or slumber,
Till I made up that happy number,
The pleasure counterpoised the cumber,
  In ev'ry part, 10
And snoov't away like three-hand omber,
  Sixpence a cart.

Of thy last poem, bearing date
August the fourth, I grant receipt;
It was sae bra, gart me look blate, 15
  'Maist tyne my senses,
And look just like poor country Kate
  In Lucky Spence's.

I shawed it to our parish priest,
Wha was as blyth as gi'm a feast; 20
He says, thou may had up thy creest,
  And craw fu' crouse,
The poets a' to thee's but jest,
  Not worth a souce.

Thy blyth and cheerfu' merry muse, 25
Of compliments is sae profuse;
For my good haivens dis me roose
  Sae very finely

4 doilt *stupid* donsie *dull*
6 sonsie *lucky*
9 cumber *trouble*
11 snoov't *whirled* omber *card game*
12 cart *card*
15 blate *bashful*
18 Lucky Spence *see Ramsay's poem*
21 creest *crest*
22 craw *crow* crouse *proud*
24 souce *blow*
27 haivens *good manners* roose *praise*

It were ill breeding to refuse
  To thank her kindly. 30

What though sometimes in angry mood,
When she puts on her barlick-hood,
Her dialect seem rough and rude;
  Let's ne'er be flee't,
But take our bit when it is good, 35
  And buffet wi't.

For gin we ettle anes to taunt her,
And dinna cawmly thole her banter,
She'll take the flings; verse may grow scanter,
  Syne wi' great shame 40
We'll rue the day that we do want her,
  Then wha's to blame?

But let us still her kindness culzie,
And wi' her never breed a toulzie,
For we'll bring aff but little spulzie 45
  In sic a barter;
And she'll be fair to gar us fulzie,
  And cry for quarter.

Sae little worth's my rhyming ware,
My pack I scarce dare apen mair, 50
Till I take better wi' the lair,
  My pen's sae blunted;
And a' for fear I file the fair,
  And be affronted.

The dull draff-drink makes me sae dowff, 55
A' I can do's but bark and yowff;
Yet set me in a claret howff,
  Wi' fowk that's chancy,

32 barlick-hood *drunken temper*
34 flee't *afraid*
35–36 bit and buffet *rough with the smooth*
37 ettle *try*
38 cawmly thole *calmly endure*
39 flings *sulks*
43 culzie *flatter*
44 toulzie *fight*
45 spulzie *plunder*
47 fulzie *defeat*
50 apen *open*
51 lair *learning*
53 file *defile*
55 draff *dregs* dowff *gloomy*
56 yowff *bark*
57 howff *pub*

My muse may len me then a gowff
  To clear my fancy. 60

Then Bacchus-like I'd bawl and bluster,
And a' the Muses 'bout me muster;
Sae merrily I'd squeeze the cluster,
  And drink the grape,
'Twad gie my verse a brighter lustre, 65
  And better shape.

The pow'rs aboon be still auspicious
To thy achievements maist delicious,
Thy poems sweet and nae way vicious,
  But blyth and kanny; 70
To see, I'm anxious and ambitious,
  Thy miscellany.

A' blessings, Ramsay, on thee row,
Lang may thou live, and thrive, and dow,
Until thou claw an auld man's pow; 75
  And through thy creed,
Be keeped frae the wirricow
  After thou's dead.

59 gowff *slap*
70 kanny *canny astute*
73 row *roll*
74 dow *go about*
75 claw *scratch* pow *head*
77 wirricow *devil*

Answer III [Ramsay to Hamilton]

Edinburgh, September 2nd, 1719.

My Trusty Trojan,

Thy last oration orthodox,
Thy innocent auldfarren jokes,
And sonsie saw of three provokes
  Me anes again,
Tod Lowrie like,[1] to loose my pocks, 5
  And pump my brain.

By a' your letters I ha'e read,
I eithly scan the man well bred,
And soger that where honour led,
  Has ventured bauld; 10
Wha now to youngsters leaves the yed
  To 'tend his fald.[2]

That bang'ster billy Cæsar July,
Wha at Pharsalia wan the tooly,
Had better sped, had he mair hooly 15
  Scampered thro' life,
And 'midst his glories sheathed his gooly,
  And kissed his wife.

Had he like you, as well he could,[3]
Upon burn banks the muses wooed, 20
Retired betimes frae 'mang the crowd,
  Wha'd been aboon him?
The senate's durks, and faction loud,
  Had ne'er undone him.

2 auldfarren *ingenious*
3 sonsie *hearty*
5 pock *bag*
9 soger *soldier*
11 yed *strife*
13 bang'ster billy *bullying fellow*
14 tooly *brawl* Pharsalia *see note*
15 hooly *carefully*
17 gooly *knife*
23 durks *dirks, knives*

[1] Tod . . . like. Like Reynard the Fox, to betake my self to some more of my wiles.

[2] Leaves . . . fald. Leaves the martial contention and retires to a country life.

[3] As . . . could. 'Tis well known he could write as well as fight.

Yet sometimes leave the riggs and bog, 25
Your howms, and braes, and shady scrog,
And helm-a-lee the claret cog,
To clear your wit:
Be blyth, and let the warld e'en shog,
As it thinks fit. 30

Ne'er fash about your neist year's state,
Nor with superior powers debate,
Nor cantrapes cast to ken your fate;
There's ills anew
To cram our days, which soon grow late; 35
Let's live just now.

When northern blasts the ocean snurl,
And gars the heights and hows look gurl,
Then left about the bumper whirl,
And toom the horn,[1] 40
Grip fast the hours which hasty hurl,
The morn's the morn.

Thus to Leuconoe[2] sang sweet Flaccus,
Wha nane e'er thought a gillygacus:
And why should we let whimsies bawk us, 45
When joy's in season,
And thole sae aft the spleen to whauk us
Out of our reason?

25 riggs *strips of farmland*
26 howms *low-lying land beside a river* scrog *undergrowth*
27 cog *pour into a cup*
29 shog *jogalong*
31 fash *worry*
33 cantrapes *spells*
34 anew *enough*
37 snurl *ruffle*
38 hows *hollows* gurl *stormy*
41 hurl *rush*
42 the morn *tomorrow*
43 Flaccus *Horace*
44 gillygacus *fool*
45 bawk *balk*
47 thole *suffer* whauk *whack*

[1] Toom . . . horn. 'Tis frequent in the country to drink beer out of horn cups, made in shape of a water glass.
[2] Thus to Leuconoe. Vide Book I, xi, Ode of Horace.

Tho I were laird of tenscore acres,
Nodding to jouks of hallenshakers,[3] 50
Yet crushed wi' humdrums, which the weaker's
Contentment ruins,
I'd rather roost wi' causey-rakers,
And sup cauld sowens.

I think, my friend, an fowk can get 55
A doll of rost beef pypin het,
And wi' red wine their wyson wet,
And cleathing clean,
And be nae sick, or drowned in debt,
They're no to mean. 60

I read this verse to my ain kimmer,
Wha kens I like a leg of gimmer,
Or sic and sic good belly timmer;
Quoth she, and leugh,
'Sicker of thae winter and simmer, 65
Ye're well enough.'

My hearty goss, there is nae help,
But hand to nive we twa maun skelp
Up Rhine and Thames, and o'er the Alp-
pines and Pyrenians, 70
The cheerfou carles do sae yelp
To ha'e 's their minions.

49 laird *lord*
50 jouks *bows*
51 humdrums *low spirits* weaker *insomniac*
53 causey-rakers *street-sweepers*
54 sowens *oats steeped in water and boiled*
56 doll *large piece* rost *roast* het *hot*
57 wyson *gullet*
60 mean *moan, complain*
61 kimmer *wife*
62 gimmer *a year-old ewe*
63 timmer *timber*
64 leugh *laughed*
67 goss *crony*
68 nive *fist* skelp *gallop*
71 carles *fellows*

[3] Hallenshakers. A hallen is a fence (built of stone, turf, or a moveable flake of heather) at the sides of the door in country places, to defend them from the wind. The trembling attendant about a forgetful great man's gate or levee is all expressed in the term hallenshaker.

Thy raffan rural rhyme sae rare,
Sic wordy, wanton, hand-wailed ware,
Sae gash and gay, gars folk gae gare[1] 75
  To ha'e them by them;
Tho gaffin they wi' sides sae sair,
  Cry, 'Wae gae by him!'[2]

Fair fa that sodger did invent
To ease the poets toil wi' print: 80
Now, William, we maun to the bent,
  And pouss our fortune,
And crack wi' lads wha're well content
  Wi' this our sporting.

Gin ony sour-mou'd girning bucky 85
Ca' me conceity keckling chucky,
That we like nags whase necks are yucky,
  Ha'e used our teeth;
I'll answer fine, 'Gae kiss yer lucky[3]
  She dwells i' Leith.' 90

I ne'er wi' lang tales fash my head,
But when I speak, I speak indeed:
Wha ca's me droll, but ony feed,
  I'll own I am sae,
And while my champers can chew bread, 95
  Yours – Allan Ramsay.

73 raffan *merry*
74 wordy *worthy* wailed *chosen*
75 gash *shrewd* gare *eager*
77 tho *then* gaffin *giddy*
81 bent *field*
82 pouss *push*
83 crack *chat*
85 sour-mou'd girning bucky *sour-mouthed whining obstinate person*
86 keckling chucky *cackling chicken*
87 yucky *itchy*
89 lucky *landlady*
90 Leith *port near Edinburgh*
93 feed *feud, quarrel*

[1] Gars . . . gare. Make people very earnest.

[2] Wi' . . . him! 'Tis usual for many, after a full laugh, to complain of sore sides and to bestow a kindly curse on the author of the jest. But the folks of more tender consciences have turned their expletives to friendly wishes such as this: or 'Sonse fa' ye', and the like.

[3] Gae . . . lucky, etc. Is a cant phrase, from what rise I know not; but 'tis made use of when one thinks it not worth while to give a direct answer, or think themselves foolishly accused.

Epistle to Robert Yarde of Devonshire, Esquire

Frae northern mountains clad with snaw,
Where whistling winds incessant blaw,
In time now when the curling-stane
Slides murm'ring o'er the icy plain,
What sprightly tale in verse can Yarde 5
Expect frae a cauld Scottish bard,
With brose and bannocks poorly fed,
In hodden gray right hashly cled,
Skelping o'er frozen hags with pingle,
Picking up peets to beet his ingle, 10
While sleet that freezes as it fa's,
Theeks as with glass the divot waws
Of a laigh hut, where sax thegither,
Ly heads and thraws on craps of heather?
  Thus, sir, of us the story gaes, 15
By our mair dull and scornfu' faes:
But let them tauk, and gowks believe,
While we laugh at them in our sleeve;
For we, nor barbarous nor rude,
Ne'er want good wine to warm our blood, 20
Have tables crowned, and hartsome biels,
And can in Cumin's, Don's or Steil's,
Be served as plenteously and civil,
As you in London at the devil.
You, sir, your self wha came and saw, 25
Owned that we wanted nought at a',
To make us as content a nation,
As any is in the creation.
  This point premised, my canty muse
Cocks up her crest without excuse, 30

7 brose *porridge* bannock *cake of oatmeal*
8 hodden *homespun wool cloth* hashly *slovenly*
9 skelping *galloping* hags *bogholes* pingle *hard work*
10 beet *add fuel to*
12 theeks *thatches* divot waws *turf walls*
13 laigh *low*
14 heads and thraws *alternating head to feet* craps *bundles*
17 gowks *fools*
21 hartsome biels *pleasant refuges*
22 Cumin's, Don's or Steil's *Edinburgh taverns*

And scorns to screen her natural flaws,
With if's and but's, and dull because;
She pukes her pens, and aims a flight
Through regions of internal light,
Frae fancy's field, these truths to bring 35
That you should hear, and she should sing.
  Langsyne, when love and innocence
Were human nature's best defence,
E'er party-jars made lateth less,
By cleathing't in a monkish dress; 40
Then poets shawed these evenly roads,
That lead to dwellings of the gods.
In these dear days, well kenned to fame,
'Divini Vates' was their name:
It was, and is, and shall be ay, 45
While they move in fair virtue's way.
Though rarely we to stipends reach,
Yet nane dare hinder us to preach.
  Believe me, sir, the nearest way
To happiness, is to be gay; 50
For spleen indulged will banish rest
Far frae the bosoms of the best;
Thousands a-year's no worth a prin,
When e'er this fashous guest gets in:
But a fair competent estate 55
Can keep a man frae looking blate,
Sae eithly it lays to his hand
What his just appetites demand.
Wha has, and can enjoy, oh wow,
How smoothly may his minutes flow? 60
A youth thus blest with manly frame,
Enlivened with a lively flame,
Will ne'er with sordid pinch control
The satisfaction of his soul.
Poor is that mind, ay discontent, 65
That canna use what God has lent;
But envious girns at a' he sees,
That are a crown richer than he's;

33 pukes *plucks* pens *quills*
37 langsyne *long ago*
39 lateth *loyalty*
44 Divini Vates *divine prophets*
53 prin *pin*
54 fashous *troublesome*
56 blate *timid*
67 girns *grumbles*

Which gars him pitifully hane,
And hell's ase-middings rake for gain; 70
Yet never kens a blythsome hour,
Is ever wanting, ever sowr.
  Yet ae extreme should never make
A man the gowden mien forsake.
It shaws as much a shallow mind, 75
And ane extravagantly blind,
If careless of his future fate,
He daftly waste a good estate,
And never thinks till thoughts are vain,
And can afford him nought but pain. 80
Thus will a joiner's shavings bleez,
Their low will for some seconds please;
But soon the glaring leam is past,
And cauldrife darkness follows fast:
While slaw the faggots large expire, 85
And warm us with a lasting fire.
Then neither, as I ken ye will,
With idle fears your pleasures spill,
Nor with neglecting prudent care,
Do skaith to your succeeding heir. 90
Thus steering cannily through life,
Your joys shall lasting be and rife:
Give a' your passions room to reel,
As lang as reason guides the wheel.
Desires, though ardent, are nae crime, 95
When they harmoniously keep time:
But when they spang o'er reason's fence,
We smart for't at our ain expence
To recreate us we're allowed,
But gaming deep boils up the blood, 100
And gars ane at Groomporters ban
The being that made him a man,
When his fair gardens, house and lands,
Are fa'n amongst the sharpers' hands.
A cheerfu' bottle soothes the mind, 105

69 hane *hoard*
70 ase-middings *ash-pits*
74 gowden mien *golden mean*
81 bleeze *blaze*
82 low *flame*
83 leam *light*
85 slaw *slow*
90 skaith *harm*
92 rife *plentiful*
97 spang *leap*
101 Groomporters *court gambling officials* ban *curse*

Gars carles grow canty, free and kind;
Defeats our care, and hales our strife,
And brawly oils the wheels of life:
But when just quantums we transgress,
Our blessing turns the quite reverse. 110
To love the bonny smiling fair,
Nane can their passions better ware;
Yet love is kittle and unruly,
And should move tentily and hooly:
For if it get o'er meikle head, 115
'Tis fair to gallop ane to dead:
O'er ilka hedge it wildly bounds,
And grazes on forbidden grounds;
Where constantly, like furies, range,
Poortith, diseases, death, revenge: 120
To toom ane's pouch to dunty clever,
Or have wranged husband probe ane's liver,
Or void ane's saul out through a shanker;
In faith 'twad any mortal canker.
Then wale a virgin worthy you, 125
Worthy your love and nuptial vow:
Syne frankly range o'er a' her charms,
Drink deep of joy within her arms;
Be still delighted with her breast,
And on her love with rapture feast. 130
May she be blooming, saft and young,
With graces melting from her tongue;
Prudent and yielding to retain
Your love, as well as you her ain.
Thus with your leave, sir, I've made free 135
To give advice to ane can gi'e
As good again; but as Mess John
Said, when the sand tald time was done,
'Ha'e patience, my dear friends, a wee,
And take ae ither glass frae me; 140
And if ye think there's doublets due,
I shanna bauk the like frae you.'

107 hales *heals*
112 ware *employ*
113 kittle *mysterious*
114 tentily and hooly *cautiously and carefully*
120 poortith *poverty*
121 dunty *mistress*
123 saul *soul* shanker *chancre*
124 canker *put in a bad temper*
125 wale *choose*
137 Mess John *name for a minister*
141 doublets *double portions*
142 shanna bauk *shall not balk*

Epistle to Mr John Gay, Author of 'The Shepherd's Week',

on hearing Her Grace the Duchess of Queensberry commend some of his Poems

Dear lad, wha linkan o'er the lee,
Sang 'Blowzalind' and 'Bowzybee',
And, like the lavrock, merrily
  Waked up the morn,
When thou didst tune, with heartsome glee, 5
  Thy bog-reed horn.

To thee, frae edge of Pentland height,
Where fawns and fairies take delight,
And revel a' the live-lang night,
  O'er glens and braes, 10
A bard that has the second sight
  Thy fortune spaes.

Now, lend thy lug, and tent me, Gay,
Thy fate appears like flow'rs in May,
Fresh flowrishing, and lasting ay, 15
  Firm as the aik,
Which envious winds, when critics bray,
  Shall never shake.

Come, shaw your loof – ay, there's the line
Foretells thy verse shall ever shine, 20
Dawted whilst living by the Nine,
  And a' the best,
And be, when past the mortal line,
  Of fame possest.

Immortal Pope, and skilfu' John,[1] 25
The learned leach frae Callidon,

1 linkan *skipping*
2 Blowzalind and Bowzybee *see note*
3 lavrock *lark*
7 Pentland height *see note*
12 spaes *predicts*
13 lug *ear* tent *heed*
16 aik *oak*
19 loof *palm*
21 dawted *adored* Nine *the Muses*
25 Pope, and skilfu' John *see note*
26 leach *doctor* Callidon *Scotland*

---

[1] Dr Arbuthnot.

With mony a witty dame and don,
  O'er lang to name,
Are of your roundels very fon,
  And sound your fame. 30

And sae do I, wha roose but few,
Which nae sma' favour is to you:
For to my friends I stand right true,
  With shanks a spar;
And my good word (ne'er gi'en but due) 35
  Gangs unko far.

Here mettled men my muse mantain,
And ilka beauty is my friend;
Which keeps me canty, brisk and bein,
  Ilk wheeling hour, 40
And a sworn fae to hatefu' spleen,
  And a' that's sour.

But bide y boy, the main's to say,
Clarinda bright as rising day,
Divinely bonny, great and gay, 45
  Of thinking even,
Whase words and looks, and smiles display
  Full views of heaven.

To rumage nature for what's braw,
Like lillies, roses, gems and snaw; 50
Compared with her's, their lustre fa',
  And bauchly tell
Her beauties: she excels them a',
  And's like her sell.

As fair a form as e'er was blest, 55
To have an angel for a guest;
Happy the prince who is possest
  Of sic a prize,
Whose vertues place her with the best
  Beneath the skies. 60

29 fon *fond*
31 roose *praise*
34 shanks a spar *legs braced*
39 bein *well-off*
44 Clarinda *see note*
52 bauchly *poorly*
54 sell *self*

O sonsy Gay, this heavenly born,
Whom ev'ry Grace strives to adorn,
Looks not upon thy lays with scorn;
  Then bend thy knees,
And bless the day that ye was born 65
  With arts to please.

She says, thy sonnet smoothly sings,
Sae ye may craw and clap your wings,
And smile at ether-capite stings
  With careless pride, 70
When sae much wit and beauty brings
  Strength to your side.

Lilt up your pipes, and rise aboon
Your 'Trivia' and your moorland tune,
And sing Clarinda late and soon, 75
  In touring strains,
Till gratefu' gods cry out 'Well done!'
  And praise thy pains.

Exalt thy voice, that all around,
May echo back the lovely sound, 80
Frae Dover cliffs, with samphire crowned,
  To Thule's shore,
Where northward no more Britain's found
  But seas that rore.

Thus sing, whil'st I frae Arthur's height, 85
O'er Chiviot glowr with tyred sight,
And langing wish, like raving wight,
  To be set down,
Frae coach and sax, baith trim and tight,
  In London town. 90

But lang I'll gove and bleer my ee,
Before, alake, that sight I see;
Then, best relief, I'll strive to be
  Quiet and content,

61 sonsy *fortunate*
68 craw *crow*
69 ether-capite *spider's*
74 'Trivia' *see note*
76 touring *towering*
81 Dover cliffs *see note*
82 Thule *see note*
85 Arthur's height *see note*
86 Cheviot *see note*
89 sax *six horses*
91 gove *stare*

And streek my limbs down easylie 95
  Upon the bent.

There sing the gowans, broom and trees,
The crystal burn and westlin breeze,
The bleeting flocks, and bisy bees,
  And blythsome swains, 100
Wha rant and dance, with kiltit dees,
  O'er mossy plains.

Farewell, but, e'er we part, let's pray,
God save Clarinda night and day,
And grant her a' she'd wish to ha'e, 105
  Withoutten end! –
Nae mair at present I've to say,
  But am your friend.

95 streek *stretch*
96 bent *open field*
97 gowans *daisies*
101 rant *romp* kiltit dees *dairy maids with skirts tucked up*

An Epistle Wrote from Mavisbank, March 1748, to a Friend in Edinburgh

Dear friend, to smoke and noise confined,
Which soils your shirt, and frets your mind,
And makes you rusty look, and crabbed,
As if you were bepoxed, or scabbed,
Or had been going through a dose 5
Of mercury, to save your nose,
Let me advise you, out of pity,
To leave the chattering, stinking city;
Where pride, and shallowness, take place
Of plain integrity, and grace, 10
Where hideous screams would kill a cat,
Of who buys this or who buys that,
And through the day from break of mornings
The buzz of bills, protests, and hornings,
Besides the everlasting squabble 15
Amongst the great and little rabble
Who tear their lungs, and deave your ears,
With all their party hopes and fears,
While rattling o'er their silly cant,
Learned from the *Mercury*, and *Courant*, 20
About the aid that comes from Russia,
And the neutrality of Prussia,
Of France's tyranny and slavery,
Of Holland's selfishness and knavery,
Of Spain, the most beloved son 25
Of the Old Whore of Babylon,
The guardian of her whips and faggots
And all her superstitious maggots,
Of all his gambols on the green
With Hungary's imperial queen, 30
Of Genoa's resolute resistance
Without Napolitan assistance,
Of passing Var, sieging Savona,
And breaking fiddles at Cremona,

6 mercury *see note*
14 hornings *proclamations of bankruptcy*
17 deave *deafen*
20 *Mercury, Courant see note*
26 Old Whore of Babylon *Roman Catholic Church*
30 Hungary's Imperial Queen *see note*

Of how much blood and dirt is cost 35
Before a town is won or lost,
Of popes, stateholders, faith's defenders,
Generals, marshals, and pretenders,
Of treaties, ministers, and kings,
And of a thousand other things, 40
Of all which their conceptions dull,
Suits with the thickness of the skull,
Yet with such stuff one must be worried
That's through the city gauntlet hurried.
But ah, ye cry, the dear, dear dances, 45
With beauties brisk, who harm our fancies,
For five or six gay hours complete
In circles of the assembly sweet.
Who can forsake so fair a field
Where all to conquering beauty yield? 50
No doubt while in this am'rous fit
Your next plea's boxes, and the pit,
Where wit, and humours of the age,
Flow entertaining from the stage,
Where, if the drama's right conducted, 55
One's both diverted and instructed.
Well, I shall grant it bears with reason,
These have their charms in proper season,
But must not be indulged too much,
Lest they the softened soul bewitch, 60
And faculties in fetters bind
That are for greater ends designed.
Then, rouse ye from these dozing dreams,
Come view with me the golden beams,
Which Phebus every morning pours 65
Upon the plains, adorned with flowers;
With me o'er springing verdures stray,
Where wimpling waters make their way;
Here, from the oak with ivy bound,
You'll hear the soft melodious sound 70
Of all the choristers on high,
Whose notes re-echo through the sky,
Better than concerts of your town,
Yet do not cost you half a crown:

52 boxes *in the theatre*
65 Phebus *the sun*
68 wimpling *rippling*

Here blackbirds, mavises and linnets, 75
Excel your fiddles, flutes, and spinets;
Next we may mount the broomy height
And wild, wide landscapes cheer our sight,
Diverted with the bleating tribe,
And plough-men whistling o'er the glebe. 80
Here we, with little labour, gain
Firm health, and all its joyful train,
Silent repose, the cheerful smile,
Which best intruding cares beguile,
And makes the springs of life to flow 85
Through every vein with kindly glow,
Giving the cheek a rosy taint,
Surpassing all the arts of paint.
The heights surveyed, we may return
Along the margin of the burn, 90
Where fishes will divert your eye,
While jumping up to catch a fly,
Which taught the angler first to wait
And hook them with the tempting bait;
Next the fair gardens we may trace 95
Where art adds life to native grace,
The walls and espaliers load, and lined
With fruits of the best chosen kind,
The borders freighted with delight,
To please the smelling, and the sight, 100
While echo entertains the ear,
When raised by notes well-tuned, and clear.
  Such morning walks, the balmy air,
Improves the gust for healthy fare,
And, when the bell for breakfast rings, 105
At heels you'll find Hermetic wings,
To reach a table, neatly crowned,
With all that's hearty, hale, and sound,
Where in the shining vessels stand
Blessings of Jacob's promised land, 110
Of which with freedom you may share,
For ceremony comes not there.
Nature refreshed, you may retire

75 mavises *song-thrushes*
77 broomy *covered in broom bushes*
80 glebe *field*
104 gust *taste*
106 Hermetic wings *see note*
110 Jacob *Biblical patriarch*

With books that jump with your desire;
If cloudy skies keep you within, 115
We've rooms neat, warm, and free from din,
Where, in the well-digested pages,
We can converse with by-past ages,
And oft, to set our dumps adrift,
We smile with Prior, Gay, and Swift; 120
Or, with great Newton, take a flight
Through all the rolling orbs of light,
Their order note, their bulk and shine
Till fired with raptures all divine;
With Milton, Pope, and all the rest, 125
Who smoothly copy Nature best,
From those inspired, we often find,
What brightens, and improves, the mind,
And carry men a pitch beyond
These views, of which low minds are fond. 130
This hinders not the jocund smile
With mirth to mix the moral style;
In conversation this being right
As is in painting shade and light.
  This is the life poets have sung 135
Most to be wished by old and young,
By the most brave, and the most fair,
Where least ambition, least of care,
Disturbs the soul, where virtuous ease
And temperance never cease to please. 140

114 jump *accord*
120 Prior, Gay and Swift *see note*
121 Newton *see note*
125 Milton, Pope *see note*

An Ode to Mr Forbes

Solvitur acris hiems . . .
Horace

Now gowans sprout and lavrocks sing,
And welcome west winds warm the spring,
O'er hill and dale they saftly blaw,
And drive the winter's cauld awa.
The ships lang gyzened at the pier 5
Now spread their sails and smoothly steer,
The nags and nowt hate wissened strae,
And frisking to the fields they gae,
Nor hynds wi' elson and hemp lingle,
Sit soling shoon out o'er the ingle. 10
Now bonny haughs their verdure boast,
That late were clade wi' snaw and frost,
With her gay train the Paphian Queen
By moon-light dances on the green,
She leads while nymphs and graces sing, 15
And trip around the fairy ring.
Mean time poor Vulcan hard at thrift,
Gets mony a sair and heavy lift,
Whilst rinnen down, his haff-blind lads
Blaw up the fire, and thump the gads. 20
Now leave your fitsted on the dew,
And busk yersell in habit new.
Be gratefu' to the guiding powers,
And blythly spend your easy hours.
O canny Forbes, tutor time, 25
And live as lang's ye're in your prime;
That ill-bred death has nae regard
To king or cottar, or a laird,

1 gowans *daisies* lavrocks *larks*
5 gyzened *with warped timbers*
7 nowt *cattle* wissened strae *withered straw*
9 hynds *farm-servants* elson *awl* lingle *shoemaker's thread*
10 shoon *shoes*
11 haughs *low-lying land by a river*
13 Paphian Queen *the goddess Venus*
17 Vulcan *blacksmith god, Venus's husband*
19 rinnen down *drenched in sweat*
20 gads *iron bars*
21 fitsted *footprint*
22 busk *dress*
25 Forbes *see note*
28 laird *lord*

As soon a castle he'll attack,
As waus of divots roofed wi' thack. 30
Immediately we'll a' take flight
Unto the mirk realms of night,
As stories gang, with gaists to roam,
In gloumie Pluto's gousty dome;
Bid fair good-day to pleasure syne 35
Of bonny lasses and red wine.
 Then deem ilk little care a crime,
Dares waste an hour of precious time;
And since our life's sae unko short,
Enjoy it a', ye've nae mair for't. 40

30 divots *turfs* thack *thatch*
32 mirk *murky*
33 gaists *ghosts*
34 Pluto *god of the underworld*
 gousty *dreary*

To R— H— B—, an Ode

Nullam Vare sacra vite prius severis arborem,
Circa mite solum Tiburis et mœnia Catili.

Horace.

O B—, could these fields of thine
Bear as in Gaul the juicy vine,
How sweet the bonny grape would shine
  On wau's where now,
Your apricocks and peaches fine 5
  Their branches bow.

Since human life is but a blink,
Why should we its short joys sink?
He disna live that canna link
  The glass about, 10
When warmed with wine, like men we think,
  And grow mair stout.

The cauldrife carlies clogged wi' care,
Wha gathering gear gang hyt and gare,
If rammed wi' red, they rant and rair 15
  Like mirthfu' men,
It soothly shaws them they can spare,
  A rowth to spend.

What soger when with wine he's bung
Did e'er complain he had been dung, 20
Or of his toil, or empty spung?
  Na, o'er his glass,
Nought but braw deeds imploy his tongue,
  Or some sweet lass.

1 B— *see note*
2 Gaul *France*
4 wau's *walls*
9 link *move briskly*
13 cauldrife carlies *spiritless fellows*
14 hyt *mad* gare *greedy*
15 red *red wine* rair *roar*
18 rowth *plenty*
19 soger *soldier* bung *tipsy*
20 dung *beaten*
21 spung *purse*

Yet trouth, 'tis proper we should stint 25
Our sells to a fresh mod'rate pint;
Why should we the blyth blessing mint
  To waste or spill,
Since, aften, when our reason's tint,
  We may do ill? 30

Let's set these hair-brained fowk in view,
That when they're stupid, mad and fow
Do brutal deeds, which aft they rue
  For a' their days,
Which frequently prove very few 35
  To such as these.

Then let us grip our bliss mair sicker,
And tape our heal, and sprightly liquor,
Which sober tane makes wit the quicker,
  And sense mair keen, 40
While graver heads that's muckle thicker
  Grane wi' the spleen.

May ne'er sic wicked fumes arise
In me shall break a' sacred ties,
And gar me like a fool despise 45
  With stiffness rude,
What ever my best friends advise
  Though ne'er so good.

'Tis best then to evite the sin
Of bending till our sauls gae blin, 50
Lest like our glass our breasts grow thin,
  And let fowk peep,
At ilka secret hid within
  That we should keep.

26 sells *selves*
27 mint *aim*
29 tint *lost*
38 tape *use sparingly* heal *health*
39 tane *taken*
49 evite *avoid*
50 bending *drinking* blin *blind*

The Vision

Compylit in Latin be a most lernit Clerk[1] in Tyme of our Hairship and Oppression, anno 1300, and translatit in 1524

I

Bedoun the bents of Banquo brae
Milane I wandert waif and wae,
  Musand our main mischaunce;
How be thay faes we ar undone,
That staw the sacred stane frae Scone,[2] 5
  And leids us sic a daunce:
Quhyle Ingland's Edert taks our tours,
  And Scotland ferst obeys,
Rude ruffians ransakk ryal bours,
  And Baliol homage pays; 10
    Throch feidom our freidom
    Is blotit with this skore,
    Quhat Romans' or no man's
    Pith culd eir do befoir

II

The air grew ruch with bousteous thuds, 15
Bauld Boreas branglit outthrow the cluds,
  Maist lyke a drunken wicht;
The thunder crakt, and flauchts did rift
Frae the blak vissart of the lift:
  The forrest schuke with fricht; 20

Title Hairship *harrying*
1 bents *fields* Banquo *see note*
2 waif *lonely*
5 staw *stole* stane frae Scone *see note*
7 Edert *see note*
10 Baliol *see note*
11 feidom *power of fate*
13 Romans *see note*
15 ruch *rough* bousteous *fierce*
16 Boreas *the north wind* branglit *shook*
18 flauchts *lightning* lift *sky*

[1] The history of the Scots' sufferings, by the unworthy condescension of Baliol to Edward I of England, till they recovered their independence by the conduct and valour of the great Bruce, is so universally known that any Argument to this antique poem seems useless.

[2] The old chair (now in Westmenister Abbey) in which the Scots kings were always crowned, wherein there is a piece of marble with this inscription:

Ni fallat fatum, SCOTI, quocunque locatum
Invenient lapidem, regnare tenentur ibidem.

Nae birds abune thair wing extenn,
  They ducht not byde the blast,
Ilk beist bedeen bangd to thair den,
  Untill the storm was past:
    Ilk creature in nature 25
    That had a spunk of sence,
    In neid then, with speid then,
    Methocht cryt 'In defence!'

III
To se a morn in May sae ill,
I deimt Dame Nature was gane will, 30
  To rair with rackles reil;
Quhairfor to put me out of pain,
And skonce my skap and shanks frae rain,
  I bure me to a beil,
Up ane hich craig that lundgit alaft, 35
  Out owre a canny cave,
A curious cruif of Nature's craft,
  Quhilk to me schelter gaif;
    Ther vexit, perplexit,
    I leint me doun to weip, 40
    In brief ther, with grief ther
    I dottard owre on sleip.

IV
Heir Somnus in his silent hand
Held all my sences at command,
  Quhyle I forget my cair; 45
The myldest meid of mortall wichts
Quha pass in peace the private nichts,
  That wauking finds it rare;
Sae in saft slumbers did I ly,
  But not my wakryfe mynd, 50
Quhilk still stude watch, and couth espy
  A man with aspeck kynd,

22 ducht *could* byde *endure*
23 bangd *hurried*
26 spunk *spark*
28 'In defence!' *the Scottish royal motto*
30 will *astray*
31 rackles *reckless*
33 skap *scalp*
34 beil *shelter*
37 cruif *enclosure*
42 dottard *staggered*
43 Somnus *sleep*
50 wakryfe *watchful*

Richt auld lyke and bauld lyke,
With baird thre quarters skant,
Sae braif lyke and graif lyke, 55
He seemt to be a sanct.

V

Grit darring dartit frae his ee,
A braid-sword schogled at his thie,
On his left arm a targe;
A shynand speir filld his richt hand, 60
Of stalwart mak, in bane and brawnd,
Of just proportions, large;
A various rainbow colourt plaid
Owre his left spaul he threw,
Doun his braid back, frae his quhyt heid, 65
The silver wymplers grew;
Amaisit, I gaisit
To se, led at command,
A strampant and rampant
Ferss lyon in his hand. 70

VI

Quhilk held a thistle in his paw,
And round his collar graift I saw
This poesie pat and plain,
'Nemo me impune lacess-
-et'—in Scots, 'Nane sall oppress 75
Me, unpunist with pain';
Still schaking, I durst naithing say,
Till he with kynd accent
Sayd, 'Fere, let nocht thy hairt affray,
I cum to hier thy plaint; 80
Thy graining and maining
Haith laitlie reikd myne eir,
Debar then affar then
All eiryness or feir.

56 sanct *saint*
58 schogled *swung*
59 targe *small round shield*
64 spaul *shoulder*
66 wymplers *waving locks*
69 strampant *tramping*
70 ferss *fierce*
74 'Nemo me . . .' *see note*
79 fere *friend*
82 reikd *reached*

VII

'For I am ane of a hie station, 85
The Warden of this auntient nation,
  And can nocht do the wrang';
I vissyt him then round about,
Syne with a resolution stout,
  Speird, 'Quhair he had bene sae lang?' 90
Quod he, 'Althocht I sum forsuke,
  Becaus they did me slicht,
To hills and glens I me betuke,
  To them that luves my richt;
    Quhase mynds yet inclynds yet 95
    To damm the rappid spate,
    Devysing and prysing
    Freidom at ony rate.

VIII

'Our trechour peirs thair tyranns treit,
Quha jyb them, and thair substance eit, 100
  And on thair honour stramp;
They, pure degenerate, bend thair baks,
The victor, Langshanks, proudly cracks
  He has blawn out our lamp:
Quhyle trew men, sair complainand, tell, 105
  With sobs, thair silent greif,
How Baliol thair richts did sell,
  With small howp of reliefe;
    Regretand and fretand
    Ay at his cursit plot, 110
    Quha rammed and crammed
    That bargin doun thair throt.

IX

'Braif gentrie sweir, and burgers ban,
Revenge is muttert be ilk clan
  That's to their nation trew; 115
The cloysters cum to cun the evil,
Mailpayers wiss it to the devil,
  With its contryving crew:

86 Warden *see note*
88 vissyt *inspected*
90 speird *asked*
100 jyb *gibe*
103 Langshanks *see note* cracks *brags*
113 ban *curse*
116 cun *learn*
117 mailpayers *rentpayers*

The hardy wald with hairty wills,
  Upon dyre vengance fall; 120
The feckless fret owre heuchs and hills,
  And eccho answers all,
    Repetand and greitand,
    With mony a sair alace,
    For blasting and casting 125
    Our honour in disgrace.'

X
'Waes me!' quod I, 'our case is bad,
And mony of us are gane mad,
  Sen this disgraceful paction.
We are felld and herryt now by forse; 130
And hardly help for't, thats yit warse,
  We are sae forfairn with faction.
Then has not he gude cause to grumble,
  Thats forst to be a slaif;
Oppression dois the judgment jumble 135
  And gars a wyse man raif.
    May cheins then, and pains then
    Infernal be thair hyre
    Quha dang us, and flang us
    Into this ugsum myre.' 140

XI
Then he with bauld forbidding luke,
And staitly air did me rebuke,
  For being of sprite sae mein:
Said he 'It's far beneath a Scot
To use weak curses quhen his lot 145
  May sumtyms sour his splein,
He rather should mair lyke a man,
  Some braif design attempt;
Gif its nocht in his pith, what than?
  Rest but a quhyle content, 150
    Nocht feirful, but cheirful,
    And wait the will of fate,
    Which mynds to desygns to
    Renew your auntient state.

121 heuchs *ravines*
129 paction *bargain (see note)*
132 forfairn *worn out*
139 dang *beat*
140 ugsum *disgusting*
149 pith *strength*

XII

'I ken sum mair than ye do all 155
Of quhat sall afterwart befall,
  In mair auspicious tymes;
For aften far abufe the mune,
We watching beings do convene,
  Frae round eard's outmost climes, 160
Quhair every warden represents
  Cleirly his nation's case,
Gif famyne, pest, or sword torments,
  Or vilains hie in place,
    Quha keip ay, and heip ay 165
    Up to themselves grit store,
    By rundging and spunging
    The leil laborious pure.'

XIII

'Say then,' said I, 'at your hie sate,
Lernt ye ocht of auld Scotland's fate, 170
  Gif eir schoil be her sell?'
With smyle celest, quod he, 'I can,
But its nocht fit an mortal man
  Sould ken all I can tell:
But part to thee I may unfold, 175
  And thou may saifly ken,
Quhen Scottish peirs slicht Saxon gold,
  And turn trew heartit men;
    Quhen knaivry and slaivrie,
    Ar equally dispysd, 180
    And loyalte and royalte,
    Universalie are prysd.

XIV

'Quhen all your trade is at a stand,
And cunyie clene forsaiks the land,
  Quhilk will be very sune, 185
Will preists without their stypands preich
For nocht will lawyers causes streich?
  Faith thatis nae easy done.

167 rundging *devouring*
168 leil *loyal*
171 schoil *she will*
177 Saxon gold *see note*
184 cunyie *coinage*

All this and mair maun cum to pass,
  To cleir your glamourit sicht; 190
And Scotland maun be made an ass
To set her jugment richt.
    Theyil jade hir and blad hir,
    Until scho brak hir tether,
    Thocht auld schois yit bauld schois, 195
    And teuch lyke barkit lether.

XV
'But mony a corss sall braithles ly,
And wae sall mony a widow cry,
  Or all rin richt again;
Owre Cheviot prancing proudly north, 200
The faes sall tak the feild neir Forthe,
  And think the day their ain:
But burns that day sall rin with blude
  Of them that now oppress;
Thair carcasses be corbys' fude, 205
  By thousands on the gress.
    A king then sall ring then,
    Of wyse renoun and braif,
    Quhase pusians and sapiens,
    Sall richt restoir and saif.' 210

XVI
'The view of freidomis sweit,' quod I,
'O say, grit tennant of the skye,
  How neiris that happie tyme?'
'We ken things but be circumstans,
Nae mair,' quod he, 'I may advance, 215
  Leist I commit a cryme.'
'Quhat eir ye pleis, gae on,' quod I,
  'I sall not fash ye moir,
Say how, and quhair ye met, and quhy,
  As ye did hint befoir.' 220

190 glamourit *bewitched*
193 jade *treat like an old horse*
  blad *harm*
195 schois *she is*
196 barkit *tanned*
197 corss *corpse*
199 or *before*
200 Cheviot *hills on the English border*
201 neir Forthe *see note*
205 corbys *ravens*
207 ring *reign*
209 pusians *power*
218 fash *trouble*

With air then sae fair then,
That glanst like rayis of glory,
Sae godlyk and oddlyk
He thus resumit his storie.

XVII

'Frae the sun's rysing to his sett, 225
All the pryme rait of wardens met,
In solemn bricht array,
With vehicles of aither cleir,
Sic we put on quhen we appeir
To sauls rowit up in clay; 230
Thair in a wyde and splendit hall,
Reird up with shynand beims,
Quhais rufe-treis wer of rainbows all,
And paist with starrie gleims,
Quhilk prinked and twinkled 235
Brichtly beyont compair,
Much famed and named
A castill in the air.

XVIII

'In midst of quhilk a tabill stude,
A spacious oval reid as blude, 240
Made of a fyre-flaucht,
Arround the dazeling walls were drawn,
With rays be a celestial hand,
Full mony a curious draucht.
Inferiour beings flew in haist, 245
Without gyd or derectour,
Millions of myles throch the wyld waste,
To bring in bowlis of nectar:
Then roundly and soundly
We drank lyk Roman gods; 250
Quhen Jove sae dois rove sae,
That Mars and Bacchus nods.

XIX

'Quhen Phebus heid turns licht as cork,
And Neptune leans upon his fork,
And limpand Vulcan blethers: 255

226 rait *row*
230 rowit *rolled*
241 fyre-flaucht *thunderbolt*

Quhen Pluto glowrs as he were wyld,
And Cupid, luve's we wingit chyld,
  Fals down and fyls his fethers.
Quhen Pan forgets to tune his reid,
  And slings it cairless bye, 260
And Hermes wingd at heils and heid,
  Can nowther stand nor lye:
    Quhen staggirand and swaggirand,
    They stoyter hame to sleip,
    Quhyle centeries at enteries 265
    Imortal watches keip.

XX

'Thus we tuke in the high browin liquour,
And bangd about the nectar biquour;
  But evir with his ods:
We neir in drink our judgments drensch, 270
Nor scour about to seik a wensch
  Lyk these auld baudy gods,
But franklie at ilk uther ask,
  Quhats proper we suld know,
How ilk ane hes performt the task, 275
  Assigned to him below.
    Our minds then sae kind then,
    Are fixt upon our care,
    Ay noting and ploting
    Quhat tends to thair weilfair. 280

XXI

'Gothus and Vandall baith lukt bluff,
Quhyle Gallus sneerd and tuke a snuff,
  Quhilk made Allmane to stare;
Latinus bad him naithing feir,
But lend his hand to haly weir, 285
  And of cowd crouns tak care;
Batavius with his paddock-face
  Luking asquint, cryd, "Pisch,

264 stoyter *stagger*
268 biquour *beaker*
269 ods *difference*
271 scour *rush*
281 Gothus, Vandall *see note*
282 Gallus *France*
283 Allmane *Germany*
284 Latinus *Italy*
285 weir *war*
286 cowd *cropped, tonsured*
287 Batavius *Holland* paddock *frog*

Your monks ar void of sence or grace,
I had leur ficht for fisch; 290
Your schule-men ar fule-men,
Carvit out for dull debates,
Decoying and destroying
Baith monarchies and states."

XXII
'Iberius with a gurlie nod 295
Cryd, "Hogan, yes we ken your god,
Its herrings ye adore";
Heptarchus, as he usd to be,
Can nocht with his ain thochts agre,
But varies bak and fore; 300
And quhyle he says, it is not richt
A monarch to resist,
Neist braith all ryall powir will slicht,
And passive homage jest;
He hitches and fitches 305
Betwein the *hic* and *hoc*,
Ay jieand and flieand
Round lyk a wedder-cock.

XXIII
'I still support my precedens
Abune them all, for sword and sens, 310
Thocht I haif layn richt now lown,
Quhylk was, becaus I bure a grudge
At sum fule Scotis, quha lykd to drudge
To princes no thair awin;
Sum thanis thair tennants pykit and squeist, 315
And pursit up all thair rent,
Syne wallopit to far courts, and bleist,
Till riggs and schaws war spent;
Syne byndging and whyndging,

290 leur *rather*
295 Iberius *Spain* gurlie *threatening*
298 Heptarchus *see note*
305 hitches *hops* fitches *fidgets*
306 *hic* and *hoc this and this*
307 jieand *shifting*
311 lown *subdued*
315 pykit *robbed*
317 bleist *blazed*
318 schaws *woods*
319 byndging *fawning*

Quhen thus redusit to howps, 320
They dander and wander
About, pure lickmadowps.

XXIV
'But now its tyme for me to draw
My shynand sword against club-law,
And gar my lyon roir; 325
He sall or lang gie sic a sound,
The ecchoe sall be hard arround
Europe, frae schore to schore;
Then lat them gadder all thair strenth,
And stryve to wirk my fall, 330
Tho numerous, yit at the lenth
I will owrecum them all,
And raise yit and blaze yit
My braifrie and renown,
By gracing and placing 335
Arright the Scottis crown.

XXV
'Quhen my braif Bruce the same sall weir
Upon his ryal heid, full cleir
The diadem will shyne;
Then sall your sair oppression ceis, 340
His intrest yours he will not fleice,
Or leif you eir inclyne:
Thocht millions to his purse be lent,
Yell neir the puirer be,
But rather richer, quhyle its spent 345
Within the Scottish se:
The field then sall yeild then
To honest husbands welth,
Gude laws then sall cause then
A sickly state haif helth.' 350

XXVI
Quhyle thus he talkit, methocht ther came
A wondir fair etherial dame,
And to our Warden sayd,

320 howps *mouthfuls*
322 lickmadowps *flatterers*
337 Bruce *see note*

'Grit Callidon I cum in serch
Of you, frae the hych starry arch, 355
The counsill wants your ayd;
Frae every quarter of the sky,
As swift as quhirl-wynd,
With spirits' speid the chiftains hy,
Sum grit thing is desygnd 360
Owre muntains be funtains,
And round ilk fairy ring,
I haif chaist ye, o haist ye,
They talk about your king.'

XXVII
With that my hand methocht he schuke, 365
And wischt I happyness micht bruke,
To eild be nicht and day;
Syne quicker than an arrow's flicht,
He mountit upwarts frae my sicht,
Straicht to the Milkie Way; 370
My mynd him followit throw the skyes,
Until the brynie streme
For joy ran trinckling frae myne eyes,
And wakit me frae dreme;
Then peiping, half sleiping, 375
Frae furth my rural beild,
It eisit me and pleisit me
To se and smell the feild.

XXVIII
For Flora in hir clene array,
New washen with a showir of May, 380
Lukit full sweit and fair;
Quhyle hir cleir husband frae aboif
Sched doun his rayis of genial luve,
Hir sweits perfumt the air;
The winds war husht, the welkin cleird, 385
The glumand clouds war fled,
And all as saft and gay appeird
As ane Elysion sched;

366 bruke *enjoy*
367 eild *age*
376 beild *shelter*
385 welkin *sky*
388 Elysion *paradise*

Quhilk heisit and bleisit
My heart with sic a fyre, 390
As raises these praises
That do to heaven aspyre.

Quod Ar. Scot.

389 heisit *lifted* bleisit *lit up*

The Gentle Shepherd
A Pastoral Comedy

THE PERSONS

Men

Sir William Worthy.
Patie, the gentle shepherd, in love with Peggy.
Roger, a rich young shepherd in love with Jenny.
Symon, an old shepherd, tenant to Sir William.
Glaud, an old shepherd, tenant to Sir William.
Bauldy, a hynd engaged with Neps.

Women

Peggy, thought to be Glaud's Niece.
Jenny, Glaud's only daughter.
Mause, an old woman supposed to be a witch.
Elspa, Symon's wife.
Madge, Glaud's sister.

SCENE
A shepherd's village and fields some few miles from Edinburgh.
Time of action: within twenty hours.

ACT I
Scene (i)

Beneath the south side of a craigy beild,
Where crystal springs the halesome waters yield,
Twa youthful shepherds on the gowans lay,
Tenting their flocks ae bonny morn of May.
Poor Roger granes till hollow echoes ring; 5
But blyther Patie likes to laugh and sing.
(*Enter Patie and Roger.*)

I(i)
1 craigy beild *rocky shelter*
2 halesome *wholesome*
3 gowans *daisies*
4 tenting *tending*
5 grane *groan*

PATIE:
Sang I (*tune: 'The Wawking of the Faulds'*):

My Peggy is a young thing,
 Just entered in her teens,
Fair as the day, and sweet as May,
Fair as the day, and always gay. 10
 My Peggy is a young thing,
  And I'm not very auld,
 Yet well I like to meet her at
  The wawking of the fauld.

My Peggy speaks sae sweetly, 15
 When e'er we meet alane.
I wish nae mair, to lay my care,
I wish nae mair, of a' that's rare.
 My Peggy speaks sae sweetly,
  To a' the lave I'm cauld; 20
 But she gars a' my spirits glow
  At wawking of the fauld.

My Peggy smiles sae kindly,
 Whene'er I whisper love,
That I look down on a' the town, 25
That I look down upon a crown.
 My Peggy smiles sae kindly,
  It makes me blyth and bauld.
 And naithing gi'es me sic delight,
  As wawking of the fauld. 30

My Peggy sings sae saftly,
 When on my pipe I play;
By a' the rest, it is confest,
By a' the rest, that she sings best,
 My Peggy sings sae saftly, 35
  And in her sangs are tald,
 With innocence the wale of sense,
  At wawking of the fauld.

14 wawking *all-night watch* fauld *sheep-fold*
20 lave *rest*
28 bauld *bold*
37 wale *choice*

This sunny morning, Roger, cheers my blood,
And puts all nature in a jovial mood. 40
How heartsome 'tis to see the rising plants,
To hear the birds chirm o'er their pleasing rants;
How halesome 'tis to snuff the cauler air,
And all the sweets it bears when void of care.
What ails thee, Roger, then? What gars thee grane? 45
Tell me the cause of thy ill-seasoned pain.

ROGER: I'm born, O Patie, to a thrawart fate;
I'm born to strive with hardships sad and great.
Tempest may cease to jaw the rowan flood,
Corbies and tods to grein for lambkin's blood; 50
But I, opprest with never-ending grief,
Maun ay despair of lighting on relief.

PATIE: The bees shall loath the flower, and quit the hive,
The saughs on boggie-ground shall cease to thrive,
Ere scornful queans, or loss of warldly gear, 55
Shall spill my rest, or ever force a tear.

ROGER: Sae might I say; but 'tis no easy done
By ane whase saul is sadly out of tune.
You have sae saft a voice, and slid a tongue,
You are the darling of baith auld and young. 60
If I but ettle at a sang, or speak,
They dit their lugs, syne up their leglens cleek;
And jeer me hameward frae the loan or bught,
While I'm confused with mony a vexing thought:
Yet I am tall, and as well built as thee, 65
Nor mair unlikely to a lass's eye.
For ilka sheep ye have, I'll number ten,
And should, as ane may think, come farer ben.

PATIE: But ablins, nibour, ye have not a heart,
And downa eithly wi' your cunzie part. 70

41 heartsome *cheerful*
42 chirm *chirp*
43 cauler *fresh*
47 thrawart *twisted, adverse*
49 jaw *gush* rowan *rolling*
50 corbies *ravens* tods *foxes* grein *yearn*
52 maun *must*
54 saughs *willows*
55 queans *girls*
56 spill *spoil*
58 whase *whose*
59 slid *smooth*
61 ettle *aim* sang *song*
62 dit *close* lugs *ears* leglens *milk pails* cleek *hook*
63 loan *milking field* bucht *ewe milking fold*
67 ilka *every*
68 farer ben *in greater favour*
69 ablins *perhaps*
70 downa eithly *cannot easily* cunzie *money*

If that be true, what signifies your gear?
A mind that's scrimpit never wants some care.
ROGER: My byar tumbled, nine braw nowt were smoored,
Three elf-shot were; yet I these ills endured:
In winter last, my cares were very sma', 75
Though scores of wathers perished in the snaw.
PATIE: Were your bein rooms as thinly stocked as mine,
Less you wad lose, and less you wad repine.
He that has just enough, can soundly sleep;
The o'ercome only fashes fowk to keep. 80
ROGER: May plenty flow upon thee for a cross,
That thou may'st thole the pangs of mony a loss.
Oh mayst thou dote on some fair paughty wench,
That ne'er will lout thy lowan drouth to quench,
'Till brised beneath the burden, thou cry dool, 85
And awn that ane may fret that is nae fool.
PATIE: Sax good fat lambs I sald them ilka clute
At the West Port, and bought a winsome flute,
Of plum-tree made, with iv'ry virles round,
A dainty whistle with a pleasant sound: 90
I'll be mair canty wi't, and ne'er cry dool,
Than you with all your cash, ye dowie fool.
ROGER: Na, Patie, na! I'm nae sic churlish beast,
Some other thing lyes heavier at my breast:
I dreamed a dreary dream this hinder night, 95
That gars my flesh a' creep yet with the fright.
PATIE: Now to a friend how silly's this pretence,
To ane wha you and a' your secrets kens:
Daft are your dreams, as daftly was ye hide
Your well-seen love, and dorty Jenny's pride. 100
Take courage, Roger, me your sorrows tell,
And safely think nane kens them but yoursell.
ROGER: Indeed now, Patie, ye have guessed o'er true,

72 scrimpit *money-wise*
73 byar *cow-shed* nowt *cattle* smoored *smothered*
74 elf-shot *made ill by fairy magic*
76 wathers *sheep*
77 bein *well-stocked*
80 o'ercome *surplus* fashes *troubles*
82 thole *suffer*
83 paughty *proud*
84 lout *stoop* lowan drouth *burning thirst*
85 brised *bruised* dool *alas*
86 awn *admit*
87 sald *sold* clute *hoof*
88 West Port *see note*
89 virles *rings*
91 canty *merry*
92 dowie *doleful*
98 kens *knows*
100 dorty *haughty*

And there is nathing I'll keep up frae you.
Me dorty Jenny looks upon a-squint; 105
To speak but till her I dare hardly mint:
In ilka place she jeers me air and late,
And gars me look bumbazed, and unko blate:
But yesterday I met her 'yont a know,
She fled as frae a shellycoat or kow. 110
She Bauldy loes, Bauldy that drives the car;
But gecks at me, and says I smell of tar.

PATIE: But Bauldy loes not her, right well I wat;
He sighs for Neps – sae that may stand for that.

ROGER: I wish I couldna loo her – but in vain; 115
I still maun dote, and thole her proud disdain.
My Bawty is a cur I dearly like,
Even while he fawned, she strak the poor dumb tyke:
If I had filled a nook within her breast,
She wad have shawn mair kindness to my beast. 120
When I begin to tune my stock and horn,
With a' her face she shaws a caulrife scorn.
Last night I played, ye never heard sic spite,
'O'er Bogie' was the spring, and her delyte;
Yet tauntingly she at her cousin speered, 125
Gif she could tell what tune I played, and sneered.
Flocks, wander where ye like, I dinna care,
I'll break my reed, and never whistle mair.

PATIE: E'en do sae, Roger, wha can help misluck,
Saebeins she be sic a thrawin-gabet chuck? 130
Yonder's a craig, since ye have tint all hope,
Gae till't your ways, and take the lover's lowp.

ROGER: I needna mak sic speed my blood to spill,
I'll warrant death come soon enough a will.

PATIE: Daft gowk! Leave off that silly whindging way; 135

106 till *to* mint *aim*
107 air *early*
108 bumbazed *confused* unko blate *strangely bashful*
109 know *knoll*
110 shellycoat *water-sprite* kow *goblin*
111 loes *loves* car *sledge*
112 gecks *mocks*
113 wat *know*
117 Bawty *dog's name*
121 stock and horn *wind instrument*
122 caulrife *cold*
124 spring *tune*
125 speered *asked*
130 saebeins *since* thrawin-gabet chuck *peevish chicken*
131 craig *cliff* tint *lost*
132 lowp *leap*
134 a will *spontaneously*
135 gowk *fool*

Seem careless, there's my hand ye'll win the day.
Hear how I served my lass I love as well
As ye do Jenny, and with heart as leel:
Last morning I was gay and early out,
Upon a dike I leaned glowring about, 140
I saw my Meg come linkan o'er the lee;
I saw my Meg, but Meggy saw na me:
For yet the sun was wading through the mist,
And she was closs upon me ere she wist;
Her coats were kiltit, and did sweetly shaw 145
Her straight bare legs that whiter were than snaw;
Her cockernony snooded up fou sleek,
Her haffet-locks hang waving on her cheek;
Her cheek sae ruddy, and her een sae clear;
And oh, her mouth's like ony hinny pear. 150
Neat, neat she was, in bustine waste-coat clean,
As she came skiffing o'er the dewy green.
Blythsome, I cried, 'My bonny Meg, come here,
I ferly wherefore ye're sae soon asteer;
But I can guess, ye're gawn to gather dew.' 155
She scoured awa, and said, 'What's that to you?'
'Then fare ye well, Meg dorts, and e'en's ye like,'
I careless cried, and lap in o'er the dike.
I trow, when that she saw, within a crack,
She came with a right thievless errand back; 160
Misca'd me first, then bade me hound my dog
To wear up three waff ews strayed on the bog.
I leugh, and sae did she; then with great haste
I clasped my arms about her neck and waist,
About her yielding waist, and took a fouth 165
Of sweetest kisses frae her glowing mouth.
While hard and fast I held her in my grips,
My very saul came lowping to my lips.

138 leel *faithful*
139 gay and *rather*
141 linkan *running*
145 kiltit *tucked up*
147 cockernonny *a woman's hair gathered up on her head* snooded *held by a ribbon*
148 haffet-locks *side locks*
150 hinny *honey*
151 bustine *cotton*
152 skiffing *skipping*
154 ferly *marvel*
156 scoured *rushed*
157 dorts *sulks*
158 dike *ditch*
160 thievless *unconvincing*
162 waff *wandering*
163 leugh *laughed*
165 fouth *abundance*

Sair, sair she flet wi' me 'tween ilka smack;
But well I kent she meant nae as she spake. 170
Dear Roger, when your jo puts on her gloom,
Do ye sae too, and never fash your thumb.
Seem to forsake her, soon she'll change her mood;
Gae woo anither, and she'll gang clean wood.

Sang II (*tune: 'Fy gar rub her o'er with Strae'*):

Dear Roger, if your Jenny geck, 175
  And answer kindness with a slight,
Seem unconcerned at her neglect,
  For women in a man delight;
But them dispise who're soon defeat,
  And with a simple face give way 180
To a repulse – then be not blate,
  Push bauldly on, and win the day.

When maidens, innocently young,
  Say aften what they never mean;
Ne'er mind their pretty lying tongue; 185
  But tent the language of their een:
If these agree, and she persist
  To answer all your love with hate,
Seek elsewhere to be better blest,
  And let her sigh when 'tis too late. 190

ROGER: Kind Patie, now fair fa' your honest heart,
Ye're ay sae cadgy, and have sic an art
To hearten ane: for now as clean's a leek,
Ye've cherished me since ye began to speak.
Sae for your pains, I'll make ye a propine, 195
My mother (rest her saul) she made it fine,
A tartan plaid, spun of good hawslock woo,
Scarlet and green the sets, the borders blew,
With sprainings like gowd and siller, crossed with black;
I never had it yet upon my back. 200

169 sair *sorely* flet *scolded* smack *kiss*
171 jo *sweetheart*
174 wood *mad*
186 tent *heed*
192 cadgy *cheerful*
195 propine *gift*
197 hawslock woo *wool from a sheep's neck*
198 sets *pattern*
199 sprainings *stripes*

Well are ye wordy o't, wha have sae kind
Red up my revelled doubts, and cleared my mind.
PATIE: Well, hald ye there – and since ye've frankly made
A present to me of your braw new plaid,
My flute's be your's, and she too that's sae nice 205
Shall come a will, gif ye'll tak my advice.
ROGER: As ye advise, I'll promise to observ't;
But ye maun keep the flute, ye best deserv't.
Now tak it out, and gie's a bonny spring,
For I'm in tift to hear you play and sing. 210
PATIE: But first we'll take a turn up to the height,
And see gif all our flocks be feeding right.
Be that time bannocks, and a shave of cheese,
Will make a breakfast that a laird might please;
Might please the daintiest gabs, were they sae wise, 215
To season meat with health instead of spice.
When we have tane the grace-drink at this well,
I'll whistle fine, and sing t'ye like mysell.
(*Exeunt.*)

Scene (ii)

A flowrie howm between twa verdent braes,
Where lasses use to wash and spread their claiths,
A trotting burnie wimpling through the ground,
Its channel peebles, shining, smooth and round; 5
Here view twa barefoot beauties clean and clear;
First please your eye, next gratify your ear,
While Jenny what she wishes discommends,
And Meg with better sense true love defends.

(*Enter Peggy and Jenny.*)
JENNY: Come, Meg, let's fa' to wark upon this green,
The shining day will bleech our linen clean; 10

201 wordy *worthy*
202 red *cleared* revelled *tangled*
203 hald *hold*
210 tift *mood*
213 bannocks *oatcakes*
214 laird *lord*
215 gabs *mouths*
217 tane *taken* grace-drink *see note*

I(ii)
1 howm *low land beside a river* braes *hills*
2 claiths *clothes*
3 burnie wimpling *small stream rippling*
4 peebles *pebbles*
9 wark *work*

The water's clear, the lift unclouded blew,
Will make them like a lilly wet with dew.
PEGGY: Go farer up the burn to Habby's How,
Where a' the sweets of spring and summer grow;
Between twa birks, out o'er a little lin 15
The water fa's, and makes a singand din;
A pool breast-deep beneath, as clear as glass,
Kisses with easy whirles the bord'ring grass:
We'll end our washing while the morning's cool,
And when the day grows het, we'll to the pool, 20
There wash oursells – 'tis healthfu' now in May,
And sweetly cauler on sae warm a day.
JENNY: Daft lassie, when we're naked, what'll ye say,
Gif our twa herds come brattling down the brae,
And see us sae? That jeering fallow Pate 25
Wad taunting say, 'Haith, lasses, ye're no blate.'
PEGGY: We're far frae ony road, and out of sight;
The lads they're feeding far beyont the height:
But tell me now, dear Jenny (we're our lane),
What gars ye plague your wooer with disdain? 30
The nibours a' tent this as well as I,
That Roger loos you, yet ye carena by.
What ails ye at him? Trowth, between us twa,
He's wordy you the best day e'er ye saw.
JENNY: I dinna like him, Peggy, there's an end; 35
A herd mair sheepish yet I never kend.
He kaims his hair indeed, and gaes right snug,
With ribbon-knots at his blew bonnet-lug;
Whilk pensily he wears a thought a-jee,
And spreads his garters diced beneath his knee. 40
He falds his owrlay down his breast with care;
And few gang trigger to the kirk or fair.
For a' that, he can neither sing nor say,
Except 'How d'ye' – or, 'There's a bonny day'.
PEGGY: Ye dash the lad with constant slighting pride; 45

11 lift *sky*
13 farer *farther* Habby's How *see note*
15 birks *birches* lin *waterfall*
20 het *hot*
24 brattling *clattering*
25 fallow *fellow*
29 our lane *alone*
31 tent *note*
37 kaims *combs*
39 whilk *which* pensily *foppishly* a-jee *to one side*
40 diced *neatly*
41 falds *folds* owrlay *cravat*
42 trigger *neater*

Hatred for love is unco sair to bide:
But ye'll repent ye, if his love grows cauld.
What like's a dorty maiden when she's auld?

Sang III (*tune: 'Polwart on the Green'*):

The dorty will repent,
  If lover's heart grow cauld, 50
And nane her smiles will tent,
  Soon as her face looks auld:
The dawted bairn thus takes the pet,
  Nor eats, though hunger crave,
Whimpers and tarrows at its meat, 55
  And's laught at by the lave,
They jest it till the dinner's past,
  Thus by itself abused,
The fool thing is obliged to fast,
  Or eat what they've refused. 60

Fy, Jenny, think, and dinna sit your time.
JENNY: I never thought a single life a crime.
PEGGY: Nor I – but love in whispers lets us ken,
That men were made for us, and we for men.
JENNY: If Roger is my jo, he kens himsell; 65
For sic a tale I never heard him tell.
He glowrs and sighs, and I can guess the cause,
But wha's obliged to spell his hums and haws?
When e'er he likes to tell his mind mair plain,
I'se tell him frankly ne'er to do't again. 70
They're fools that slavery like, and may be free:
The cheils may a' knit up themsells for me.
PEGGY: Be doing your ways; for me, I have a mind
To be as yielding as my Patie's kind.
JENNY: Heh, lass, how can ye loo that rattle-skull, 75
A very deel that ay maun hae his will?
We'll soon here tell what a poor fighting life
You twa will lead, sae soon's ye're man and wife.

46 sair *sore* bide *endure*
48 dorty *haughty*
53 dawted bairn *spoiled child*
55 tarrows *spurns*
72 cheils *young men*
76 deel *devil*

Sang IV (*tune: 'O dear Mother, what shall I do?'*):

O dear Peggy love's beguiling,
  We ought not to trust his smiling. 80
Better far to do as I do,
  Lest a harder luck betyde you.
Lasses when their fancy's carried,
  Think of nought but to be married;
Running to a life destroys 85
  Heartsome, free, and youthfu' joys.

PEGGY: I'll rin the risk; nor have I ony fear,
  But rather think ilk langsome day a year,
  Till I with pleasure mount my bridal-bed,
  Where on my Patie's breast I'll lean my head. 90
  There we may kiss as lang as kissing's good,
  And what we do, there's nane dare call it rude.
  He's get his will: why no? 'Tis good my part
  To give him that; and he'll give me his heart.
JENNY: He may indeed, for ten or fifteen days, 95
  Mak meikle o' ye, with an unco fraise;
  And daut ye baith afore fowk and your lane:
  But soon as his newfangleness is gane,
  He'll look upon you as his tether-stake,
  And think he's tint his freedom for your sake. 100
  Instead then of lang days of sweet delite,
  Ae day be dumb, and a' the neist he'll flite:
  And may be, in his barlickhoods, ne'er stick
  To lend his loving wife a loundering lick.
PEGGY: Sic coarse-spun thoughts as thae want pith
    to move 105
  My settled mind, I'm o'er far gane in love.
  Patie to me is dearer than my breath;
  But want of him I dread nae other skaith.
  There's nane of a' the herds that tread the green
  Has sic a smile, or sic twa glancing een. 110
  And then he speaks with sic a taking art,

87 rin *run*
88 ilk langsome *each tedious*
96 fraise *flattery*
97 daut *caress* your lane *on your own*
102 flite *complain*
103 barlickhoods *drunken temper*
104 loundering lick *resounding blow*
105 pith *strength*
108 skaith *harm*

His words they thirle like music through my heart.
How blythly can he sport, and gently rave,
And jest at feckless fears that fright the lave?
Ilk day that he's alane upon the hill, 115
He reads fell books that teach him meikle skill.
He is – but what need I say that or this?
I'd spend a month to tell you what he is!
In a' he says or does, there's sic a gait,
The rest seem coofs compared with my dear Pate. 120
His better sense will lang his love secure:
Ill nature heffs in sauls are weak and poor.
JENNY: Hey, bonny lass of Branksome, or't be lang,
Your witty Pate will put you in a sang.
Oh, 'tis a pleasant thing to be a bride; 125
Syne whindging getts about your ingle-side,
Yelping for this or that with fasheous din,
To mak them brats then ye maun toil and spin.
Ae wean fa's sick, ane scads itsell wi' broe,
Ane breaks his shin, anither tynes his shoe; 130
The deil gaes o'er John Wobster, hame grows hell,
When Pate misca's ye war than tongue can tell.
PEGGY:

Sang v (*tune: 'How can I be sad on my Wedding-Day?'*):

How shall I be sad when a husband I hae,
That has better sense than any of thae
Sour weal silly fellows, that study like fools 135
To sink their ain joy, and make their wives snools?
The man who is prudent ne'er lightlies his wife,
Or with dull reproaches encourages strife;
He praises her virtues, and ne'er will abuse
Her for a small failing, but find an excuse. 140

112 thirle *pierce*
113 rave *rove*
116 fell *remarkable*
119 gait *way*
120 coofs *fools*
122 heffs *acclimatises*
123 bonny lass of Branksome *see note* or *before*
125 getts *offspring*
127 fasheous *troublesome*
128 brats *rags*
129 wean *child* scads *scalds* broe *hot liquid*
130 tynes *loses*
131 The deil gaes o'er John Wobster *see note*
132 war *worse*
136 snools *pitiful weaklings*
137 lightlies *disparages*

Yes, 'tis a heartsome thing to be a wife,
When round the ingle-edge young sprouts are rife.
Gif I'm sae happy, I shall have delight,
To hear their little plaints, and keep them right.
Wow, Jenny, can there greater pleasure be, 145
Than see sic wee tots toolying at your knee;
When a' they ettle at, their greatest wish,
Is to be made of, and obtain a kiss?
Can there be toil in tenting day and night,
The like of them, when love makes care delight? 150

JENNY: But poortith, Peggy, is the warst of a',
Gif o'er your heads ill chance should beggary draw:
But little love, or canty cheer can come,
Frae duddy doublets, and a pantry toom.
Your nowt may die; the spate may bear away 155
Frae aff the howms your dainty rucks of hay.
The thick blawn wreaths of snaw, or blashy thows,
May smoor your wathers, and may rot your ews.
A dyvour buys your butter, woo and cheese,
But, or the day of payment, breaks and flees. 160
With glooman brow the laird seeks in his rent:
'Tis no to gi'e; your merchant's to the bent;
His honour mauna want, he poinds your gear:
Syne, driven frae house and hald, where will ye steer?
Dear Meg, be wise, and live a single life; 165
Troth 'tis nae mows to be a married wife.

PEGGY: May sic ill luck befa' that silly she,
Wha has sic fears; for that was never me.
Let fowk bode well, and strive to do their best;
Nae mair's required, let Heaven make out the rest. 170
I've heard my honest uncle aften say,
That lads should a' for wives that's virtuous pray:
For the maist thrifty man could never get
A well stored room, unless his wife wad let:
Wherefore nocht shall be wanting on my part, 175
To gather wealth to raise my shepherd's heart.

146 toolying *quarrelling*
149 tenting *caring*
151 poortith *poverty*
154 duddy *ragged* toom *empty*
156 rucks *stacks*
157 blashy thows *rainy thaws*
159 dyvour *debtor* woo *wool*
161 glooman *scowling*
162 to the bent *fled from creditors*
163 mauna *must not* poinds *distrains* gear *possessions*
164 hald *hold* steer *go*
166 mows *joke*
169 bode *expect*

What e'er he wins, I'll guide with canny care,
And win the vogue, at market, tron, or fair,
For halesome, clean, cheap and sufficient ware.
A flock of lambs, cheese, butter, and some woo, 180
Shall first be sald, to pay the laird his due;
Syne a' behind's our ain. Thus, without fear,
With love and rowth we through the warld will steer:
And when my Pate in bairns and gear grows rife,
He'll bless the day he gat me for his wife. 185

JENNY: But what if some young giglit on the green,
With dimpled cheeks, and twa bewitching een,
Should gar your Patie think his haff-worn Meg,
And her kend kisses, hardly worth a feg?

PEGGY: Nae mair of that. Dear Jenny, to be free, 190
There's some men constanter in love than we:
Nor is the ferly great, when nature kind
Has blest them with solidity of mind.
They'll reason calmly, and with kindness smile,
When our short passions wad our peace beguile. 195
Sae whensoe'er they slight their maiks at hame,
'Tis ten to ane the wives are maist to blame.
Then I'll employ with pleasure a' my art
To keep him cheerfu', and secure his heart.
At even, when he comes weary frae the hill, 200
I'll have a' things made ready to his will.
In winter, when he toils through wind and rain,
A bleezing ingle, and a clean hearth-stane.
And soon as he flings by his plaid and staff,
The seething pot's be ready to take aff. 205
Clean hagabag I'll spread upon his board,
And serve him with the best we can afford.
Good humour and white bigonets shall be
Guards to my face, to keep his love for me.

JENNY: A dish of married love right soon grows cauld, 210
And dosens down to nane, as fowk grow auld.

PEGGY: But we'll grow auld togither, and ne'er find
The loss of youth, when love grows on the mind.

177 canny *prudent*
178 vogue *reputation* tron *town centre*
183 rowth *plenty*
186 giglit *girl*
189 feg *fig*
196 maiks *mates*
206 hagabag *huckabuck, linen*
208 bigonets *caps*
211 dosens *cools*

Bairns, and their bairns, make sure a firmer ty,
Than ought in love the like of us can spy. 215
See yon twa elms that grow up side by side,
Suppose them, some years syne, bridegroom and bride;
Nearer and nearer ilka year they've prest,
Till wide their spreading branches are increast,
And in their mixture now are fully blest. 220
This shields the other frae the eastlin blast,
That in return defends it frae the west.
Sic as stand single – a state sae liked by you! –
Beneath ilk storm, frae ev'ry airth, maun bow.

JENNY: I've done – I yield – dear lassie, I maun yield, 225
Your better sense has fairly won the field,
With the assistance of a little fae
Lyes darned within my breast this mony a day.

Sang VI (*tune: 'Nansy's to the Green Wood gane'*):

I yield, dear lassie, you have won,
And there is nae denying, 230
That sure as light flows frae the sun,
Frae love proceeds complying;
For a' that we can do or say,
'Gainst love nae thinker heeds us,
They ken our bosoms lodge the fae, 235
That by the heart-strings leads us.

PEGGY: Alake, poor prisoner! Jenny, that's no fair,
That ye'll no let the wee thing tak the air:
Haste, let him out, we'll tent as well's we can,
Gif he be Bauldy's or poor Roger's man. 240

JENNY: Anither time's as good, for see the sun
Is right far up, and we're no yet begun
To freath the graith; if cankered Madge our aunt
Come up the burn, she'll gie's a wicked rant:
But when we've done, I'll tell ye a' my mind; 245
For this seems true – nae lass can be unkind.

(*Exeunt.*)

End of the first act

224 airth *direction*
227 fae *foe*
228 darned *concealed*
243 freath *froth* graith *lather*

ACT II
Scene (i)

A snug thack-house, before the door a green;
Hens on the midding, ducks in dubs are seen.
On this side stands a barn, on that a byre;
A peat-stack joins, and forms a rural square.
The house is Glaud's; there you may see him lean, 5
And to his divot-seat invite his frien'.
(*Enter Glaud and Symon.*)

GLAUD: Good-morrow, nibour Symon, come sit down,
And gie's your cracks. What's a' the news in town?
They tell me ye was in the ither day,
And sald your Crummock and her bassend quey. 10
I'll warrant ye've coft a pund of cut and dry;
Lug out your box, and gie's a pipe to try.
SYMON: With a' my heart; and tent me now, auld boy,
I've gathered news will kittle your mind with joy.
I couldna rest till I came o'er the burn, 15
To tell ye things have taken sic a turn,
Will gar our vile oppressors stend like flaes,
And skulk in hidlings on the hether braes.
GLAUD: Fy, blaw! Ah, Symie, rattling chiels ne'er stand
To cleck and spread the grossest lies aff hand, 20
Whilk soon flies round like will-fire far and near:
But loose your poke, be't true or fause, let's hear.
SYMON: Seeing's believing, Glaud, and I have seen
Hab, that abroad has with our master been –
Our brave good master, wha right wisely fled, 25
And left a fair estate, to save his head:
Because ye ken fou well he bravely chose
To stand his liege's friend with great Montrose.
Now Cromwell's gane to Nick; and ane ca'd Monk

II(i)
1 thack *thatched*
2 midding *dunghill* dubs *ponds*
6 divot *turf*
8 cracks *gossip*
10 Crummock *name of a cow* bassend quey *heifer with a white face-mark*
11 coft *bought* pund *pound* cut and dry *tobacco*
14 kittle *tickle*
17 stend *leap* flaes *fleas*
18 hidlings *hiding places*
19 rattling *lively, wild*
20 cleck *chatter*
21 will-fire *wild-fire*
22 poke *bag* fause *false*
27 fou *full*
28–29 Montrose, Cromwell, Monk *see note*
29 Nick *the Devil*

Has played the Rumple a right slee begunk, 30
Restored King Charles, and ilka thing's in tune:
And Habby says we'll see Sir William soon.
GLAUD: That makes me blyth indeed; but dinna flaw:
Tell o'er your news again, and swear till't a'!

Sang VII (*tune: 'Cald Kale in Aberdeen'*):

Cauld be the rebel's cast, 35
Oppressors base and bloody,
I hope we'll see them at the last
Strung a' up in a woody.
Blest be he of worth and sense,
And ever high his station, 40
That bravely stands in the defence
Of conscience, king and nation.

And saw ye Hab! And what did Halbert say?
They have been e'en a dreary time away.
Now God be thanked that our laird's come hame, 45
And his estate, say, can he eithly claim?
SYMON: They that hag-raid us till our guts did grane,
Like greedy bairs, dare nae mair do't again;
And good Sir William sall enjoy his ain.
GLAUD: And may he lang; for never did he stent 50
Us in our thriving, with a racket rent:
Nor grumbled, if ane grew rich; or shored to raise
Our mailens, when we pat on Sunday's claiths.
SYMON: Nor wad he lang, with senseless saucy air,
Allow our lyart noddles to be bare. 55
'Put on your bonnet, Symon – Tak a seat –
How's all at hame? – How's Elspa? How does Kate?
How sells black cattle? – What gie's woo this year?' –
And sic like kindly questions wad he speer.

30 Rumple *see note* slee begunk *sly trick*
31 King Charles *Charles II*
33 flaw *lie*
35 cast *fate*
38 woody *gallow's rope*
47 hag-raid *oppressed*
49 sall *shall* ain *own*
50 stent *tax*
51 racket *inflated*
52 shored *threatened*
53 mailens *land-rents* pat *put*
55 lyart *grey-haired*
58 gie's woo *price wool*

Sang VIII (*tune: 'Mucking of Geordy's Byer'*):

The laird who in riches and honour 60
  Wad thrive, should be kindly and free,
Nor rack the poor tenants, who labour
  To rise aboon poverty:
Else like the pack horse that's unfothered
  And burdened, will tumble down faint; 65
Thus virtue by hardship is smothered,
  And rackers aft tine their rent.

GLAUD: Then wad he gar his butler bring bedeen
The nappy bottle ben, and glasses clean,
Whilk in our breast raised sic a blythsome flame, 70
As gart me mony a time gae dancing hame.
My heart's e'en raised! Dear nibour, will ye stay,
And tak your dinner here with me the day?
We'll send for Elspath too – and upo' sight,
I'll whistle Pate and Roger frae the height: 75
I'll yoke my sled, and send to the neist town,
And bring a draught of ale baith stout and brown,
And gar our cottars a', man, wife and wean,
Drink till they tine the gate to stand their lane.
SYMON: I wad na bauk my friend his blyth design, 80
Gif that it hadna first of a' been mine:
For heer-yestreen I brewed a bow of maut,
Yestreen I slew twa wathers prime and fat;
A firlot of good cakes my Elspa beuk,
And a large ham hings reesting in the nook: 85
I saw mysell, or I came o'er the loan,
Our meikle pot that scads the whey put on,
A mutton-bouk to boil – and ane we'll roast;
And on the haggis Elspa spares nae cost;
Sma' are they shorn, and she can mix fu' nice 90

64 unfothered *unfed*
67 rackers *greedy landlords*
68 bedeen *at once*
69 nappy *strong ale* ben *in*
78 cottars *farmworkers* wean *child*
79 gate *way* their lane *alone*
80 bauk *balk*
82 heer-yestreen *the night before last* bow *boll* maut *malt*
83 yestreen *last night* wathers *wethers*
84 firlot *a quarter of a boll* beuk *baked*
85 reesting *smoking* nook *fireside*
88 bouk *carcase*
90 shorn *minced*

The gusty ingans with a curn of spice:
Fat are the puddings, heads and feet well sung.
And we've invited nibours auld and young,
To pass this afternoon with glee and game,
And drink our master's health and welcome-hame. 95
Ye mauna then refuse to join the rest,
Since ye're my nearest friend that I like best.
Bring wi' ye a' your family, and then,
Whene'er you please, I'll rant wi' you again.

GLAUD: Spoke like yersell, auld-birky, never fear 100
But at your banquet I shall first appear.
Faith we shall bend the bicker, and look bauld,
Till we forget that we are failed or auld.
Auld, said I! Troth, I'm younger be a score,
With your good news, than what I was before. 105
I'll dance or een! Hey, Madge! Come forth: d'ye hear?

(*Enter Madge.*)

MADGE: The man's gane gyte! Dear Symon, welcome here.
What wad ye, Glaud, with a' this haste and din?
Ye never let a body sit to spin. 109

GLAUD: Spin! Snuff – gae break your wheel, and burn your tow,
And set the meiklest peat-stack in a low.
Syne dance about the bane-fire till ye die,
Since now again we'll soon Sir William see.

MADGE: Blyth news indeed! And wha has tald you o't?

GLAUD: What's that to you? Gae get my Sunday's coat; 115
Wale out the whitest of my bobbit bands,
My white-skin hose, and mittons for my hands;
Then frae their washing cry the bairns in haste,
And make yoursells as trig, head, feet and waist,
As ye were a' to get young lads or e'en; 120
For we're gaun o'er to dine with Sym bedeen.

SYMON: Do, honest Madge: and, Glaud, I'll o'er the gate,
And see that a' be done as I wad hae't.

(*Exeunt.*)

91 gusty ingans *tasty onions* curn *grain*
92 sung *singed*
99 rant *chat*
100 birky *fellow*
102 bend the bicker *drink heartily*
107 gyte *crazy*
110 tow *unspun fibre*
111 low *flame*
112 bane-fire *bonfire*
116 wale *choose* bobbit *tasselled*
119 trig *neat*
120 or e'en *before evening*

Scene (ii)

The open field – a cottage in a glen,
An auld wife spinning at the sunny end –
At a small distance, by a blasted tree,
With falded arms, and haff raised look ye see –

(Bauldy his lane.)
BAULDY: What's this! I canna bear't! 'Tis war than Hell, 5
To be sae burnt with love, yet darna tell!
O Peggy, sweeter than the dawning day,
Sweeter than gowany glens, or new mawn hay;
Blyther than lambs that frisk out o'er the knows,
Straighter than ought that in the forest grows: 10
Her een the clearest blob of dew outshines;
The lilly in her breast its beauty tines.
Her legs, her arms, her cheeks, her mouth, her een,
Will be my dead, that will be shortly seen!
For Pate loes her – wae's me! – and she loes Pate; 15
And I with Neps, by some unlucky fate,
Made a daft vow: oh, but ane be a beast
That makes rash aiths till he's afore the priest!
I dare na speak my mind, else a' the three,
But doubt, wad prove ilk ane my enemy. 20
'Tis sair to thole – I'll try some witchcraft art,
To break with ane, and win the other's heart.
Here Mausy lives, a witch, that for sma' price
Can cast her cantraips, and give me advice.
She can o'ercast the night, and cloud the moon, 25
And mak the deils obedient to her crune.
At midnight hours, o'er the kirk-yards she raves,
And howks unchristened weans out of their graves;
Boils up their livers in a warlock's pow,
Rins withershins about the hemlock low; 30
And seven times does her prayers backward pray,

II(ii)
5 war *worse*
6 darna *dare not*
8 gowany *daisy-covered*
mawn *mown*
18 aiths *oaths*
21 thole *endure*
24 cantraips *magic spells*
26 deils *devils* crune *crooning*
28 howks *digs* weans *children*
29 pow *head*
30 rins *runs* withershins *anti-clockwise*

Till Plotcock comes with lumps of Lapland clay,
Mixt with the venom of black taids and snakes;
Of this unsonsy pictures aft she makes
Of ony ane she hates, and gars expire 35
With slaw and racking pains afore a fire;
Stuck fu' of prins, the devilish pictures melt,
The pain, by fowk they represent, is felt.
And yonder's Mause: ay, ay, she kens fu' well,
When ane like me comes rinning to the Deil. 40
She and her cat sit beeking in her yard,
To speak my errand, faith, amaist I'm feared:
But I maun do't, though I should never thrive;
They gallop fast that deils and lasses drive.

(*Exit.*)

Scene (iii)

A green kail-yard, a little fount,
Where water popilan springs;
There sits a wife with wrinkle-front.
And yet she spins and sings.

MAUSE:

Sang IX (*tune: 'Carle and the King come'*):

Peggy, now the king's come, 5
  Peggy, now the king's come;
Thou may dance, and I shall sing,
  Peggy, since the king's come.
Nae mair the hawkies shalt thou milk,
  But change thy plaiding-coat for silk, 10
And be a lady of that ilk,
  Now, Peggy, since the king's come.

(*Enter Bauldy.*)

BAULDY: How does auld honest lucky of the glen?
Ye look baith hale and fere at threescore ten.

32 Plotcock *a devil*
33 taids *toads*
34 unsonsy *ill-omened*
36 slaw *slow*
37 prins *pins*
41 beeking *warming*

II(iii)
2 popilan *bubbling*
9 hawkies *cows*
11 ilk *kind*
13 lucky *see note*
14 fere *sturdy*

MAUSE: E'en twining out a threed with little din, 15
And beeking my cauld limbs afore the sun.
What brings my bairn this gate sae air at morn?
Is there nae muck to lead – to thresh nae corn?
BAULDY: Enough of baith – but something that requires
Your helping hand employs now all my cares. 20
MAUSE: My helping hand! Alake, what can I do,
That underneath baith eild and poortith bow?
BAULDY: Ay, but ye're wise, and wiser far than we,
Or maist part of the parish tells a lie.
MAUSE: Of what kind wisdom think ye I'm possest, 25
That lifts my character aboon the rest?
BAULDY: The word that gangs, how ye're sae wise and fell,
Ye'll may be take it ill gif I should tell.
MAUSE: What fowk says of me, Bauldy, let me hear;
Keep nathing up, ye nathing have to fear. 30
BAULDY: Well, since ye bid me, I shall tell ye a',
That ilk ane talks about you, but a flaw.
When last the wind made Glaud a roofless barn;
When last the burn bore down my mither's yarn;
When Brawny elf-shot never mair came hame; 35
When Tibby kirned, and there nae butter came;
When Bessy Freetock's chuffy-cheeked wean
To a fairy turned, and could na stand its lane;
When Watie wandered ae night through the shaw,
And tint himsell amaist amang the snaw; 40
When Mungo's mear stood still, and swat with fright,
When he brought east the howdy under night;
When Bawsy shot to dead upon the green,
And Sara tint a snood was nae mair seen:
You, lucky, gat the wyte of a' fell out, 45
And ilka ane here dreads you round about.
And sae they may that mint to do ye skaith:
For me to wrang ye, I'll be very laith;

15 twining *separating*
threed *thread*
17 air *early*
18 muck *dung* lead *transport*
22 eild *old age*
32 flaw *lie*
35 elf-shot *enchanted*
36 kirned *churned*
37 chuffy *chubby*
38 its lane *on its own*
39 shaw *thicket*
41 mear *mare* swat *sweated*
42 howdy *midwife*
43 shot *bled*
44 snood *hair-ribbon*
45 lucky *old woman* wyte *blame*
47 mint *aim* skaith *harm*
48 laith *loath*

But when I neist make grots, I'll strive to please
You with a firlot of them mixt with pease. 50

MAUSE: I thank ye, lad. Now tell me your demand,
And, if I can, I'll lend my helping hand.

BAULDY: Then, I like Peggy – Neps is fond of me –
Peggy likes Pate – and Patie's bauld and slee,
And loes sweet Meg – but Neps I downa see. 55
Could ye turn Patie's love to Neps, and than
Peggy's to me, I'd be the happiest man.

MAUSE: I'll try my art to gar the bowls row right;
Sae gang your ways, and come again at night:
'Gainst that time I'll some simple things prepare, 60
Worth all your pease and grots; tak ye nae care.

BAULDY: Well, Mause, I'll come, gif I the road can find:
But if ye raise the Deil, he'll raise the wind;
Syne rain and thunder maybe, when 'tis late,
Will make the night sae rough, I'll tine the gate. 65
We're a' to rant in Symie's at a feast,
Oh, will ye come like Badrans, for a jest,
And there ye can our different haviours spy?
There's nane shall ken o't there but you and I.

MAUSE: 'Tis like I may – but let na on what's past 70
'Tween you and me, else fear a kittle cast.

BAULDY: If I ought of your secrets e'er advance,
May ye ride on me ilka night to France.

(*Exit Bauldy*.)

(*Mause her lane*.)

MAUSE: Hard luck, alake, when poverty and eild,
Weeds out of fashion, and a lanely beild, 75
With a sma' cast of wiles, should in a twitch,
Gi'e ane the hatefu' name a wrinkled witch.
This fool imagines, as do mony sic,
That I'm a wretch in compact with Auld Nick;
Because by education I was taught 80
To speak and act aboon their common thought.
Their gross mistake shall quickly now appear;
Soon shall they ken what brought, what keeps me here;

49 grots *milled oats*
58 row *roll*
67 Badrans *name for a cat*
71 kittle cast *awkward fate*
75 weeds *fades* bield *refuge*

Nane kens but me, and if the morn were come,
I'll tell them tales will gar them a' sing dumb. 85
(*Exit.*)

Scene (iv)

Behind a tree, upon the plain,
Pate and his Peggy meet;
In love, without a vicious stain,
The bonny lass and cheerfu' swain
Change vows and kisses sweet. 5

(*Enter Patie and Peggy.*)
PEGGY: O Patie, let me gang, I mauna stay,
We're baith cried hame, and Jenny she's away.
PATIE: I'm laith to part sae soon; now we're alane,
And Roger he's awa with Jenny gane:
They're as content, for ought I hear or see, 10
To be alane themsells, I judge, as we.
Here, where primroses thickest paint the green,
Hard by this little burnie let us lean.
Hark how the lavrocks chant aboon our heads,
How saft the westlin winds sough through the reeds. 15
PEGGY: The scented meadows, birds, and healthy breeze,
For ought I ken, may mair than Peggy please.
PATIE: Ye wrang me sair, to doubt my being kind;
In speaking sae, ye ca' me dull and blind.
Gif I could fancy ought's sae sweet or fair 20
As my dear Meg, or worthy of my care.
Thy breath is sweeter than the sweetest brier,
Thy cheek and breast the finest flowers appear.
Thy words excel the maist delightfu' notes,
That warble through the merl or mavis' throats. 25
With thee I tent nae flowers that busk the field,
Or ripest berries that our mountains yield.
The sweetest fruits that hing upon the tree,
Are far inferior to a kiss of thee.
PEGGY: But Patrick, for some wicked end, may fleech, 30
And lambs should tremble when the foxes preach.

II(iv)
7 cried *called*
14 lavrocks *larks*
15 sough *sigh*
25 merl *blackbird* mavis *song-thrush*
26 busk *adorn*
30 fleech *flatter*

I dare na stay – ye joker, let me gang,
Anither lass may gar ye change your sang;
Your thoughts may flit, and I may thole the wrang.

PATIE: Sooner a mother shall her fondness drap, 35
And wrang the bairn sits smiling on her lap;
The sun shall change, the moon to change shall cease,
The gaits to clim, the sheep to yield the fleece,
Ere ought by me be either said or done,
Shall skaith our love; I swear by all aboon. 40

PEGGY: Then keep your aith: but mony lads will swear,
And be mansworn to twa in haff a year.
Now I believe ye like me wonder well;
But if a fairer face your heart should steal,
Your Meg forsaken, bootless might relate, 45
How she was dauted anes by faithless Pate.

PATIE: I'm sure I canna change, ye needna fear;
Though we're but young, I've looed you mony a year.
I mind it well, when thou coud'st hardly gang,
Or lisp out words, I choosed ye frae the thrang 50
Of a' the bairns, and led thee by the hand,
Aft to the tansy-know, or rashy strand.
Thou smiling by my side, I took delite,
To pou the rashes green, with roots sae white,
Of which, as well as my young fancy could, 55
For thee I plet the flowry belt and snood.

Sang x (*tune: 'Winter was cauld, and my Cleathing was thin'*):

PEGGY: When first my dear laddie gade to the green hill,
And I at ew-milking first seyd my young skill,
To bear the milk-bowie, nae pain was to me,
When I at the bughting forgathered with thee. 60

PATIE: When corn-riggs waved yellow, and blew hether-bells
Bloomed bonny on moorland and sweet rising fells,
Nae birns, brier, or breckens, gave trouble to me,
If I found the berries right ripened for thee.

35 drap *drop*
38 gaits *goats*
45 bootless *unrewarded*
46 dauted *adored*
50 thrang *throng*
52 rashy *rushy*
56 plet *plaited*
58 seyd *tried*
59 milk-bowie *milk-bucket*
60 bughting *ewe-milking*
63 birns *scorched patches of heather* breckens *bracken*

PEGGY: When thou ran, or wrestled, or putted the stane, 65
And came aff the victor, my heart was ay fain:
Thy ilka sport manly, gave pleasure to me;
For nane can put, wrestle or run swift as thee.

PATIE: Our Jenny sings saftly the 'Cowden Broom-Knows',
And Rosie lilts sweetly 'The Milking the Ews'; 70
There's few 'Jenny Nettles' like Nansy can sing,
At 'Through the Wood, Laddie' Bess gars our lugs ring:

But when my dear Peggy sings with better skill,
'The Boat-man', 'Tweed-side', or 'The Lass of the Mill',
'Tis many times sweeter and pleasing to me; 75
For though they sing nicely, they cannot like thee.

PEGGY: How easy can lasses trow what they desire?
And praises sae kindly increases love's fire;
Give me still this pleasure, my study shall be
To make my self better and sweeter for thee. 80

PATIE: Wert thou a giglit gawky like the lave,
That little better than our nowt behave;
At nought they'll ferly – senseless tales believe;
Be blyth for silly heghts, for trifles grieve.
Sic ne'er could win my heart, that kenna how 85
Either to keep a prize, or yet prove true.
But thou, in better sense, without a flaw,
As in thy beauty far excells them a',
Continue kind; and a' my care shall be,
How to contrive what pleasing is for thee. 90
PEGGY: Agreed – but harken, yon's auld aunty's cry;
I ken they'll wonder what can make us stay.
PATIE: And let them ferly. Now, a kindly kiss,
Or fivescore good anes wad not be amiss;
And syne we'll sing the sang with tunefu' glee, 95
That I made up last owk on you and me.
PEGGY: Sing first, syne claim your hire.
PATIE: Well, I agree.

65 stane *stone*
72 lugs *ears*
77 trow *believe*
81 giglit *girl*
83 ferly *marvel*
84 heghts *promises*
96 owk *week*

Sang XI (*tune: 'By the delicious warmness of thy mouth'*):

PATIE: By the delicious warmness of thy mouth,
And rowing eyes that smiling tell the truth,
I guess, my lassie, that as well as I, 100
You're made for love; and why should ye deny?
PEGGY: But ken ye, lad, gin we confess o'er soon,
Ye think us cheap, and syne the wooing's done?
The maiden that o'er quickly tines her power,
Like unripe fruit, will taste but hard and sowr. 105
PATIE: But gin they hing o'er lang upon the tree,
Their sweetness they may tine; and sae may ye.
Red cheeked you completely ripe appear;
And I have tholed and wooed a lang haff year.
PEGGY [falls into Patie's arms]:
Then dinna pu' me, gently thus I fa' 110
Into my Patie's arms, for good and a'.
But stint your wishes to this kind embrace;
And mint nae farther till we've got the grace.
PATIE [with his left hand about her waist]:
O charming armfu', hence ye cares away,
I'll kiss my treasure a' the live lang day; 115
All night I'll dream my kisses o'er again,
Till that day come that ye'll be a' my ain.

Sung by both:
Sun, gallop down the westlin skies,
Gang soon to bed, and quickly rise;
O lash your steeds, post time away, 120
And haste about our bridal day:
And if ye're wearied, honest light,
Sleep, gin ye like, a week that night.

End of the second act.

ACT III
Scene (i)

Now turn your eyes beyond yon spreading lime,
And tent a man whase beard seems bleeched with time;
An elvand fills his hand, his habit mean:

99 rowing *roving*
113 mint *aim*

III(i)
2 tent *observe*
3 elvand *ellwand*

Nae doubt ye'll think he has a pedlar been.
But whisht! It is the knight in masquerade, 5
That comes hid in this cloud to see his lad.
Observe how pleased the loyal sufferer moves
Through his auld av'news, anes delightfu' groves.

(*Enter Sir William solus.*)

SIR WILLIAM: The gentleman thus hid in low disguise,
I'll for a space unknown delight mine eyes, 10
With a full view of every fertile plain,
Which once I lost – which now are mine again.
Yet 'midst my joys, some prospects pain renew,
Whilst I my once fair seat in ruins view.
Yonder, ah me, it desolately stands, 15
Without a roof; the gates fal'n from their bands;
The casements all broke down; no chimney left;
The naked walls of tap'stry all bereft:
My stables and pavilions, broken walls,
That with each rainy blast decaying falls: 20
My gardens, once adorned the most complete,
With all that nature, all that art makes sweet;
Where, round the figured green, and peeble walks,
The dewy flowers hung nodding on their stalks:
But, overgrown with nettles, docks and brier, 25
No jaccacinths or eglintines appear.
How do those ample walls to ruin yield,
Where peach and nect'rine branches found a beild,
And basked in rays, which early did produce
Fruit fair to view, delightfu' in the use! 30
All round in gaps, the most in rubbish lie,
And from what stands the withered branches fly.
These soon shall be repaired. And now my joy
Forbids all grief, when I'm to see my boy,
My only prop, and object of my care, 35
Since Heaven too soon called hame his mother fair.
Him, ere the rays of reason cleared his thought,
I secretly to faithful Symon brought,
And charged him strictly to conceal his birth,
'Till we should see what changing times brought forth. 40
Hid from himself, he starts up by the dawn,

16 bands *hinges*
23 peeble *pebble*
26 jaccacinths *hyacinths*
28 beild *shelter*

And ranges careless o'er the height and lawn,
After his fleecy charge, serenely gay,
With other shepherds whistling o'er the day.
Thrice happy life, that's from ambition free; 45
Removed from crowns and courts, how cheerfully
A quiet contented mortal spends his time
In hearty health, his soul unstained with crime.

Sang XII (*tune: 'Happy Clown'*):

Hid from himself, now by the dawn
He starts as fresh as roses blawn, 50
And ranges o'er the heights and lawn,
  After his bleeting flocks.
Healthful, and innocently gay
He chants, and whistles out the day;
Untaught to smile, and then betray, 55
  Like courtly weathercocks.

Life happy from ambition free,
Envy and vile hypocrisie,
Where truth and love with joys agree,
  Unsullied with a crime: 60
Unmoved with what disturbs the great,
In propping of their pride and state;
He lives, and unafraid of fate,
  Contented spends his time.

Now tow'rds good Symon's house I'll bend my way, 65
And see what makes yon gamboling to day,
All on the green, in a fair wanton ring,
My youthful tenants gayly dance and sing.
(*Exit.*)

Scene (ii)

'Tis Symon's house, please to step in,
  And vissy't round and round;
There's nought superfluous to give pain,
  Or costly to be found.

50 blawn *blown*

III(ii)
2 vissy *inspect*

Yet all is clean: a clear peat-ingle 5
Glances amidst the floor;
The green-horn spoons, beech-luggies mingle,
On skelfs foregainst the door.
While the young brood sport on the green,
The auld anes think it best, 10
With the brown cow to clear their een,
Snuff, crack, and take their rest.

(*Enter Symon, Glaud and Elspa.*)

GLAUD: We anes were young oursells. I like to see
The bairns bob round with other merrilie.
Troth, Symon, Patie's grown a strapan lad, 15
And better looks than his I never bade.
Amang our lads, he bears the gree awa',
And tells his tale the cleverest of them a'.

ELSPA: Poor man! He's a great comfort to us baith:
God mak him good, and hide him ay frae skaith. 20
He is a bairn, I'll say't, well worth our care,
That ga'e us ne'er vexation late or air.

GLAUD: I trow, goodwife, if I be not mistane,
He seems to be with Peggy's beauty tane,
And troth, my niece is a right dainty wean, 25
As ye well ken: a bonnier needna be,
Nor better – be't she were nae kin to me.

SYMON: Ha, Glaud, I doubt that ne'er will be a match;
My Patie's wild, and will be ill to catch:
And or he were, for reasons I'll no tell, 30
I'd rather be mixt with the mools mysell.

GLAUD: What reason can ye have? There's nane, I'm sure,
Unless ye may cast up that she's but poor:
But gif the lassie marry to my mind,
I'll be to her as my ain Jenny kind. 35
Fourscore of breeding ews of my ain birn,
Five ky that at ae milking fills a kirn,
I'll gi'e to Peggy that day she's a bride;

5 ingle *hearth*
7 luggies *wooden bowls*
8 skelfs *shelves*
11 brown cow *liquor container*
12 crack *gossip*
16 bade *desired*
17 gree *first place*
23 mistane *mistaken*
25 wean *child*
31 mools *earth*
36 birn *summer pasture*
37 ky *cattle* kirn *churn*

By and attour, gif my good luck abide,
Ten lambs at spaining-time, as lang's I live, 40
And twa quey cawfs I'll yearly to them give.

ELSPA: Ye offer fair, kind Glaud; but dinna speer
What may be is not fit ye yet should hear.

SYMON: Or this day eight days likely he shall learn,
That our denial disna slight his bairn. 45

GLAUD: Well, nae mair o't. Come, gie's the other bend;
We'll drink their healths, whatever way it end.
(*Their healths gae round.*)

SYMON: But will ye tell me, Glaud, by some 'tis said,
Your niece is but a fundling that was laid
Down at your hallon-side, ae morn in May, 50
Right clean rowed up, and bedded on dry hay?

GLAUD: That clatteran Madge, my titty, tells sic flaws,
When e'er our Meg her cankart humour gaws.
(*Enter Jenny.*)

JENNY: O father, there's an auld man on the green,
The fellest fortune-teller e'er was seen: 55
He tents our loofs, and syne whops out a book,
Turns o'er the leaves, and gie's our brows a look;
Syne tells the oddest tales that e'er ye heard.
His head is gray, and lang and gray his beard.

SYMON: Gae bring him in; we'll hear what he can say: 60
Nane shall gang hungry by my house to day.
(*Exit Jenny.*)
But for his telling fortunes, troth I fear,
He kens nae mair of that than my gray mare.

GLAUD: Spae-men! The truth of a' their saws I doubt;
For greater liars never ran there out. 65

(*Jenny returns, bringing in Sir William; with them Patie.*)

SYMON: Ye're welcome, honest carle – here take a seat.

SIR WILLIAM: I give ye thanks, goodman; I'se no be blate.

39 attour *in addition*
40 spaining *weaning*
41 quey cawfs *heifer calves*
46 bend *drink*
49 fundling *foundling*
50 hallon *porch*
51 rowed *rolled*
52 titty *sister* flaws *lies*
53 gaws *galls*
55 fellest *cleverest*
56 loofs *palms* whops *whips*
64 spae-men *fortune-tellers*
66 carle *fellow*
67 blate *shy*

GLAUD (*drinking*): Come t'ye, friend; how far came ye the day?
SIR WILLIAM: I pledge ye, nibour; e'en but little way:
Rousted with eild, a wee piece gate seems lang; 70
Twa miles or three's the maist that I dow gang.
SYMON: Ye're welcome here to stay all night with me,
And take sic bed and board as we can gi'ye.
SIR WILLIAM: That's kind unsought. Well, gin ye have a bairn
That ye like well, and wad his fortune learn, 75
I shall employ the farthest of my skill,
To spae it faithfully, be't good or ill.
SYMON (*pointing to Patie*): Only that lad – alake, I have nae mae,
Either to make me joyful now, or wae.
SIR WILLIAM: Young man, let's see your hand – what
gars ye sneer? 80
PATIE: Because your skill's but little worth I fear.
SIR WILLIAM: Ye cut before the point. But, billy, bide:
I'll wager there's a mouse mark on your side.
ELSPA: Betooch-us-to! And well I wat that's true:
Awa, awa, the Deil's o'er grit wi' you! 85
Four inch aneath his oxter is the mark,
Scarce ever seen since he first wore a sark.
SIR WILLIAM: I'll tell ye mair: if this young lad be spared
But a short while, he'll be a braw rich laird.
ELSPA: A laird! Hear ye, goodman! What think ye now? 90
SYMON: I dinna ken: strange auld man, what art thou?
Fair fa' your heart; 'tis good to bode of wealth:
Come turn the timmer to laird Patie's health.
(*Patie's health gaes round.*)
PATIE: A laird of twa good whistles, and a kent,
Twa curs, my trusty tenants, on the bent, 95
Is all my great estate – and like to be:
Sae, cunning carle, ne'er break your jokes on me.
SYMON: Whisht, Patie, let the man look o'er your hand,
Aftimes as broken a ship has come to land.

(*Sir William looks a little at Patie's hand, then counterfeits falling into a trance, while they endeavour to lay him right.*)

70 rousted *parched* eild *age*
gate *way*
71 dow *can*
77 spae *predict*
78 mae *more*
84 betooch-us-to *commend-us-to* *[God]*
85 grit *great*
86 aneath *underneath* oxter *armpit*
93 timmer *wooden cups*
94 kent *long staff*
95 bent *pasture*

ELSPA: Preserve's! The man's a warlock, or possest 100
With some nae good – or second sight, at least:
Where is he now?
GLAUD: He's seeing a' that's done
In ilka place, beneath or yont the moon.
ELSPA: These second-sighted fowk – His peace be here! –
See things far aff, and things to come, as clear 105
As I can see my thumb – wow, can he tell
(Speer at him, soon as he comes to himsell)
How soon we'll see Sir William? Whisht, he heaves,
And speaks out broken words like ane that raves.
SYMON: He'll soon grow better. Elspa, haste ye, gae, 110
And fill him up a tass of usquebae.
SIR WILLIAM (*starts up, and speaks*):
A knight that for a lyon fought,
Against a herd of bears,
Was to lang toil and trouble brought,
In which some thousands shares. 115
But now again the lyon rares,
And joy spreads o'er the plain:
The lyon has defeat the bears,
The knight returns again.
That knight, in a few days, shall bring 120
A shepherd frae the fauld,
And shall present him to his king,
A subject true and bauld.
He Mr Patrick shall be called:
All you that hear me now, 125
May well believe what I have tald;
For it shall happen true.
SYMON: Friend, may your spaeing happen soon and weel;
But, faith, I'm redd you've bargained with the Deil,
To tell some tales that fowks wad secret keep: 130
Or do ye get them tald you in your sleep?
SIR WILLIAM: Howe'er I get them, never fash your beard;
Nor come I to redd fortunes for reward:
But I'll lay ten to ane with ony here,
That all I prophesy shall soon appear. 135

104 second-sighted *clairvoyant*
107 speer *enquire*
111 tass *cup* usquebae *whisky*
112 lyon *see note*
116 rares *roars*
129 redd *afraid*
132 fash *trouble*
133 redd *sort out*

SYMON: You prophesying fowks are odd kind men!
They're here that ken, and here that disna ken,
The wimpled meaning of your unco tale,
Whilk soon will mak a noise o'er moor and dale.
GLAUD: 'Tis nae sma' sport to hear how Sym believes, 140
And takes't for gospel what the spae-man gives
Of flawing fortunes, whilk he evens to Pate:
But what we wish, we trow at ony rate.
SIR WILLIAM: Whisht, doubtfu' carle; for ere the sun
Has driven twice down to the sea, 145
What I have said ye shall see done
In part, or nae mair credit me.
GLAUD: Well, be't sae, friend, I shall say nathing mair;
But I've twa sonsy lasses young and fair,
Plump ripe for men: I wish ye could foresee 150
Sic fortunes for them might prove joy to me.
SIR WILLIAM: Nae mair through secrets can I sift,
Till darkness black the bent:
I have but anes a day that gift;
Sae rest a while content. 155
SYMON: Elspa, cast on the claith, fetch butt some meat,
And, of your best, gar this auld stranger eat.
SIR WILLIAM: Delay a while your hospitable care;
I'd rather enjoy this evening calm and fair,
Around yon ruined tower, to fetch a walk 160
With you, kind friend, to have some private talk.
SYMON: Soon as you please I'll answer your desire:
And, Glaud, you'll take your pipe beside the fire;
We'll but gae round the place, and soon be back,
Syne sup together, and tak our pint, and crack. 165
GLAUD: I'll out a while, and see the young anes play.
My heart's still light, abeit my locks be gray.
(*Exeunt.*)

138 wimpled *twisted*
142 flawing *lying* evens *applies*
149 sonsy *handsome*
156 butt *out*

Scene (iii)

Jenny pretends an errand hame,
  Young Roger draps the rest,
To whisper out his melting flame,
  And thow his lassie's breast.
Behind a bush, well hid frae sight, they meet: 5
See Jenny's laughing; Roger's like to greet.
    Poor shepherd!
    (*Enter Roger and Jenny.*)

ROGER: Dear Jenny, I wad speak to ye, wad ye let;
And yet I ergh, ye're ay sae scornfu' set.
JENNY: And what would Roger say, if he could speak? 10
Am I obliged to guess what ye're to seek?
ROGER: Yes, ye may guess right eith for what I grein,
Baith by my service, sighs, and langing een.
And I maun out wi't, though I risk your scorn;
Ye're never frae my thoughts baith ev'n and morn. 15
Ah, could I loo ye less, I'd happy be;
But happier far, could ye but fancy me.
JENNY: And wha kens, honest lad, but that I may?
Ye canna say that e'er I said ye nay.
ROGER: Alake, my frighted heart begins to fail, 20
When e'er I mint to tell ye out my tale,
For fear some tighter lad, mair rich than I,
Has win your love, and near your heart may lie.
JENNY: I loo my father, cousin Meg I love;
But to this day, nae man my mind could move: 25
Except my kin, ilk lad's alike to me;
And frae ye all I best had keep me free.
ROGER: How lang, dear Jenny? Sayna that again;
What pleasure can ye tak in giving pain?
I'm glad, however, that ye yet stand free: 30
Wha kens but ye may rue, and pity me?
JENNY: Ye have my pity else, to see ye set
On that whilk makes our sweetness soon foryet.
Wow, but we're bonny, good, and everything;

III(iii)
4 thow *thaw*
6 greet *weep*
9 ergh *hesitate*
12 eith *easily* grein *yearn*
21 mint *try*
33 foryet *forgotten*

How sweet we breathe, when e'er we kiss, or sing! 35
But we're nae sooner fools to give consent,
Than we our daffine and tint power repent:
When prisoned in four waws, a wife right tame,
Although the first, the greatest drudge at hame.

ROGER: That only happens, when for sake of gear, 40
Ane wales a wife, as he wad buy a mear;
Or when dull parents bairns together bind
Of different tempers, that can ne'er prove kind.
But love, true downright love, engages me,
Though thou should scorn, still to delight in thee. 45

JENNY: What sugared words frae woers lips can fa'!
But girning marriage comes and ends them a'.
I've seen with shining fair the morning rise,
And soon the sleety clouds mirk a' the skies.
I've seen the silver spring a while rin clear, 50
And soon in mossy puddles disappear.
The bridegroom may rejoice, the bride may smile;
But soon contentions a' their joys beguile.

ROGER: I've seen the morning rise with fairest light,
The day unclouded sink in calmest night. 55
I've seen the spring rin wimpling through the plain,
Increase and join the ocean without stain.
The bridegroom may be blyth, the bride may smile;
Rejoice through life, and all your fears beguile.

Sang XIII (*tune: 'Leith-Wynd'*):

JENNY:

Were I assured you'll constant prove, 60
You should nae mair complain,
The easy maid beset with love,
Few words will quickly gain;
For I must own, now since you're free,
This too fond heart of mine 65
Has lang, a black-sole true to thee,
Wished to be paired with thine.

37 daffine *folly* tint *lost*
41 wales *chooses*
47 girning *grumbling*
49 mirk *darken*
66 black-sole *lovers' go-between*

ROGER:
I'm happy now, ah! let my head
  Upon thy breast recline;
The pleasure strikes me near-hand dead! 70
  Is Jenny then sae kind? –
O let me briss thee to my heart!
  And round my arms entwine:
Delytful thought; we'll never part!
  Come press thy mouth to mine. 75

JENNY: With equal joy my easy heart gi'es way,
To own thy well-tried love has won the day.
Now by these warmest kisses thou has tane,
Swear thus to love me, when by vows made ane.
ROGER: I swear by fifty thousand yet to come, 80
Or may the first ane strike me deaf and dumb,
There shall not be a kindlier dawted wife,
If you agree with me to lead your life.
JENNY:
Sang XIV (*tune: 'O'er Bogie'*):

Well I agree, ye're sure of me;
  Next to my father gae. 85
Make him content to give consent,
  He'll hardly say you nay:
For you have what he wad be at,
  And will commend you well,
Since parents auld think love grows cauld, 90
  Where bairns want milk and meal.

Should he deny, I carena by,
  He'd contradict in vain.
Though a' my kin had said and sworn,
  But thee I will have nane. 95
Then never range, or learn to change,
  Like these in high degree:
And if you prove faithful in love,
  You'll find nae fault in me.

72 briss *press* 82 dawted *adored*

ROGER: My faulds contain twice fifteen forrow nowt, 100
As mony newcal in my byers rowt;
Five pack of woo I can at Lammas sell,
Shorn frae my bob-tailed bleeters on the fell:
Good twenty pair of blankets for our bed,
With meikle care, my thrifty mither made. 105
Ilk thing that makes a heartsome house and tight,
Was still her care, my father's great delight.
They left me all; which now gi'es joy to me,
Because I can give a', my dear, to thee:
And had I fifty times as meikle mair, 110
Nane but my Jenny should the samen skair.
My love and all is yours; now had them fast,
And guide them as ye like, to gar them last.
JENNY: I'll do my best. But see wha comes this way,
Patie and Meg – besides, I mauna stay: 115
Let's steal frae ither now, and meet the morn;
If we be seen, we'll drie a deal of scorn.
ROGER: To where the saugh-trees shades the mennin-pool,
I'll frae the hill come down, when day grows cool:
Keep triste, and meet me there – there let us meet, 120
To kiss, and tell our love – there's nought sae sweet.
(*Exeunt.*)

Scene (iv)

This scene presents the knight and Sym
Within a gallery of the place,
Where all looks ruinous and grim;
Nor has the baron shown his face,
But joking with his shepherd leel, 5
Aft speers the gate he kens fu' well.

(*Enter Sir William and Symon.*)
SIR WILLIAM: To whom belongs this house so much decayed?
SYMON: To ane that lost it, lending generous aid,

100 forrow nowt *cattle not in calf*
101 newcal *with calf* rowt *roar*
102 Lammas *1 August*
106 heartsome *pleasant*
111 samen skair *same share*
112 had *hold*
117 drie *suffer*
118 saugh *willow* mennin *minnow*
120 triste *tryst*

III(iv)
2 place *mansion*
5 leel *loyal*
6 speers the gate *asks the way*

To bear the head up, when rebellious tail
Against the laws of nature did prevail. 10
Sir William Worthy is our master's name,
Whilk fills us all with joy, now he's come hame.
(Sir William draps his masking beard,
Symon transported sees
The welcome knight with fond regard, 15
And grasps him round the knees.)
My master! My dear master! Do I breathe,
To see him healthy, strong, and free frae skaith;
Returned to cheer his wishing tenants sight,
To bless his son, my charge, the world's delight! 20
SIR WILLIAM: Rise, faithful Symon; in my arms enjoy
A place, thy due, kind guardian of my boy:
I came to view thy care in this disguise,
And am confirmed thy conduct has been wise;
Since still the secret thou'st securely sealed, 25
And ne'er to him his real birth revealed.
SYMON: The due obedience to your strict command
Was the first lock; neist, my ain judgment fand
Out reasons plenty, since, without estate,
A youth, though sprung frae kings, looks baugh and blate. 30
SIR WILLIAM: And aften vain and idly spend their time,
'Till grown unfit for action, past their prime,
Hang on their friends – which gie's their sauls a cast,
That turns them downright beggars at the last.
SYMON: Now well I wat, sir, ye have spoken true; 35
For there's Laird Kytie's son, that's looed by few:
His father steght his fortune in his wame,
And left his heir nought but a gentle name.
He gangs about sornan frae place to place,
As scrimp of manners, as of sense and grace; 40
Oppressing all as punishment of their sin,
That are within his tenth degree of kin:
Rins in ilk trader's debt, wha's sae unjust
To his ain fam'ly, as to give him trust.
SIR WILLIAM: Such useless branches of a common-wealth, 45
Should be lopt off, to give a state mair health,
Unworthy bare reflection. Symon, run

28 fand *found*
30 baugh *indifferent* blate *timid*
36 Kytie *corpulent*
37 steght *stuffed* wame *stomach*
39 sornan *scrounging*
40 scrimp *short*

O'er all your observations on my son;
A parent's fondness easily finds excuse:
But do not with indulgence truth abuse. 50

SYMON: To speak his praise, the langest simmer day
Wad be o'er short – could I them right display.
In word and deed he can sae well behave,
That out of sight he runs before the lave;
And when there's e'er a quarrel or contest, 55
Patrick's made judge to tell whase cause is best;
And his decreet stands good – he'll gar it stand:
Wha dares to grumble, finds his correcting hand;
With a firm look, and a commanding way,
He gars the proudest of our herds obey. 60

SIR WILLIAM: Your tale much pleases. My good friend, proceed:
What learning has he? Can he write and read?

SYMON: Baith wonder well; for, troth, I didna spare
To gi'e him at the school enough of lair;
And he delites in books: he reads, and speaks 65
With fowks that ken them, Latin words and Greeks.

SIR WILLIAM: Where gets he books to read, and of what kind?
Though some give light, some blindly lead the blind.

SYMON: Whene'er he drives our sheep to Edinburgh port,
He buys some books of history, sangs or sport: 70
Nor does he want of them a rowth at will,
And carries ay a poutchfu' to the hill.
About ane Shakspear, and a famous Ben,
He aften speaks, and ca's them best of men.
How sweetly Hawthrenden and Stirling sing, 75
And ane ca'd Cowley, loyal to his king,
He kens fu' well, and gars their verses ring.
I sometimes thought he made o'er great a frase,
About fine poems, histories and plays.
When I reproved him anes, a book he brings, 80
'With this,' quoth he, 'on braes I crack with kings.'

SIR WILLIAM: He answered well; and much ye glad my ear,
When such accounts I of my shepherd hear.

57 decreet *decision*
64 lair *learning*
69 port *gateway*
71 rowth *plenty*
73 Ben *Jonson see note*
75–76 Hawthrenden, Stirling, Cowley *see note*
78 frase *fuss*
81 crack *talk*

Reading such books can raise a peasant's mind
Above a lord's that is not thus inclined. 85

SYMON: What ken we better, that sae sindle look,
Except on rainy Sundays, on a book;
When we a leaf or twa haff read, haff spell,
Till a' the rest sleep round, as well's oursell?

SIR WILLIAM: Well jested, Symon; but one question more 90
I'll only ask ye now, and then give o'er.
The youth's arrived the age when little loves
Flighter around young hearts like cooing doves:
Has nae young lassie, with inviting mien,
And rosy cheek, the wonder of the green, 95
Engaged his look, and caught his youthfu' heart?

SYMON: I feared the warst, but kend the smallest part,
Till late I saw him twa three times mair sweet,
With Glaud's fair neice, than I thought right or meet:
I had my fears; but now have nought to fear, 100
Since like yoursell your son will soon appear.
A gentleman, enriched with all these charms,
May bless the fairest best-born lady's arms.

SIR WILLIAM: This night must end his unambitious fire,
When higher views shall greater thoughts inspire. 105
Go, Symon, bring him quickly here to me;
None but yourself shall our first meeting see.
Yonder's my horse and servants nigh at hand,
They come just at the time I gave command;
Straight in my own apparel I'll go dress: 110
Now ye the secret may to all confess.

SYMON: With how much joy I on this errand flee,
There's nane can know, that is not downright me!

(*Exit Symon.*)

SIR WILLIAM (*solus*): When the event of hopes successfully appears,
One happy hour cancels the toil of years. 115
A thousand toils are lost in Lethe's stream,
And cares evanish like a morning dream;
When wished-for pleasures rise like morning light,
The pain that's past enhances the delight.

86 sindle *seldom*
93 flighter *flutter*
112 flee *fly*
114 event *outcome*
116 Lethe *river of forgetting*
117 evanish *vanish*

These joys I feel that words can ill express, 120
I ne'er had known without my late distress.

Sang XV (*tune: 'Wat ye wha I met Yestreen?'*):

Now from rusticity, and love,
  Whose flames but over lowly burn
My gentle shepherd must be drove,
  His soul must take another turn: 125
As the rough diamond from the mine,
  In breakings only shews its light.
'Till polishing has made it shine,
  Thus learning makes the genius bright.
(*Exit.*)

End of the third act.

ACT IV
Scene (i)

The scene described in former page,
Glaud's onset. Enter Mause and Madge.

MAUSE: Our laird's come hame! And owns young Pate his heir!
  That's news indeed!
MADGE: As true as ye stand there.
  As they were dancing all in Symon's yard, 5
  Sir William, like a warlock, with a beard
  Five nives in length, and white as driven snaw,
  Amang us came, cried, 'Had ye merry a'.'
  We ferlied meikle at his unco look,
  While frae his pouch he whirled forth a book. 10
  As we stood round about him on the green,
  He viewed us a', but fixed on Pate his een;
  Then pawkily pretended he could spae,
  Yet for his pains and skill wad nathing ha'e.
MAUSE: Then sure the lasses, and ilk gaping coof, 15
  Wad rin about him, and had out their loof.

IV(i)
2 onset *farmstead*
7 nives *fists*
9 ferlied *marvelled*
13 pawkily *craftily*
15 coof *fool*
16 loof *palm*

MADGE: As fast as flaes skip to the tate of woo,
Whilk slee Tod Lawrie hads without his mow,
When he to drown them, and his hips to cool,
In simmer days slides backward in a pool: 20
In short he did, for Pate, braw things fortell,
Without the help of conjuring or spell.
At last, when well diverted, he withdrew,
Powed aff his beard to Symon, Symon knew
His welcome master, round his knees he gat, 25
Hang at his coat, and syne for blythness grat.
Patrick was sent for – happy lad is he!
Symon tald Elspa, Elspa tald it me.
Ye'll hear out a' the secret story soon;
And troth 'tis e'en right odd when a' is done, 30
To think how Symon ne'er afore wad tell,
Na, no sae meikle as to Pate himsell.
Our Meg, poor thing, alake, has lost her jo.
MAUSE: It may be sae; wha kens? And may be no.
To lift a love that's rooted is great pain; 35
Even kings have tane a queen out of the plain:
And what has been before, may be again.
MADGE: Sic nonsense! Love tak root, but tocher-good,
'Tween a herd's bairn, and ane of gentle blood!
Sic fashions in King Bruce's days might be; 40
But siccan ferlies now we never see.
MAUSE: Gif Pate forsakes her, Bauldy she may gain;
Yonder he comes, and wow but he looks fain!
Nae doubt he thinks that Peggy's now his ain.
MADGE: He get her! Slaverin doof, it sets him weil 45
To yoke a plough where Patrick thought to till.
Gif I were Meg, I'd let young master see –
MAUSE: Ye'd be as dorty in your choice as he:
And so wad I. But whisht, here Bauldy comes.
(*Enter Bauldy singing.*)

BAULDY:
Jenny said to Jocky, gin ye winna tell, 50
Ye shall be the lad, I'll be the lass mysell;

17 flaes *fleas* tate *tuft*
18 Tod Lawrie *the fox*
26 grat *wept*
33 jo *sweetheart*
38 tocher *dowry*
40 King Bruce *see note*
41 ferlies *wonders*
43 fain *joyful*
45 slaverin doof *chattering fool*
48 dorty *haughty*
49 s.d. Bauldy singing *see note*
50 winna *will not*

Ye're a bonny lad, and I'm a lassie free;
Ye're welcomer to tak me than to let me be.
MADGE: Well liltit, Bauldy, that's a dainty sang.
BAULDY: I'll gie ye't a', 'tis better than 'tis lang. 55
(*Bauldy sings again.*)
I hae gowd and gear, I have land enough,
I hae seven good owsen ganging in a pleugh;
Gangin in a pleugh, and linkan o'er the lee,
And gin ye winna tak me, I can let ye be.

I hae a good ha'-house, a barn and a byre, 60
A peatstack 'fore the door, we'll make a rantin fire;
I'll make a rantin fire, and merry sall we be,
And gin ye winna take me, I can let ye be.

I trow sae. Lasses will come to at last,
Though for a while they maun their snaw-ba's cast. 65
MAUSE: Well, Bauldy, how gaes a'?
BAULDY: Faith, unco right:
I hope we'll a' sleep sound but ane this night.
MADGE: And wha's the unlucky ane, if we may ask?
BAULDY: To find out that is nae difficult task;
Poor bonny Peggy, wha maun think nae mair 70
On Pate, turned Patrick, and Sir William's heir.
Now, now, good Madge, and honest Mause, stand be,
While Meg's in dumps, put in a word for me.
I'll be as kind as ever Pate could prove;
Less wilful, and ay constant in my love. 75
MADGE: As Neps can witness, and the bushy thorn,
Where mony a time to her your heart was sworn:
Fy, Bauldy, blush, and vows of love regard;
What other lass will trow a mansworn herd?
The curse of Heaven hings ay aboon their heads, 80
That's ever guilty of sic sinfu' deeds.
I'll ne'er advise my niece sae gray a gate;
Nor will she be advised, fu' well I wate.
BAULDY: Sae gray a gate! Mansworn! and a' the rest:
Ye leed, auld roudes – and, in faith, had best 85

57 owsen *oxen*
58 linkan *skipping*
60 ha'-house *manor house*
65 snaw-ba's *snow-balls*
79 mansworn *perjured*
82 sae gray a gate *a disastrous course*
83 wate *know*
85 leed *babble* roudes *hag*

Eat in your words; else I shall gar ye stand
With a het face afore the haly band.
MADGE: Ye'll gar me stand! Ye sheveling-gabit brock;
Speak that again, and, trembling, dread my rock,
And ten sharp nails, that when my hands are in, 90
Can flyp the skin o' yer cheeks out o'er your chin.
BAULDY: I tak ye witness, Mause, ye heard her say,
That I'm mansworn – I winna let it gae.
MADGE: Ye're witness to, he ca'd me bonny names,
And should be served as his good breeding claims. 95
Ye filthy dog!
(*Madge flees to his hair like a fury. A stout battle. Mause endeavours to redd them.*)
MAUSE: Let gang your grips, fy, Madge! Howt, Bauldy, leen:
I wadna wish this tulzie had been seen;
'Tis sae daft like.
(*Bauldy gets out of Madge's clutches with a bleeding nose.*)
MADGE: 'Tis dafter like to thole
An ether-cap, like him, to blaw the coal: 100
It sets him well, with vile unscrapit tongue,
To cast up whether I be auld or young;
They're aulder yet than I have married been,
And or they died their bairns' bairns have seen.
MAUSE: That's true; and Bauldy ye was far to blame, 105
To ca' Madge ought but her ain christened name.
BAULDY: My lugs, my nose, and noddle finds the same.
MADGE: Auld roudes! Filthy fallow; I shall auld ye.
MAUSE: Howt no! Ye'll e'en be friends with honest Bauldy.
Come, come, shake hands; this maun nae farder gae: 110
Ye maun forgi'e 'm. I see the lad looks wae.
BAULDY: In troth now, Mause, I have at Madge nae spite;
But she abusing first was a' the wite
Of what has happened: and should therefore crave
My pardon first, and shall acquittance have. 115
MADGE: I crave your pardon! Gallows-face, gae greet,
And own your faut to her that ye wad cheat,

87 haly band *the Kirk Session*
88 sheveling-gabit brock *wry-mouthed badger*
89 rock *distaff*
91 flyp *peel*
96 s.d. redd *part*
97 leen *desist*
98 tulzie *fight*
99 thole *endure*
100 ether-cap *spider*
107 lugs *ears* noddle *head*
110 farder *farther*
113 wite *blame*
116 greet *weep*

Gae, or be blasted in your health and gear,
'Till ye learn to perform, as well as swear.
Vow, and lowp back! Was e'er the like heard tell? 120
Swith, tak him, Deil; he's o'er lang out of Hell.

BAULDY (*running off*): His presence be about us! Curst were he
That were condemned for life to live with thee.
(*Exit Bauldy*.)

MADGE (*laughing*): I think I've towzled his harigalds a wee;
He'll no soon grein to tell his love to me. 125
He's but a rascal that wad mint to serve
A lassie sae, he does but ill deserve.

MAUSE: Ye towined him tightly – I commend ye for't;
His blooding snout gave me nae little sport:
For this forenoon he had that scant of grace, 130
And breeding baith, to tell me to my face,
He hoped I was a witch, and wadna stand,
To lend him in this case my helping hand.

MADGE: A witch! How had ye patience this to bear,
And leave him een to see, or lugs to hear? 135

MAUSE: Auld withered hands, and feeble joints like mine,
Obliges fowk resentment to decline;
Till aft 'tis seen, when vigour fails, then we
With cunning can the lake of pith supplie.
Thus I pat aff revenge till it was dark, 140
Syne bade him come, and we should gang to wark:
I'm sure he'll keep his triste; and I came here
To seek your help, that we the fool may fear.

MADGE: And special sport we'll have, as I protest;
Ye'll be the witch, and I shall play the ghaist; 145
A linen sheet wond round me like ane dead,
I'll cawk my face, and grane, and shake my head.
We'll fleg him sae, he'll mint nae mair to gang
A-conjuring, to do a lassie wrang.

MAUSE: Then let us go; for see, 'tis hard on night, 150
The westlin cloud shines red with setting light.
(*Exeunt*.)

120 lowp back *renege*
121 swith *quick*
124 towzled *ruffled* harigalds *entrails*
125 grein *yearn*
126 mint *aim*
128 towined *beat*
139 lake *lack*
146 wond *wound*
147 cawk *chalk*
148 fleg *frighten*

Scene (ii)

When birds begin to nod upon the bough,
And the green swaird grows damp with falling dew,
While good Sir William is to rest retired,
The gentle shepherd, tenderly inspired,
Walks through the broom with Roger ever leel, 5
To meet, to comfort Meg, and tak farewell.

ROGER: Wow, but I'm cadgie, and my heart lowps light,
Oh, Mr Patrick, ay your thoughts were right:
Sure gentle fowk are farther seen than we,
That naithing ha'e to brag of pedigree. 10
My Jenny now, wha brak my heart this morn,
Is perfect yielding, sweet, and nae mair scorn.
I spake my mind – she heard – I spake again,
She smiled – I kissed – I wooed, nor wooed in vain.
PATIE: I'm glad to hear't – but oh, my change this day 15
Heaves up my joy, and yet I'm sometimes wae.
I've found a father, gently kind as brave,
And an estate that lifts me 'boon the lave.
With looks all kindness, words that love confest;
He all the father to my soul exprest, 20
While close he held me to his manly breast.
'Such were the eyes,' he said, 'thus smiled the mouth
Of thy loved mother, blessing of my youth,
Who set too soon!' – and while he praise bestowed,
Adown his graceful cheek a torrent flowed. 25
My new-born joys, and this his tender tale,
Did, mingled thus, o'er a' my thoughts prevail:
That speechless lang, my late kend sire I viewed,
While gushing tears my panting breast bedewed.
Unusual transports made my head turn round, 30
Whilst I myself with rising raptures found
The happy son of ane sae much renowned.
But he has heard! Too faithful Symon's fear
Has brought my love for Peggy to his ear:
Which he forbids. Ah, this confounds my peace, 35
While thus to beat, my heart shall sooner cease.
ROGER: How to advise ye, troth I'm at a stand:
But were't my case, ye'd clear it up aff hand.

IV(ii)
2 swaird *sward*
5 leel *faithful*
7 cadgie *cheerful*

PATIE:
Sang XVI (*tune: 'Kirk wad let me be'*):

Duty and part of reason,
  Plead strong on the parent's side, 40
Which love superior calls treason;
  The strongest must be obeyed:
For now though I'm one of the gentry,
  My constancy falsehood repels;
For change in my heart is no entry, 45
  Still there my dear Peggy excels.

ROGER: Enjoy them baith. Sir William will be won:
Your Peggy's bonny – you're his only son.
PATIE: She's mine by vows, and stronger ties of love;
And frae these bands nae change my mind shall move. 50
I'll wed nane else; through life I will be true:
But still obedience is a parent's due.
ROGER: Is not our master and yoursell to stay
Amang us here, or are ye gawn away
To London court, or ither far aff parts, 55
To leave your ain poor us with broken hearts?
PATIE: To Edinburgh straight tomorrow we advance,
To London neist, and afterwards to France,
Where I must stay some years, and learn – to dance,
And twa three other monkey-tricks. That done, 60
I come hame strutting in my red-heeled shoon.
Then 'tis designed, when I can well behave,
That I maun be some petted thing's dull slave,
For some few bags of cash, that I wat weel
I nae mair need nor carts do a third wheel. 65
But Peggy, dearer to me than my breath,
Sooner than hear sic news, shall hear my death.
ROGER: 'They wha have just enough, can soundly sleep;
The o'ercome only fashes fowk to keep.'
Good Mr Patrick, tak your ain tale hame. 70
PATIE: What was my morning thought, at night's the same.
The poor and rich but differ in the name.
Content's the greatest bliss we can procure
Frae 'boon the lift. Without it kings are poor.
ROGER: But an estate like yours yields braw content, 75

68–69 *Act I.(i).* 79–80   74 lift *sky*

When we but pick it scantly on the bent:
Fine claiths, saft beds, sweet houses, and red wine,
Good cheer, and witty friends, whene'er ye dine;
Obeysant servants, honour, wealth and ease:
Wha's no content with these are ill to please. 80

PATIE: Sae Roger thinks, and thinks not far amiss;
But mony a cloud hings hovering o'er the bliss.
The passions rule the roast, and, if they're sowr,
Like the lean ky, will soon the fat devour.
The spleen, tint honour, and affronted pride, 85
Stang like the sharpest goads in gentry's side,
The gouts and gravels, and the ill disease,
Are frequentest with fowk o'erlaid with ease;
While o'er the moor the shepherd, with less care,
Enjoys his sober wish, and halesome air. 90

ROGER: Lord, man, I wonder ay, and it delights
My heart, whene'er I hearken to your flights.
How gat ye a' that sense, I fain wad lear,
That I may easier disappointments bear.

PATIE: Frae books, the wale of books, I gat some skill; 95
These best can teach what's real good and ill.
Ne'er grudge ilk year to ware some stanes of cheese,
To gain these silent friends that ever please.

ROGER: I'll do't, and ye shall tell me which to buy:
Faith, I'se ha'e books, though I should sell my ky. 100
But now let's hear how you're designed to move,
Between Sir William's will, and Peggy's love.

PATIE: Then here it lies. His will maun be obeyed;
My vows I'll keep, and she shall be my bride:
But I some time this last design maun hide. 105
Keep you the secret close, and leave me here;
I sent for Peggy, yonder comes my dear.

ROGER: Pleased that ye trust me with the secret, I
To wyle it frae me a' the deils defy.

(*Exit Roger.*)

76 bent *field*
79 obeysant *obedient*
84 ky *cattle*
85 tint *lost*
86 stang *sting*
93 lear *learn*
95 wale *choice*
97 ware *sell*

PATIE (*solus*): With what a struggle must I now impart 110
My father's will to her that hads my heart!
I ken she loves, and her saft saul will sink,
While it stands trembling on the hated brink
Of disappointment. Heaven support my fair,
And let her comfort claim your tender care! 115
Her eyes are red!

(*Enter Peggy.*)

My Peggy, why in tears?
Smile as ye wont, allow nae room for fears:
Though I'm nae mair a shepherd, yet I'm thine.

PEGGY: I dare not think sae high: I now repine
At the unhappy chance, that made not me 120
A gentle match, or still a herd kept thee.
Wha can, withoutten pain, see frae the coast
The ship that bears his all like to be lost?
Like to be carried, by some rever's hand,
Far frae his wishes, to some distant land? 125

PATIE: Ne'er quarrel fate, whilst it with me remains,
To raise thee up, or still attend these plains.
My father has forbid our loves, I own:
But love's superior to a parent's frown.
I falsehood hate: come, kiss thy cares away; 130
I ken to love, as well as to obey.
Sir William's generous; leave the task to me,
To make strict duty and true love agree.

PEGGY:
Sang XVII (*tune: 'Woes my heart that we shou'd sunder'*):

Speak on, speak thus, and still my grief,
Hold up a heart that's sinking under 135
These fears, that soon will want relief,
When Pate must from Peggy sunder.
A gentler face and silk attire,
A lady rich in beauty's blossom,
Alake, poor me, will now conspire, 140
To steal thee from thy Peggy's bosom.

No more the shepherd who excelled
The rest, whose wit made them to wonder,

124 rever *pirate*

Shall now his Peggy's praises tell,
  Ah, I can die, but never sunder. 145
Ye meadows where we often strayed,
  Ye banks where we were wont to wander,
Sweet scented rucks round which we played,
  You'll loss your sweets when we're asunder.

Again, ah, shall I never creep 150
  Around the know with silent duty,
Kindly to watch thee while asleep,
  And wonder at thy manly beauty?
Hear, Heaven, while solemnly I vow,
  Though thou shouldst prove a wandering lover, 155
Through life to thee I shall prove true,
  Nor be a wife to any other.

PATIE: Sure Heaven approves – and be assured of me,
I'll ne'er gang back of what I've sworn to thee:
And time, though time maun interpose a while, 160
And I maun leave my Peggy and this isle;
Yet time, nor distance, nor the fairest face,
If there's a fairer, e'er shall fill thy place.
I'd hate my rising fortune, should it move
The fair foundation of our faithful love. 165
If at my foot were crowns and sceptres laid,
To bribe my soul frae thee, delightful maid;
For thee I'd soon leave these inferior things
To sic as have the patience to be kings.
Wherefore that tear? Believe, and calm thy mind. 170
PEGGY:
Sang XVIII (*tune: 'Tweed-side'*):

When hope was quite sunk in despair,
  My heart it was going to break;
My life appeared worthless my care,
  But now I will sav't for thy sake.
Where'er my love travels by day, 175
  Wherever he lodges by night,
With me his dear image shall stay,
  And my soul keep him e'er in sight.

148 rucks *haystacks*

With patience I'll wait the long year,
And study the gentlest charms; 180
Hope time away till thou appear,
To lock thee for ay in those arms.
Whilst thou wast a shepherd, I prized
No higher degree in this life;
But now I'll endeavour to rise 185
To a height is becoming thy wife.

For beauty that's only skin deep,
Must fade like the gowans of May,
But inwardly rooted, will keep
For ever, without a decay. 190
Nor age, nor the changes of life,
Can quench the fair fire of love,
If virtue's ingrained in the wife,
And the husband have sense to approve.

PATIE: That's wisely said, 195
And what he wares that way shall be well paid.
Though without a' the little helps of art,
Thy native sweets might gain a prince's heart:
Yet now, lest in our station, we offend,
We must learn modes, to innocence unkend; 200
Affect aftimes to like the thing we hate,
And drap serenity, to keep up state:
Laugh, when we're sad; speak, when we've nought to say;
And, for the fashion, when we're blyth, seem wae:
Pay compliments to them we aft have scorned; 205
Then scandalize them, when their backs are turned.
PEGGY: If this is gentry, I had rather be
What I am still – but I'll be ought with thee.
PATIE: No, no, my Peggy, I but only jest
With gentry's apes; for still amangst the best, 210
Good manners give integrity a bleez,
When native virtues join the arts to please.
PEGGY: Since with nae hazard, and sae small expense,
My lad frae books can gather siccan sense;
Then why, ah, why should the tempestuous sea, 215
Endanger thy dear life, and frighten me?
Sir William's cruel, that wad force his son,

188 gowans *daisies*
196 wares *spends*
211 bleez *beacon*

For watna-whats sae great a risk to run.
PATIE: There is nae doubt, but travelling does improve,
Yet I would shun it for thy sake, my love. 220
But soon as I've shook aff my landwart cast
In foreign cities, hame to thee I'll haste.
PEGGY:
Sang XIX (*tune: 'Bush aboon Traquair'*):

At setting day and rising morn,
With soul that still shall love thee,
I'll ask of heaven thy safe return, 225
With all that can improve thee.
I'll visit oft the birken-bush,
Where first thou kindly told me,
Sweet tales of love, and hid my blush,
Whilst round thou didst enfold me. 230

To all our haunts I will repair,
By greenwood-shaw or fountain;
Or where the summer-day I'd share
With thee, upon yon mountain.
There will I tell the trees and flowers, 235
From thoughts unfeigned and tender.
By vows you're mine, by love is yours
A heart which cannot wander.

PATIE: My dear, allow me, frae thy temples fair,
A shining ringlet of thy flowing hair; 240
Which, as a sample of each lovely charm,
I'll aften kiss, and wear about my arm.
PEGGY: Were't in my power with better boons to please,
I'd give the best I could with the same ease;
Nor wad I, if thy luck had faln to me, 245
Been in ae jot less generous to thee.
PATIE: I doubt it not; but since we've little time
To ware't on words, wad border on a crime:
Love's safter meaning better is exprest,
When 'tis with kisses on the heart imprest. 250
(*Exeunt.*)

End of the fourth act

218 watna-whats *don't-know-whats*
221 landwart *rustic*
227 birken-bush *birch-bush*
232 shaw *thicket*

ACT V
Scene (i)

See how poor Bauldy stares like ane possest,
And roars up Symon frae his kindly rest.
Bare legged, with night-cap, and unbuttoned coat,
See, the auld man comes forward to the sot.

SYMON: What want ye, Bauldy, at this early hour, 5
While drowsy sleep keeps a' beneath its pow'r?
Far to the north, the scant approaching light
Stands equal 'twixt the morning and the night.
What gars ye shake and glowr, and look sae wan?
Your teeth they chitter, hair like bristles stand. 10
BAULDY: Oh, len me soon some water, milk or ale,
My head's grown giddy – legs with shaking fail;
I'll ne'er dare venture forth at night my lane:
Alake! I'll never be mysell again.
I'll ne'er o'erput it! Symon! O Symon! Oh! 15
(Symon gives him a drink.)
SYMON: What ails thee, gowk, to make sae loud ado?
You've waked Sir William, he has left his bed;
He comes, I fear ill pleased: I hear his tread.

(Enter Sir William.)
SIR WILLIAM: How goes the night? Does day-light yet appear?
Symon, you're very timeously asteer. 20
SYMON: I'm sorry, sir, that we've disturbed your rest:
But some strange thing has Bauldy's sp'rit oppress;
He's seen some witch, or wrestled with a ghaist.
BAULDY: Oh ay! Dear sir, in troth 'tis very true;
And I am come to make my plaint to you. 25
SIR WILLIAM (*smiling*): I lang to hear't.
BAULDY: Ah sir, the witch ca'd Mause,
That wins aboon the mill amang the haws,
First promised that she'd help me with her art,
To gain a bonny thrawart lassie's heart.
As she had tristed, I met wi'er this night; 30
But may nae friend of mine get sic a fright!

v(i)
15 o'erput *get over*
16 gowk *fool*
23 witch *see note*
27 wins *lives* haws *hawthorns*
29 thrawart *perverse*

For the cursed hag, instead of doing me good,
(The very thought o't's like to freeze my blood!)
Raised up a ghaist or deil, I kenna whilk,
Like a dead corse in sheet as white as milk, 35
Black hands it had, and face as wan as death,
Upon me fast the witch and it fell baith,
And gat me down; while I, like a great fool,
Was laboured as I wont to be at school.
My heart out of its hool was like to lowp; 40
I pithless grew with fear, and had nae hope,
Till, with an elritch laugh, they vanished quite:
Syne I, haff dead with anger, fear and spite,
Crap up, and fled straight frae them, sir, to you,
Hoping your help, to gi'e the Deil his due. 45
I'm sure my heart will ne'er gi'e o'er to dunt,
Till in a fat tar-barrel Mause be burnt.

SIR WILLIAM: Well, Bauldy, whate'er's just shall granted be;
Let Mause be brought this morning down to me.

BAULDY: Thanks to your honour, soon shall I obey; 50
But first I'll Roger raise, and twa three mae,
To catch her fast, or she get leave to squeel,
And cast her cantraips that bring up the Deil.

(*Exit Bauldy.*)

SIR WILLIAM: Troth, Symon, Bauldy's more afraid than hurt,
The witch and ghaist have made themselves good sport. 55
What silly notions crowd the clouded mind,
That is through want of education blind!

SYMON: But does your honour think there's nae sic thing
As witches raising deils up through a ring?
Syne playing tricks, a thousand I could tell, 60
Could never be contrived on this side Hell.

SIR WILLIAM: Such as the devil's dancing in a moor
Amongst a few old women crazed and poor,
Who are rejoiced to see him frisk and lowp
O'er braes and bogs, with candles in his dowp; 65
Appearing sometimes like a black-horned cow,
Aftimes like Bawty, Badrans, or a sow:
Then with his train through airy paths to glide,
While they on cats, or clowns, or broom-staffs ride;

40 hool *skin*
42 elritch *weird*
44 crap *crept*
53 cantraips *spells*
65 dowp *bottom*
67 Bawty, Badrans *a dog, a cat*

Or in the egg-shell skim out o'er the main, 70
To drink their leader's health in France or Spain:
Then aft by night, bumbaze hare-hearted fools,
By tumbling down their cup-board, chairs and stools.
Whate'er's in spells, or if there witches be,
Such whimsies seem the most absurd to me. 75

SYMON: 'Tis true enough, we ne'er heard that a witch
Had either meikle sense, or yet was rich.
But Mause, though poor, is a sagacious wife,
And lives a quiet and very honest life;
That gars me think this hobleshew that's past 80
Will land in naithing but a joke at last.

SIR WILLIAM: I'm sure it will. But see increasing light
Commands the imps of darkness down to night;
Bid raise my servants, and my horse prepare,
Whilst I walk out to take the morning air. 85

Sang XX (*tune: 'Bonny gray ey'd Morn'*):

The bonny gray eyed morning begins to peep,
And darkness flies before the rising ray,
The hearty hynd starts from his lazy sleep,
To follow healthful labours of the day,
Without a guilty sting to wrinkle his brow, 90
The lark and the linnet tend his levee,
And he joins their concert, driving his plow,
From toil of grimace and pageantry free.

While flustered with wine, or maddened with loss,
Of half an estate, the prey of a main, 95
The drunkard and gamester tumble and toss,
Wishing for calmness and slumber in vain.
Be my portion health and quietness of mind,
Placed at due distance from parties and state,
Where neither ambition or avarice blind, 100
Reach him who has happiness linked to his fate.

(*Exeunt.*)

72 bumbaze *bewilder*
80 hobleshew *uproar*
95 main *dice-throw*

Scene (ii)

While Peggy laces up her bosom fair,
With a blew snood Jenny binds up her hair;
Glaud by his morning ingle takes a beek,
The rising sun shines motty through the reek,
A pipe his mouth; the lasses please his een, 5
And now and than his joke maun intervene.

GLAUD: I wish, my bairns, it may keep fair till night;
Ye do not use sae soon to see the light.
Nae doubt now ye intend to mix the thrang,
To take your leave of Patrick or he gang. 10
But do ye think that now when he's a laird,
That he poor landwart lasses will regard?
JENNY: Though he's young master now, I'm very sure
He has mair sense than slight auld friends, though poor.
But yesterday he ga'e us mony a tug, 15
And kissed my cousin there frae lug to lug.
GLAUD: Ay, ay, nae doubt o't, and he'll do't again;
But, be advised, his company refrain:
Before he, as a shepherd, sought a wife,
With her to live a chaste and frugal life; 20
But now grown gentle, soon he will forsake
Sic godly thoughts, and brag of being a rake.
PEGGY: A rake! What's that? Sure if it means ought ill,
He'll never be't; else I have tint my skill.
GLAUD: Daft lassie, ye ken nought of the affair, 25
Ane young and good and gentle's unco rare.
A rake's a graceless spark, that thinks nae shame,
To do what like of us thinks sin to name:
Sic are sae void of shame, they'll never stap
To brag how aften they have had the clap. 30
They'll tempt young things, like you, with youdith flushed,
Syne make ye a' their jest, when ye're debauched.
Be warry then, I say, and never gi'e
Encouragement, or bourd with sic as he.

v(ii)
2 snood *ribbon*
3 beek *warming*
4 motty *flecked* reek *smoke*
10 or *before*
16 lug *ear*
24 tint *lost*
29 stap *stop*
30 clap *venereal disease*
31 youdith *youth*
32 warry *wary*
34 bourd *frolic*

PEGGY: Sir William's virtuous, and of gentle blood; 35
And may not Patrick too, like him, be good?
GLAUD: That's true, and mony gentry mae than he,
As they are wiser, better are than we,
But thinner sawn: they're sae puft up with pride,
There's mony of them mocks ilk haly guide, 40
That shaws the gate to Heaven. I've heard mysell,
Some of them laugh at Doomsday, sin and Hell.
JENNY: Watch o'er us, Father! Heh, that's very odd!
Sure him that doubts a Doomsday, doubts a God.
GLAUD: Doubt! Why, they neither doubt, nor judge,
nor think, 45
Nor hope, nor fear; but curse, debauch and drink:
But I'm no saying this, as if I thought
That Patrick to sic gates will e'er be brought.
PEGGY: The Lord forbid! Na, he kens better things:
But here comes aunt; her face some ferly brings. 50
(*Enter Madge.*)

MADGE: Haste, haste ye; we're a' sent for o'er the gate,
To hear, and help to redd some odd debate
'Tween Mause and Bauldy, 'bout some witchcraft spell,
At Symon's house: the knight sits judge himsell.
GLAUD: Lend me my staff. Madge, lock the outer-door, 55
And bring the lasses wi' ye; I'll step before.
(*Exit Glaud.*)

MADGE: Poor Meg! Look, Jenny, was the like e'er seen,
How bleered and red with greeting look her een?
This day her brankan wooer takes his horse,
To strut a gentle spark at Edinburgh Cross; 60
To change his kent, cut frae the branchy plain,
For a nice sword, and glancing-headed cane;
To leave his ram-horn spoons, and kitted whey,
For gentler tea, that smells like new-won hay;
To leave the green-swaird dance, when we gae milk, 65
To rustle amang the beauties clad in silk.

39 sawn *sown*
40 haly *holy*
51 gate *way*
52 redd *sort out*
58 bleered *dimmed* greeting *crying*
59 brankan *prancing*
60 Cross *market cross*
61 kent *staff*
63 kitted *in a wooden bowl*

But Meg, poor Meg, maun with the shepherd stay,
And tak what God will send, in hodden-gray.
PEGGY: Dear aunt, what need ye fash us wi' your scorn?
That's no my faut that I'm nae gentler born. 70
Gif I the daughter of some laird had been,
I ne'er had noticed Patie on the green:
Now since he rises, why should I repine?
If he's made for another, he'll ne'er be mine:
And then, the like has been, if the decree 75
Designs him mine, I yet his wife may be.
MADGE: A bonny story, trowth! But we delay:
Prin up your aprons baith, and come away.
(*Exeunt.*)

Scene (iii)

Sir William fills the twa-armed chair,
While Symon, Roger, Glaud and Mause,
Attend, and with loud laughter hear
Daft Bauldy bluntly plead his cause:
For now 'tis telled him that the taz 5
Was handled by revengefu' Madge,
Because he brak good breeding's laws,
And with his nonsense raised their rage.

SIR WILLIAM: And was that all? Well, Bauldy, ye was served
No otherwise than what ye well deserved. 10
Was it so small a matter, to defame,
And thus abuse an honest woman's name?
Besides your going about to have betrayed
By perjury an innocent young maid.
BAULDY: Sir, I confess my faut through a' the steps, 15
And ne'er again shall be untrue to Neps.
MAUSE: Thus far, sir, he obliged me on the score;
I kend not that they thought me sic before.
BAULDY: An't like your honour, I believed it well;
But trowth I was e'en doilt to seek the Deil: 20
Yet, with your honour's leave, though she's nae witch,
She's baith a slee and a revengefu' bitch,

68 hodden *homespun*
78 prin *pin*

v(iii)
5 taz *punishment belt*
20 doilt *stupid*

And that my some-place finds; but I had best
Had in my tongue; for yonder comes the ghaist,
And the young bonny witch, whase rosy cheek 25
Sent me, without my wit, the Deil to seek.

(*Enter Madge, Peggy, and Jenny.*)

SIR WILLIAM (*looking at Peggy*): Whose daughter's she
that wears th'aurora gown,
With face so fair, and locks a lovely brown?
How sparkling are her eyes! What's this? I find
The girl brings all my sister to my mind. 30
Such were the features once adorned a face,
Which death too soon deprived of sweetest grace.
Is this your daughter, Glaud?
GLAUD: Sir, she's my niece;
And yet she's not – but I should hald my peace.
SIR WILLIAM: This is a contradiction: what d'ye mean? 35
She is, and is not! Pray thee, Glaud, explain.
GLAUD: Because I doubt if I should make appear
What I have kept a secret thirteen year.
MAUSE: You may reveal what I can fully clear.
SIR WILLIAM: Speak soon; I'm all impatience!
PATIE: So am I! 40
For much I hope, and hardly yet know why.
GLAUD: Then, since my master orders, I obey.
This bonny fundling, ae clear morn of May,
Close by the lee-side of my door I found,
All sweet and clean, and carefully hapt round, 45
In infant-weeds of rich and gentle make.
What could they be, thought I, did thee forsake?
Wha, warse than brutes, could leave exposed to air
Sae much of innocence sae sweetly fair,
Sae hopeless young? For she appeared to me 50
Only about twa towmands auld to be.
I took her in my arms, the bairnie smiled
With sic a look wad made a savage mild.
I hid the story: she has past sincesyne
As a poor orphan, and a niece of mine. 55
Nor do I rue my care about the wean,
For she's well worth the pains that I have tane.

24 had *hold*
45 hapt *wrapped*
51 towmands *years*

Ye see she's bonny, I can swear she's good,
And am right sure she's come of gentle blood:
Of whom I kenna. Nathing ken I mair, 60
Than what I to your honour now declare.

SIR WILLIAM: This tale seems strange!

PATIE: The tale delights my ear;

SIR WILLIAM: Command your joys, young man, till truth appear.

MAUSE: That be my task. Now, sir, bid all be hush;
Peggy may smile; thou hast nae cause to blush. 65
Long have I wished to see this happy day,
That I might safely to the truth give way;
That I may now Sir William Worthy name,
The best and nearest friend that she can claim:
He saw't at first, and with quick eye did trace 70
His sister's beauty in her daughter's face.

SIR WILLIAM: Old woman, do not rave – prove what you say;
'Tis dangerous in affairs like this to play.

PATIE: What reason, sir, can an old woman have
To tell a lie, when she's sae near her grave? 75
But how, or why, it should be truth, I grant,
I every thing looks like a reason want.

OMNES: The story's odd! We wish we heard it out.

SIR WILLIAM: Mak haste, good woman, and resolve each doubt.

MAUSE (*going forward, leading Peggy to Sir William*):
Sir, view me well: has fifteen years so plowed 80
A wrinkled face that you have often viewed,
That here I as an unknown stranger stand,
Who nursed her mother that now holds my hand?
Yet stronger proofs I'll give, if you demand.

SIR WILLIAM: Ha! Honest nurse, where were my eyes before! 85
I know thy faithfulness, and need no more;
Yet, from the lab'rinth to lead out my mind,
Say, to expose her who was so unkind.
(*He embraces Peggy, and makes her sit by him.*)
Yes, surely thou'rt my niece; truth must prevail:
But no more words, till Mause relate her tale. 90

PATIE: Good nurse, go on; nae music's haff sae fine,
Or can give pleasure like these words of thine.

69 friend *relation*

MAUSE: Then, it was I that saved her infant-life,
Her death being threat'ned by an uncle's wife.
The story's lang; but I the secret knew, 95
How they pursued, with avaricious view,
Her rich estate, of which they're now possest:
All this to me a confidant confest.
I heard with horror, and with trembling dread,
They'd smoor the sakeless orphan in her bed! 100
That very night, when all were sunk in rest,
At midnight hour, the floor I saftly prest,
And staw the sleeping innocent away;
With whom I traveled some few miles e'er day:
All day I hid me; when the day was done, 105
I kept my journey, lighted by the moon,
Till eastward fifty miles I reached these plains,
Where needful plenty glads your cheerful swains;
Afraid of being found out, I to secure
My charge, e'en laid her at this shepherd's door, 110
And took a neighbouring cottage here, that I,
Whate'er should happen to her, might be by.
Here honest Glaud himsell, and Symon may
Remember well, how I that very day
Frae Roger's father took my little crove. 115
GLAUD (*with tears of joy happing down his beard*):
I well remember't. Lord reward your love:
Lang have I wished for this; for aft I thought,
Sic knowledge sometime should about be brought.
PATIE: 'Tis now a crime to doubt – my joys are full,
With due obedience to my parent's will. 120
Sir, with paternal love survey her charms,
And blame me not for rushing to her arms.
She's mine by vows; and would, though still unknown,
Have been my wife, when I my vows durst own.
SIR WILLIAM: My niece, my daughter, welcome to
my care, 125
Sweet image of thy mother good and fair,
Equal with Patrick: now my greatest aim
Shall be, to aid your joys, and well-matched flame.
My boy, receive her from your father's hand,
With as good will as either would demand. 130

100 smoor *smother*
sakeless *innocent*
103 staw *stole*
115 crove *hovel*

(*Patie and Peggy embrace, and kneel to Sir William.*)

PATIE: With as much joy this blessing I receive,
As ane wad life, that's sinking in a wave.

SIR WILLIAM (*raising them*): I give you both my blessing: may your love
Produce a happy race, and still improve.

PEGGY: My wishes are complete, my joys arise, 135
While I'm haff dizzy with the blest surprise.
And am I then a match for my ain lad,
That for me so much generous kindness had?
Lang may Sir William bless these happy plains,
Happy while Heaven grant he on them remains. 140

PATIE: Be lang our guardian, still our master be;
We'll only crave what you shall please to gi'e:
The estate be your's, my Peggy's ane to me.

GLAUD: I hope your honour now will take amends
Of them that sought her life for wicked ends. 145

SIR WILLIAM: The base unnatural villain soon shall know,
That eyes above watch the affairs below.
I'll strip him soon of all to her pertains,
And make him reimburse his ill-got gains.

PEGGY: To me the views of wealth and an estate, 150
Seem light when put in balance with my Pate:
For his sake only, I'll ay thankful bow
For such a kindness, best of men, to you.

SYMON: What double blythness wakens up this day!
I hope now, sir, you'll no soon haste away. 155
Sall I unsaddle your horse, and gar prepare
A dinner for ye of hale country fare?
See how much joy unwrinkles every brow;
Our looks hing on the twa, and dote on you:
Even Bauldy the bewitched has quite forgot 160
Fell Madge's taz, and pawky Mause's plot.

SIR WILLIAM: Kindly old man, remain with you this day?
I never from these fields again will stray:
Masons and wrights shall soon my house repair,
And busy gardners shall new planting rear; 165
My father's hearty table you soon shall see
Restored, and my best friends rejoyce with me.

SYMON: That's the best news I heard this twenty year;
New day breaks up, rough times begin to clear.

GLAUD: God save the king, and save Sir William lang, 170
To enjoy their ain, and raise the shepherd's sang.

ROGER: Wha winna dance? Wha will refuse to sing?
What shepherd's whistle winna lilt the spring?
BAULDY: I'm friends with Mause, with very Madge I'm 'greed,
Although they skelpit me when woodly fleid: 175
I'm now fu' blyth, and frankly can forgive,
To join and sing, lang may Sir William live.
MADGE: Lang may he live: and, Bauldy, learn to steek
Your gab a wee, and think before ye speak;
And never ca' her auld that wants a man, 180
Else ye may yet some witches' fingers ban.
This day I'll wi' the youngest of ye rant,
And brag for ay, that I was ca'd the aunt
Of our young lady – my dear bonny bairn!
PEGGY: No other name I'll ever for you learn. 185
And, my good nurse, how shall I gratefu' be,
For a' thy matchless kindness done for me?
MAUSE: The flowing pleasures of this happy day
Does fully all I can require repay.
SIR WILLIAM: To faithful Symon, and, kind Glaud,
to you, 190
And to your heirs I give in endless feu,
The mailens ye posses, as justly due,
For acting like kind fathers to the pair,
Who have enough besides, and these can spare.
Mause, in my house in calmness close your days, 195
With nought to do, but sing your maker's praise.
OMNES: The Lord of Heaven return your honour's love,
Confirm your joys, and a' your blessings roove.
PATIE (*presenting Roger to Sir William*): Sir, here's my
trusty friend, that always shared
My bosom-secrets, ere I was a laird; 200
Glaud's daughter Janet (Jenny, thinkna shame)
Raised and maintains in him a lover's flame:
Lang was he dumb, at last he spake, and won,
And hopes to be our honest uncle's son:
Be pleased to speak to Glaud for his consent, 205
That nane may wear a face of discontent.
SIR WILLIAM: My son's demand is fair; Glaud, let me crave,

173 spring *tune*
175 skelpit *beat* woodly fleid *madly afraid*
178 steek *shut*
181 ban *curse*
191 feu *tenure*
192 mailens *holdings*
198 roove *rivet*

That trusty Roger may your daughter have,
With frank consent; and while he does remain
Upon these fields, I make him chamberlain. 210
GLAUD: You crowd your bounties, sir, what can we say,
But that we're dyvours that can ne'er repay?
Whate'er your honour wills, I shall obey.
Roger, my daughter, with my blessing, take,
And still our master's right your business make, 215
Please him, be faithful, and this auld gray head
Shall nod with quietness down amang the dead.
ROGER: I ne'er was good a speaking a' my days,
Or ever looed to make o'er great a fraise:
But for my master, father and my wife, 220
I will employ the cares of all my life.
SIR WILLIAM: My friends, I'm satisfied you'll all behave,
Each in his station, as I'd wish or crave.
Be ever virtuous, soon or late you'll find
Reward, and satisfaction to your mind. 225
The maze of life sometimes looks dark and wild,
And oft when hopes are highest, we're beguiled.
Aft, when we stand on brinks of dark despair,
Some happy turn with joy dispels our care.
Now all's at rights, who sings best let me hear. 230
PEGGY: When you demand, I readiest should obey:
I'll sing you ane, the newest that I ha'e.

Sang XXI (*tune: 'Corn-riggs are Bonny'*):

My Patie is a lover gay,
His mind is never muddy;
His breath is sweeter than new hay, 235
His face is fair and ruddy:
His shape is handsome, middle size,
He's comely in his wauking;
The shining of his een surprise,
'Tis heaven to hear him tawking. 240
Last night I met him on a bawk,
Where yellow corn was growing,
There mony a kindly word he spake,
That set my heart a glowing.

210 chamberlain *estate manager*
212 dyvours *debtors*
219 fraise *oration*
241 bawk *field-ridge*

He kissed, and vowed he wad be mine, 245
  And looed me best of ony,
That gars me like to sing since syne,
  Oh, corn-riggs are bonny.
Let lasses of a silly mind
  Refuse what maist they're wanting; 250
Since we for yielding were designed,
  We chastely should be granting.
Then I'll comply, and marry Pate,
  And syne my cockernonny
He's free to touzel air or late, 255
  Where corn-riggs are bonny.

(Exeunt omnes.)

248 riggs *field-strips*
254 cockernonny *topknot*
255 touzel *ruffle*

ROBERT CRAWFORD (1695–1733)

The Broom of Cowdenknowes

When summer comes, the swains on Tweed
  Sing their successful loves;
Around the ewes and lambkins feed,
  And music fills the groves.

But my loved song is then the broom 5
  So fair on Cowdenknowes;
For sure so sweet, so soft a bloom
  Elsewhere there never grows.

There Colin tuned his oaten reed,
  And won my yielding heart; 10
No shepherd e'er that dwelt on Tweed
  Could play with half such art.

He sung of Tay, of Forth, and Clyde,
  The hills and dales all round,
Of Leaderhaughs and Leaderside – 15
  Oh, how I blessed the sound!

Yet more delightful is the broom
  So fair on Cowdenknowes;
For sure so fresh, so bright a bloom
  Elsewhere there never grows. 20

Not Teviot braes so green and gay
  May with this broom compare,
Not Yarrow banks in flowery May,
  Nor the bush aboon Traquair.

More pleasing far are Cowdenknowes, 25
  My peaceful happy home,
Where I was wont to milk my ewes
  At ev'n among the broom.

1 Tweed *see note*   24 Traquair *see note*

Ye powers that haunt the woods and plains
  Where Tweed with Teviot flows, 30
Convey me to the best of swains,
  And my loved Cowdenknowes.

The Bush Aboon Traquair

Hear me, ye nymphs, and every swain,
  I'll tell how Peggy grieves me:
Though thus I languish, thus complain,
  Alas, she ne'er believes me.
My vows and sighs, like silent air, 5
  Unheeded never move her –
At the bonny bush aboon Traquair,
  'Twas there I first did love her.

That day she smiled, and made me glad,
  No maid seemed ever kinder; 10
I thought myself the luckiest lad,
  So sweetly there to find her.
I tried to soothe my am'rous flame,
  In words that I thought tender;
If more there passed I'm not to blame, 15
  I meant not to offend her.

Yet now she scornful flies the plain,
  The fields we then frequented;
If e'er we meet, she shows disdain,
  She looks as ne'er acquainted. 20
The bonny bush bloomed fair in May,
  Its sweets I'll ay remember;
But now her frowns make it decay,
  It fades as in December.

Ye rural powers, who hear my strains, 25
  Why thus should Peggy grieve me?
Oh, mak her partner in my pains,
  Then let her smiles relieve me.
If not, my love will turn despair,
  My passion nae mair tender; 30
I'll leave the bush aboon Traquair,
  To lonely wilds I'll wander.

ALEXANDER ROSS (1699–1784)

Married and Wooed an' A'

Married an' wooed an' a',
Married an' wooed an' a',
The dandilly toss of the parish,
Is married and wooed an' a'.
The wooers will now ride thinner, 5
And by, when they wonted to ca'.
'Tis needless to speer for the lassie
That's married an' wooed an' a'.

The girss had na freedom of growing,
As lang as she wasna awa'; 10
Nor i' the town could there be stowing,
For wooers that wonted to ca'.
For drinking an' dancing an' brulzies,
An' boxing an' shaking o' fa's,
The town was forever in tulzies; 15
But now the lassie's awa'.

But had they but kend her as I did,
Their errand it wad hae been sma';
She neither kend spinning nor carding,
Nor brewing nor baking ava'. 20
But the wooers ran a' mad upon her,
Because she was bonny an' bra',
An' sae I dread will be seen on her,
When she's by-hand and awa'.

He'll roose her but sma' that has married her, 25
Now when he's gotten her a',
And wish, I fear, he had miscarried her,
Tocher and ribbons an' a'.

3 dandilly *pampered* toss *toast*
9 girss *grass*
11 stowing *stuffing, eating*
13 brulzies *broils*
14 fa's *wrestling*
15 tulzies *fights*
20 ava' *at all*
24 by-hand *settled*
25 roose *praise*
28 tocher *dowry*

For her art it lay a' in her dressing,
But gin her bras anes were awa', 30
I fear she'll turn out o' the fesson,
An' knit up her muggans wi' straw.

For yesterday I yeed to see her,
An' oh, she was wonderous bra',
Yet she cried till her husband to gee her 35
An ell of red ribbons, or twa.
He up, and he set down beside her
A reel and a wheelie to ca';
She said, 'Was he this gate to guide her?'
An' out at the door, an' awa'. 40

Her neist road was hame till her mither,
Who speered at her, 'Now how was a'?'
She says till her, 'Was't for nae ither,
That I was married awa',
But gae an' sit down till a wheelie, 45
An' at it baith night an' day ca',
An' then hae it reeled by a cheelie
That ever was crying to draw?'

Her mither says till her: 'Hegh, lassie,
He's wyssest, I fear, o' the twa; 50
Ye'll hae little to put i' the bassie,
Gin ye be awkward to draw.
'Tis now ye should work like a tiger,
An' at it baith wallop an' ca',
As lang's ye hae youthit an' vigor, 55
An' little-anes an' debt are awa'.

Your thrift it will look little bouked,
An ye had a red weam or twa;
An' think yoursell stressed when ye're souked,
Though ye sud do nae mair ava', 60

30 bras *fine clothes*
31 fesson *fashion*
32 muggans *leggings*
33 yeed *went*
38 wheelie *spinning-wheel* ca' *turn*
47 cheelie *fellow*
50 wyssest *wisest*
51 bassie *dish*
54 wallop *bustle* ca' *drive*
55 youthit *youth*
57 bouked *bulked*
58 red weam *birth*
59 souked *sucked*
60 sud *should*

But sit i' the flet like a midden,
An' for your necessities ca'.
An' sae ye had best to do bidding,
As lang's ye hae feauto to ca'.

Sae swyth awa' hame to your hadding, 65
Mair fool than when ye came awa';
Ye maunna now keep ilka wedding,
Nor gae sae clean-fingered an' bra';
But mind wi' a neiper ye're yoked,
And that ye your end o't maun draw, 70
Or else ye deserve to be docked,
Sae that is an answer for a'.'

Young luckie now finds hersell niddered,
An' wist na well what gate to ca',
But wi' hersell even considered, 75
That hamewith were better to draw;
An e'en tak her chance o' her landing,
However the matter might fa'.
Fouk need no on fraits to be standing,
That's married and wooed an' a'. 80

61 flet *house* midden *dunghill*
64 feauto *see note*
65 swyth *quickly* hadding *holding*
69 neiper *partner*
71 docked *spanked*
73 niddered *brought down*
74 ca' *proceed*
76 hamewith *homeward*
79 fraits *trifles*

What Ails the Lasses at Me?

I am a batchelor winsome,
A farmer by rank and degree,
An' few I see gang out mair handsome
To kirk or to market than me.
I have outsight and insight and credit, 5
And from any eelist I'm free,
I'm well enough boarded and bedded,
And what ails the lasses at me?

My boughts of good store are no scanty,
My byres are well stocked wi' ky, 10
Of meal i' my girnels is plenty,
An' twa or three easments forby,
An' horse to ride out when they're weary,
An' cock with the best they can see,
An' then be ca'd dawty and deary – 15
I ferly what ails them at me.

Behind backs, afore fouk, I've wooed them,
An' a' the gates o't that I ken,
An' when they leugh o' me, I trowed them,
An' thought I had won, but what then? 20
When I speak of matters they grumble,
Nor are condescending and free,
But at my proposals ay stumble.
I wonder what ails them at me.

I've tried them baith Highland an' Lowland, 25
Where I a good bargain cud see,
But nane o' them fand I wad fall in
Or say they wad buckle wi' me.
With jooks an' wi' scraps I've addressed them,

5 outsight *implements used outside*
insight *household goods*
6 eelist *defect*
9 boughts *sheep-folds*
11 girnels *meal-chests*
12 easments *properties*
14 cock *show off*
15 dawty *darling*
16 ferly *marvel*
19 leugh *laughed*
26 cud *could*
27 fand *found*
29 jooks *bows* scraps *scrapes*

Been with them baith modest and free, 30
But whatever way I caressed them,
There's something still ails them at me.

Oh, if I kend but how to gain them,
How fond of the knack wad I be!
Or what an address could obtain them, 35
It should be twice welcome to me.
If kissing and clapping wad please them,
That trade I should drive till I die;
But however I study to ease them,
They've still an exception at me. 40

There's wratacks an' cripples an' cranshaks,
An' a' the wandoghts that I ken,
No sooner they speak to the wenches
But they are ta'en far enough ben.
But when I speak to them that's stately, 45
I find them ay ta'en with the gee,
An' get the denial right flatly –
What think ye can ail them at me?

I have yet but ae offer to make them,
If they wad but hearken to me, 50
And that is, I'm willing to tak them,
If they their consent wad but gee.
Let her that's content write a billet,
An' get it transmitted to me;
I hereby engage to fulfil it, 55
Though cripple, though blind she sud be.

37 clapping *fondling*
41 wratacks *dwarves*
cranshaks *cripples*
42 wandoghts *weaklings*
44 ben *inside*
46 gee *ill-temper*
56 sud *should*

Billet by Jeany Gradden

Dear batchelor, I've read your billet,
Your strait an' your hardships I see;
An' tell you it shall be fulfilled,
Though it were by none other but me.
These forty years I've been neglected, 5
An' nane has had pity on me;
Such offer should not be rejected,
Whoever the offerer be.

For beauty, I lay no claim to it,
Or maybe I had been away; 10
Though tocher or kindred could do it,
I have no pretensions to thae;
The most I can say, I'm a woman,
An' that I a wife want to be;
An' I'll tak exception at no man 15
That's willing to tak nane at me.

And now I think I may be cocky,
Since fortune has smurtled on me;
I'm Jenny, an' ye shall be Jockie;
'Tis right we together sud be; 20
For nane of us cud find a marrow,
So sadly forfairn were we,
Fouk sud no at any thing tarrow,
Whose chance looked naething to be.

On Tuesday speer for Jeany Gradden. 25
When I i' my pens ween to be,
Just at the sign of The Old Maiden,
Where ye shall be sure to meet me.
Bring with you the priest for the wedding,
That a' things just ended may be, 30
An' we'll close the whole with the bedding,
An' wha'll be sae merry as we?

11 tocher *dowry*
12 thae *those*
18 smurtled *smirked*
19 Jenny, Jockie *see note*
20 sud *should*
21 cud *could* marrow *spouse*
22 forfairn *abused*
23 fouk *folk* tarrow *spurn*
26 i' my pens *looking my best*
ween *expect*

A cripple I'm not, ye forsta' me,
Though lame of a hand that I be;
Nor blind is there reason to ca' me, 35
Although I see but with ae eye;
But I'm just the chap that you wanted,
So tightly our state doth agree;
For nane wad hae you, ye have granted;
As few, I confess, wad hae me. 40

33 forsta' *see note*

WILLIAM HAMILTON OF BANGOUR (1704–54)

The Braes of Yarrow

'Busk ye, busk ye, my bonnie, bonnie bride!
Busk ye, busk ye, my winsome marrow;
Busk ye, busk ye, my bonnie, bonnie bride,
And think nae mair on the braes of Yarrow.'

'Where got ye that bonnie, bonnie bride? 5
Where got ye that winsome marrow?'
'I got her where I durst not well be seen,
Pu'ing the birks on the braes of Yarrow.

Weep not, weep not, my bonnie, bonnie bride!
Weep not, weep not, my winsome marrow; 10
Nor let thy heart lament to leave
Pu'ing the birks on the braes of Yarrow.'

'Why does she weep, thy bonnie, bonnie bride?
Why does she weep, thy winsome marrow?
And why dare ye nae mair well be seen 15
Pu'ing the birks on the braes of Yarrow?'

'Lang maun she weep, lang maun she, maun she weep,
Lang maun she weep with dule and sorrow;
And lang maun I nae mair weel be seen
Pu'ing the birks on the braes of Yarrow. 20

For she has tint her lover, lover dear,
Her lover dear, the cause of sorrow;
And I have slain the comeliest swain
That e'er pu'd birks on the braes of Yarrow.

1 busk *adorn*
2 marrow *partner*
8 pu'ing *pulling* birks *birches*
18 dule *grief*
21 tint *lost*

Why runs thy stream, o Yarrow, Yarrow, reid? 25
Why on thy braes heard the voice of sorrow?
And why yon melancholious weeds
Hung on the bonnie birks of Yarrow?

What yonder floats on the rueful, rueful flood?
What yonder floats? Oh, dule and sorrow! 30
'Tis he, the comely swain I slew
Upon the duleful braes of Yarrow.

Wash, oh wash his wounds, his wounds in tears,
His wounds in tears of dule and sorrow;
And wrap his limbs in mourning weeds, 35
And lay him on the braes of Yarrow.

Then build, then build, ye sisters, sisters sad,
Ye sisters sad, his tomb with sorrow,
And weep around, in woeful wise,
His hapless fate on the braes of Yarrow. 40

Curse ye, curse ye, his useless, useless shield,
My arm that wrought the deed of sorrow,
The fatal spear that pierced his breast,
His comely breast, on the braes of Yarrow.

Did I not warn thee not to, not to love, 45
And warn from fight? But, to my sorrow,
Too rashly bold, a stronger arm
Thou met'st, and fell on the braes of Yarrow.

Sweet smells the birk, green grows, green grows the grass,
Yellow on Yarrow's braes the gowan; 50
Fair hangs the apple frae the rock,
Sweet the wave of Yarrow flowan.

Flows Yarrow sweet? As sweet, as sweet flows Tweed,
As green its grass, its gowan as yellow;
As sweet smells on its braes the birk, 55
The apple from its rocks as mellow.

50 gowan *daisy*

Fair was thy love, fair, fair indeed thy love,
In flowery bands thou didst him fetter;
Though he was fair and well beloved again,
Than me he never loved thee better. 60

Busk ye then, busk, my bonnie, bonnie bride!
Busk ye, busk ye, my winsome marrow;
Busk ye, and lo'e me on the banks of Tweed,
And think nae mair on the braes of Yarrow.'

'How can I busk a bonnie, bonnie bride? 65
How can I busk a winsome marrow?
How lo'e him on the banks of Tweed,
That slew my love on the braes of Yarrow?

O Yarrow fields, may never, never rain,
Nor dew thy tender blossoms cover, 70
For there was basely slain my love,
My love, as he had not been a lover.

The boy put on his robes, his robes of green,
His purple vest, 'twas my ain sewing;
Ah, wretched me, I little, little knew 75
He was in these to meet his ruin!

The boy took out his milk-white, milk-white steed,
Unheedful of my dule and sorrow;
But ere the to-fall of the night
He lay a corpse on the braes of Yarrow. 80

Much I rejoiced that woeful, woeful day,
I sang, my voice the woods returning;
But lang ere night the spear was flown
That slew my love, and left me mourning.

What can my barbarous, barbarous father do, 85
But with his cruel rage pursue me?
My lover's blood is on thy spear,
How canst thou, barbarous man, then woo me?

79 to-fall *dusk*

My happy sisters may be, may be proud,
With cruel, and ungentle scoffin', 90
May bid me seek on Yarrow's braes
My lover nailed in his coffin.

My brother Douglas may upbraid,
And strive with threatening words to move me:
My lover's blood is on thy spear, 95
How canst thou ever bid me love thee?

Yes, yes, prepare the bed, the bed of love,
With bridal sheets my body cover;
Unbar, ye bridal maids, the door,
Let in the expected husband lover. 100

But who the expected husband, husband is?
His hands, methinks, are bathed in slaughter;
Ah me, what ghastly spectre's yon,
Comes, in his pale shroud bleeding, after?

Pale as he is, here lay him, lay him down, 105
O lay his cold head on my pillow;
Take aff, take aff these bridal weeds,
And crown my careful head with willow.

Pale though thou art, yet best, yet best beloved,
O, could my warmth to life restore thee! 110
Ye'd lie all night between my breasts,
No youth lay ever there before thee.

Pale, pale indeed, o lovely, lovely youth!
Forgive, forgive so foul a slaughter;
And lie all night between my breasts, 115
No youth shall ever lie there after.'

'Return, return, O mournful, mournful bride,
Return and dry thy useless sorrow;
Thy lover heeds nought of thy sighs,
He lies a corpse on the braes of Yarrow.' 120

Inscription on a Dog

Calm though not mean, courageous without rage,
Serious not dull, and without thinking sage;
Pleased at the lot that nature has assigned,
Snarl as I list, and freely bark my mind,
As churchman wrangle not with jarring spite, 5
Nor statesman-like caressing whom I bite;
View all the canine kind with equal eyes,
I dread no mastiff, and no cur despise.
True from the first, and faithful to the end,
I balk no mistress, and forsake no friend. 10
My days and nights one equal tenor keep,
Fast but to eat, and only wake to sleep.
Thus stealing along life I live incog.,
A very plain and downright honest dog.

4 list *please* 13 incog. *incognito, unknown*

DAVID MALLET (1705–65)

The Birks of Invermay

The smiling morn, the breathing spring,
Invite the tuneful birds to sing;
And while they warble from each spray,
Love melts the universal lay.

Let us, Amanda, timely wise, 5
Like them improve the hour that flies,
And in soft raptures waste the day
Among the birks of Invermay.

For soon the winter of the year,
And age, life's winter, will appear; 10
At this, thy living bloom will fade,
As that will strip the verdant shade.

Our taste of pleasure then is o'er,
The feathered songsters love no more;
And when they droop, and we decay, 15
Adieu the birks of Invermay.

8 birks *birches*

ALISON RUTHERFORD COCKBURN (1712–94)

The Flowers of the Forest

I've seen the smiling of Fortune beguiling,
  I've tasted her favours, and felt her decay;
Sweet is her blessing, and kind her caressing,
  But soon it is fled – it is fled far away.

I've seen the forest adorned the foremost, 5
  With flowers of the fairest, most pleasant and gay;
Full sweet was their blooming, their scent the air perfuming,
  But now they are withered and a' wede away.

I've seen the morning with gold the hills adorning,
  And the red tempest storming before parting day; 10
I've seen Tweed's silver streams, glittering in the sunny beams,
  Grow drumly and dark as they rolled on their way.

O fickle Fortune, why this cruel sporting?
  Why thus perplex us poor sons of a day?
Thy frowns cannot fear me, thy smiles cannot cheer me, 15
  Since the flowers of the forest are a' wede away.

8 wede *faded* 12 drumly *muddy*

HENRY ERSKINE (1720–65)

Highland March

Such our love of liberty, our country and our laws,
That like our ancestors of old, we'll stand in freedom's cause;
We'll bravely fight like heroes bold, for honour and applause,
And defy the French, with all their art, to alter our laws.

In the garb of old Gaul, wi' the fire of old Rome, 5
From the heath-covered mountains of Scotia we come,
Where the Romans endeavoured our country to gain,
But our ancestors fought, and they fought not in vain.

No effeminate customs our sinews unbrace,
No luxurious tables enervate our race, 10
Our loud-sounding pipe bears the true martial strain,
So do we the old Scottish valour retain.

We're tall as the oak on the mount of the vale,
Are swift as the roe which the hound doth assail,
As the full moon in autumn our shields do appear, 15
Minerva would dread to encounter our spear.

As a storm in the ocean when Boreas blows,
So are we enraged when we rush on our foes;
We sons of the mountains, tremendous as rocks,
Dash the force of our foes with our thundering strokes. 20

Quebec and Cape Breton, the pride of old France,
In their troops fondly boasted till we did advance;
But when our claymores they saw us produce,
Their courage did fail, and they sued for a truce.

In our realm may the fury of faction long cease, 25
May our councils be wise, and our commerce increase;

5 Gaul *see note*
7 Romans *see note*
16 Minerva *goddess of war*
17 Boreas *north wind*
21 Quebec, Cape Breton *see note*
23 claymores *swords*

And in Scotia's cold climate may each of us find
That our friends still prove true, and our beauties prove kind.

Then we'll defend our liberty, our country, and our laws,
And teach our late posterity to fight in freedom's cause, 30
That they like our ancestors bold, for honour and applause,
May defy the French, with all their art, to alter our laws.

JOHN SKINNER (1721–1807)

Tullochgorum

Come, gie's a sang, Montgomery cried,
And lay your disputes all aside,
What signifies't for folks to chide
For what was done before them?
Let Whig and Tory all agree, 5
Whig and Tory, Whig and Tory,
Whig and Tory all agree,
To drop their Whig-mig-morum;
Let Whig and Tory all agree
To spend the night wi' mirth and glee, 10
And cheerfu' sing alang wi' me
The Reel o' Tullochgorum.

Oh, Tullochgorum's my delight,
It gars us a' in ane unite,
And ony sumph that keeps a spite, 15
In conscience I abhor him;
For blyth and cheerie we'll be a',
Blyth and cheerie, blyth and cheerie,
Blyth and cheerie we'll be a',
And mak a happy quorum; 20
For blyth and cheerie we'll be a'
As lang as we hae breath to draw,
And dance till we be like to fa'
The Reel o' Tullochgorum.

What needs there be sae great a fraise 25
Wi' dringing dull Italian lays?
I wadna gie our ain strathspeys
For half a hunder score o' them;
They're dowf and dowie at the best,
Dowf and dowie, dowf and dowie, 30

5 Whig and Tory *see note*
15 sumph *blockhead*
25 fraise *fuss, fancy talk*
26 dringing *slowly sung*
27 strathspeys *Scottish dances*
29 dowf *gloomy* dowie *sad*

Dowf and dowie at the best,
Wi' a' their variorum;
They're dowf and dowie at the best,
Their allegros and a' the rest,
They canna please a Scottish taste 35
Compared wi' Tullochgorum.

Let warldly worms their minds oppress
Wi fears o' want and double cess,
And sullen sots themsells distress
Wi' keeping up decorum; 40
Shall we sae sour and sulky sit,
Sour and sulky, sour and sulky,
Sour and sulky shall we sit,
Like old philosophorum?
Shall we sae sour and sulky sit, 45
Wi' neither sense, nor mirth, nor wit,
Nor ever try to shake a fit
To th' Reel o' Tullochgorum?

May choicest blessings aye attend
Each honest, open-hearted friend, 50
And calm and quiet be his end,
And a' that's good watch o'er him;
May peace and plenty be his lot,
Peace and plenty, peace and plenty,
Peace and plenty be his lot, 55
And dainties a great store o' them;
May peace and plenty be his lot,
Unstained by any vicious spot,
And may he never want a groat,
That's fond o' Tullochgorum! 60

But for the sullen frumpish fool,
That loves to be oppression's tool,
May envy gnaw his rotten soul,
And discontent devour him;
May dool and sorrow be his chance, 65
Dool and sorrow, dool and sorrow,
Dool and sorrow be his chance,
And nane say 'wae's me' for him!

38 cess *land tax*
47 fit *foot*
65 dool *grief*

May dool and sorrow be his chance,
Wi' a' the ills that come frae France, 70
Wha e'er he be that winna dance
    The Reel o' Tullochgorum.

TOBIAS SMOLLETT (1721–71)

Ode to Leven-Water

On Leven's banks, while free to rove,
And tune the rural pipe to love,
I envied not the happiest swain
That ever trod th' Arcadian plain.
Pure stream, in whose transparent wave 5
My youthful limbs I wont to lave,
No torrents stain thy limpid source,
No rocks impede thy dimpling course,
That sweetly warbles o'er its bed,
With white, round, polished pebbles spread, 10
While, lightly poised, the scaly brood
In myriads cleave thy crystal flood:
The springing trout in speckled pride,
The salmon, monarch of the tide,
The ruthless pike intent on war, 15
The silver eel, and mottled parr.
Devolving from thy parent lake,
A charming maze thy waters make,
By bowers of birch and groves of pine,
And hedges flowered with eglantine. 20
Still on thy banks, so gaily green,
May numerous herds and flocks be seen,
And lasses chanting o'er the pail,
And shepherds piping in the dale,
And ancient faith that knows no guile, 25
And industry embrowned with toil,
And hearts resolved, and hands prepared,
The blessings they enjoy to guard.

4 Arcadian *see note* 6 lave *bathe*

WILLIAM WILKIE (1721–72)

The Hare and the Partan

A canny man will scarce provoke
Ae creature livin, for a joke;
For be they weak or be they strang,
A jibe leaves after it a stang
To mak them think on't; and a laird 5
May find a beggar sae prepared,
Wi pawks and wiles, whar pith is wantin,
As soon will mak him rue his tauntin.

Ye hae my moral; if A'm able
A'll fit it nicely wi a fable. 10

A hare, ae morning, chanced to see
A partan creepin on a lee,
A fishwife wha was early oot
Had drapt the creature thereaboot.
Mawkin, bumbased and frighted sair 15
To see a thing but hide and hair,
Which if it sturred not might be taen
For naething ither than a stane,
Asquunt-wise wambling, sair beset
Wi gerse and rashes like a net, 20
First thought to rin for't (for by kind
A hare's nae fechter, ye maun mind)
But seeing that wi aw its strength
It scarce could creep a tether length,
The hare grew baulder and cam near, 25
Turned playsome, and forgat her fear.
Quoth Mawkin, 'Was there ere in nature

4 stang *sting*
7 pawks *tricks* pith *strength*
9 A *I*
12 partan *edible crab* lee *lea*
15 mawkin *hare* bumbased *confused*
17 sturred *stirred*
19 asquunt *sideways* wambling *staggering*
20 gerse *grass* rashes *rushes*
22 fechter *fighter*
23 aw *all*

Sae feckless and sae poor a creature?
It scarcely kens, or A'm mistaen,
The way to gang or stand its lane. 30
See how it steitters; A'll be bund
To rin a mile of up-hill grund
Before it gets a rig-braid frae
The place it's in, though doon the brae.'

Mawkin wi this began to frisk, 35
And thinkin there was little risk,
Clapt baith her feet on partan's back,
And turned him awald in a crack.
To see the creature sprawl, her sport
Grew twice as good, yet proved but short. 40
For patting wi her fit, in play,
Just whar the partan's nippers lay,
He gript it fast, which made her squeel,
And think she bourded wi the Deil.
She strave to rin, and made a fistle; 45
The tither catched a tough burr thristle,
Which held them baith, till o'er a dyke
A herd came stending wi his tyke,
And felled poor Mawkin, sairly ruein,
Whan forced to drink of her ain brewin. 50

28 feckless *feeble*
29 mistaen *mistaken*
30 its lane *on its own*
31 steitters *stumbles* bund *bound*
32 grund *ground*
33 rig-braid *width of a strip of farmland*
38 awald *on its back*
41 fit *foot*
44 bourded *sported*
45 strave *strove* fistle *whistle*
46 tither *other* thristle *thistle*
47 dyke *ditch, wall*
48 stending *leaping* tyke *dog*

JEAN ELLIOT (1727–1805)

The Flowers of the Forest

I've heard the lilting at our ewe-milking,
  Lasses a-lilting before dawn of day;
But now they are moaning on ilka green loaning –
  The flowers of the forest are a' wede away.

At buchts, in the morning, nae blythe lads are scorning, 5
  Lasses are lonely, and dowie, and wae;
Nae daffin', nae gabbin', but sighing and sabbing,
  Ilk ane lifts her leglin and hies her away.

In hairst, at the shearing, nae youths now are jeering,
  Bandsters are runkled, and lyart or grey; 10
At fair or at preaching, nae wooing, nae fleeching –
  The flowers of the forest are a' wede away.

At e'en, in the gloaming, nae younkers are roaming
  'Bout stacks with the lasses at bogle to play;
But ilk maid sits dreary, lamenting her dearie – 15
  The flowers of the forest are a' wede away.

Dool and wae for the order sent our lads to the Border!
  The English for ance by guile wan the day;
The flowers of the forest, that foucht aye the foremaist,
  The prime of our land, are cauld in the clay. 20

We'll hear nae mair lilting at the ewe-milking,
  Women and bairns are heartless and wae;
Sighing and moaning on ilka green loaning –
  The flowers of the forest are a' wede away.

3 loaning *milking-field*
4 wede *faded*
5 buchts *ewe-milking fold*
6 dowie *doleful, sad*
7 daffin' *fun* gabbin' *chatting* sabbing *sobbing*
8 leglin *milk-pail*
9 hairst *harvest*
10 bandsters *sheaf-binders* runkled *wrinkled* lyart *grey-haired*
11 fleeching *flattering*
13 gloaming *dusk* younkers *youngsters*
17 dool *grief*

JAMES BEATTIE (1735–1803)

To Mr Alexander Ross

O Ross, thou wale of hearty cocks,
Sae crouse and canty with thy jokes,
Thy hamely auldwarld muse provokes
  Me for awhile
To ape our guid plain countra folks 5
  In verse and style.

Sure never carle was haff sae gabby,
E'er since the winsome days o' Habby;
Oh mayst thou ne'er gang clung, or shabby,
  Nor miss thy snaker, 10
Or I'll ca' fortune 'nasty drabby',
  And say 'Pox take her.'

Oh, may the roupe ne'er roust thy weason,
May thirst thy thrapple never gizzen,
But bottled ale in mony a dizzen, 15
  Aye lade thy gantry,
And fouth o' vivres a' in season
  Plenish thy pantry.

Lang may thy stevin fill wi' glee
The glens and mountains of Lochlee, 20
Which were right gowsty but for thee,
  Whase sangs enamor
Ilk lass, and teach wi' melody
  The rocks to yamour.

1 wale *choice*
2 crouse *confident* canty *cheerful*
7 carle *fellow* gabby *chatty*
8 Habby *see note*
9 clung *hungry*
10 snaker *small bowl of punch*
11 drabby *whore*
13 roupe *hoarseness* roust *parch* weason *throat*
14 thrapple *throat* gizzen *shrivel*
15 dizzen *dozen*
16 lade *load* gantry *beer bar*
17 fouth *plenty* vivres *victuals*
19 stevin *voice*
20 Lochlee *see note*
21 gowsty *dreary*
24 yamour *cry out*

Ye shak your head, but, o' my fegs, 25
Ye've set old Scota on her legs,
Lang had she lyen wi' beffs and flegs,
  Bumbazed and dizzie;
Her fiddle wanted strings and pegs,
  Waes me, poor hizzie! 30

Since Allan's death naebody cared
For anes to speer how Scota fared,
Nor plack nor thristled turner wared
  To quench her drouth;
For frae the cottar to the laird 35
  We a' rin south.

The Southland chiels indeed hae mettle,
And brawly at a sang can ettle,
Yet we right couthily might settle
  O' this side Forth; 40
The devil pay them wi' a pettle
  That slight the north.

Our countra leed is far frae barren,
It's even right pithy and aulfarren,
Oursells are neiper-like, I warran', 45
  For sense and smergh;
In kittle times when faes are yarring,
  We're no thought ergh.

Oh, bonny are our greensward hows,
Where through the birks the birny rows, 50
And the bee bums, and the ox lows,

25 fegs *faith*
27 beffs *blows* flegs *kicks*
28 bumbazed *confused*
30 hizzie *hussy*
31 Allan *Allan Ramsay*
33 plack *small coin* turner *small coin* wared *spent*
34 drouth *thirst*
35 cottar *farm labourer*
37 chiels *fellows*
38 ettle *try*
39 couthily *agreeably*
40 Forth *see note*
41 pettle *plough-staff*
43 leed *language*
44 aulfarren *ingenious*
45 neiper *neighbour*
46 smergh *energy*
47 kittle *puzzling* yarring *snarling*
48 ergh *timorous*
49 hows *hollows*
50 rows *rolls*
51 bums *hums*

And saft winds rustle;
And shepherd lads on sunny knows
Blaw the blythe fusle.

It's true, we Norlans manna fa' 55
To eat sae nice or gang sae bra',
As they that come from far awa,
Yet sma's our skaith;
We've peace (and that's well worth it a')
And meat and claith. 60

Our fine newfangle sparks, I grant ye,
Gie poor auld Scotland mony a taunty;
They're grown sae ugertfu and vaunty,
And capernoited,
They guide her like a cankered aunty 65
That's deaf and doited.

Sae comes of ignorance I trow,
It's this that crooks their ill fa'red mou'
Wi' jokes sae coorse, they gar fouk spue
For downright skonner; 70
For Scotland wants na sons enew
To do her honour.

I here might gie a skreed o' names,
Dawties of Heliconian dames!
The foremost place Gawin Douglas claims, 75
That canty priest;
And wha can match the fifth King James
For sang or jest?

Montgomery grave, and Ramsay gay,
Dunbar, Scott, Hawthornden, and mae 80

53 knows *knolls*
54 fusle *whistle*
55 Norlans manna fa' *northerners may not happen*
58 skaith *harm*
63 ugertfu *squeamish* vaunty *proud*
64 capernoited *irritable*
66 doited *crazy*
68 fa'red *favoured*
69 coorse *coarse*
70 skonner *disgust*
71 enew *enough*
73 skreed *long list*
74 dawties *darlings* Heliconian dames *the Muses*
75 Gawin Douglas *see note*
77 King James *see note*
79 Montgomery, Ramsay *see note*
80 Dunbar, Scott, Hawthornden *see note* mae *more*

Than I can tell; for o' my fay,
  I maun break aff;
'Twould take a live-lang simmer day
  To name the haff.

The saucy chiels – I think they ca' them 85
Critics, the muckle sorrow claw them,
(For mense nor manners ne'er could awe them
  Frae their presumption) –
They need nae try thy jokes to fathom;
  They want rumgumption. 90

But ilka Mearns and Angus bairn,
Thy tales and sangs by heart shall learn,
And chiels shall come frae yont the Cairn-
  A-Mounth, right yousty,
If Ross will be so kind as share in 95
  Their pint at Drousty.

81 o' my fay *by my faith*
87 mense *discretion*
90 rumgumption *common sense*
91 Mearns, Angus *see note*
93 Cairn-a-Mounth *see note*
94 yousty *chatty*
96 Drousty *an alehouse in Glenlee*

ISOBEL PAGAN (1741–1821)

Ca' the Yowes to the Knowes

Ca' the yowes to the knowes,
Ca' them whare the heather grow,
Ca' them whare the burnie rows,
  My bonnie dearie!

As I gaed doun the water side, 5
There I met my shepherd lad;
He rowed me sweetly in his plaid,
  And he ca'd me his dearie.

'Will ye gang doun the water side,
And see the waves sae sweetly glide 10
Beneath the hazels spreading wide?
  The mune it shines fu' clearly.'

'I was bred up at nae sic schule,
My shepherd lad, to play the fool,
And a' the day to sit in dule, 15
  And naebody to see me.'

'Ye shall get gowns and ribbons meet,
Cawf-leather shoon to thy white feet,
And in my arms ye'se lie and sleep,
  And ye shall be my dearie.' 20

'If ye'll but stand to what ye've said,
I'se gang wi' you, my shepherd lad;
And ye may row me in your plaid,
  And I shall be your dearie.'

1 ca' *drive* yowes *ewes*
  knowes *knolls*
3 burnie rows *stream rolls*
7 rowed *rolled* plaid *blanket-cloak*
12 mune *moon*
13 schule *school*
15 dule *grief*
18 shoon *shoes*

'While waters wimple to the sea, 25
While day blinks i' the lift sae hie,
Till clay-cauld death shall blin my e'e,
  Ye aye shall be my dearie.'

25 wimple *ripple*
26 lift sae hie *sky so high*
27 blin *blind*

ALEXANDER, DUKE OF GORDON (1743–1827)

Cauld Kail in Aberdeen

There's cauld kail in Aberdeen,
  And castocks in Stra'bogie;
Gin I hae but a bonnie lass,
  Ye're welcome to your cogie.
And ye may sit up a' the night, 5
And drink till it be braid daylight;
Gie me a lass baith clean and tight
  To dance the reel o' Bogie.

In cotillons the French excel;
  John Bull loves country dances; 10
The Spaniards dance fandangoes well;
  Mynheer an allemande prances;
In foursome reels the Scots delight,
At threesomes they dance wondrous light,
But twasomes ding a' out o' sight, 15
  Danced to the reel o' Bogie.

Come lads, and view your partners weel;
  Wale each a blithesome rogie;
I'll tak this lassie to mysel,
  She looks sae keen and vogie. 20
Now, piper lads, bang up the spring,
The country fashion is the thing,
To prie their mou's ere we begin
  To dance the reel o' Bogie.

Now ilka lad has got a lass, 25
  Save yon auld doited fogey,

2 castocks *cabbage stalks*
  Stra'bogie *see note*
3 cogie *small wooden bowl*
15 ding *beat*
18 wale *choose*
20 vogie *glad*
21 bang *play* spring *tune*
23 prie *taste, sample*
26 doited *crazy*

And ta'en a fling upon the grass,
  As they do in Stra'bogie.
But a' the lasses look sae fain,
We canna think oursels to hain, 30
For they maun hae their come-again,
  To dance the reel o' Bogie.

Now a' the lads hae done their best,
  Like true men o' Stra'bogie;
We'll stop a while, and tak a rest, 35
  And tipple out a cogie.
Come now, my lads, and tak your glass,
And try ilk ither to surpass,
In wishing health to every lass
  To dance the reel o' Bogie. 40

27 fling *dance*
29 fain *eager*
30 hain *hold back*
31 come-again *kiss at the end of a dance*

HECTOR MACNEILL (1746–1818)

The Scottish Muse

Jamaica, 1798.

Now, good Cesario, but that piece of song,
That old and antique song we heard last night:
Methought it did relieve my passion much;
More than light airs, and recollected terms
Of these more brisk and giddy-paced times.
Shakespeare.

O welcome, simply soothing treasure!
In midst o' pain my lanely pleasure!
Tutored by thee, and whispering leisure,
  I quit the thrang,
And, wrapt in blessed retirement, measure 5
  Thy varied sang!

Kind, leil companion, without thee,
Ah, welladay, what should I be!
Whan jeered by fools wha canna see
  My inward pain, 10
Aneath thy sheltering wing I flee,
  And mak my mane.

There seated, smiling by my side,
For hours thegither wilt thou bide,
Chanting auld tales o' martial pride, 15
  And luve's sweet smart!
Till glowing warm thy numbers glide
  Streight to the heart.

'Tis then, wi' powerfu' plastic hand
Thou wavest thy magic-working wand; 20
And stirring up ideas grand
  That fire the brain,

2 pain *see note*
7 leil *faithful*
9 wha *who*
12 mane *moan*
19 plastic *moulding*

Aff whirlst me swift to fairy land
  'Mang Fancy's train.

Scared by disease whan balmy rest 25
Flees trembling frae her downy nest;
Starting frae horror's dreams oppress,
  I see thee come
Wi' radiance mild that cheers the breast,
  And lights the gloom! 30

Heart'ning thou com'st, wi' modest grace,
Hope, luve, and pity, in thy face,
And gliding up wi' silent pace
  My plaints to hear,
Whisper'st in turn thae soothing lays 35
  Saft in my ear.

'Ill-fated wand'rer, doomed to mane!
Wan suff'rer bleached wi' care and pain!
How changed, alas, since vogie vain,
  Wi' spirits light, 40
Ye hailed me first in untaught strain
  On Strevlin's height!

Ah me, how stark, how blithe, how bauld
Ye brattled then through wind and cauld!
Reckless, by stream, by firth and fauld 45
  Ye held your way;
By passion ruled, by love enthralled,
  Ye poured the lay.

'Twas then, entranced in am'rous sang,
I marked you midst the rural thrang; 50
Ardent and keen, the hail day lang
  Wi' Nature ta'en,
Slip frae the crowd, and mix amang
  Her simple train.

23 aff *off*
39 vogie *vaunting*
42 Strevlin *Stirling*
44 brattled *clattered*
51 hail *whole*

'Twas then I saw (alas, owre clear!) 55
Your future thriftless, lost career!
And while some blamed, wi' boding fear,
  The tunefu' art,
Your moral pride and truth sincere
  Aye wan my heart. 60

He ne'er can lout, I musing said,
To ply the fleeching, fawning trade;
Nor bend the knee, nor bow the head,
  To walth or power!
But backward turn, wi' scornfu' speed, 65
  Frae flatt'ry's door.

He'll never learn his bark to steer
'Mid passion's sudden, wild career;
Nor try at times to tack or veer
  To int'rest's gale, 70
But hoist the sheet, unawed by fear,
  Though storms prevail.

Owre proud to ask, owre bauld to yield!
Whar will he find a shelt'ring beild?
Whan poortith's blast drifts cross the field 75
  Wi' wintry cauld,
Whar will he wone – poor feckless chield! –
  Whan frail and auld!

Year after year, in youtheid's prime,
Wander he will frae clime to clime, 80
Sanguine wi' hope on wing sublime
  Mount heigh in air!
But than, waes me, there comes a time
  O' dool and care!

There comes a time, or soon, or late, 85
O' serious thought and sad debate;

55 owre *over*
60 wan *won*
61 lout *stoop*
62 fleeching *flattering*
74 beild *refuge*
75 poortith *poverty*
77 wone *live*
79 youtheid *youth*
84 dool *grief*

Whan blighted hope and adverse fate
  Owrespread their gloom,
And mirk despair, in waefu' state,
  Foresees the doom! 90

And maun he fa' (I sighing cried)
Wi' guardian honour by his side!
Shall fortune frown on guiltless pride,
  And straits owrtake him?
Weel, blame wha like, whate'er betide 95
  I'se ne'er forsake him!

Ardent I spake, and frae the day
Ye hailed me smiling, youthfu' gay
On Aichil's whin-flowered fragrant brae,
  I strave to cheer ye! 100
Frae morn's first dawn to e'en's last ray
  I ay was near ye.

Frae west to east, frae isle to isle,
To India's shore and sultry soil;
'Mid tumult, battle, care, and toil, 105
  I following flew;
Ay smoothed the past, and waked the smile
  To prospects new.

Whan warfare ceased its wild uproar,
To Elephanta's far-famed shore 110
I led ye, ardent to explore,
  Wi' panting heart,
Her idol monuments o' yore,
  And sculptured art.

Sweet flew the hours (the toil your boast) 115
On smiling Salsett's cave-wrought coast:
Though hope was tint, though a' was crossed,
  Nae dread alarms
Ye felt – fond fool!—in wonder lost
  And nature's charms! 120

89 mirk *dark*
91 maun *must*
99 Aichil *see note* brae *hill*
110 Elephanta *see note*
116 Salsett *see note*
117 hope *see note* tint *lost*

Frae east to west, frae main to main,
To Carib's shores returned again;
In sickness, trial, hardship, pain,
  Ye ken yoursell,
Drapt frae the muse's melting strain 125
  Peace balmy fell.

Fell sweet, for, as she warbling flew,
Hope lent her heaven-refreshing dew;
Fair virtue close, and closer drew,
  To join the lay; 130
While conscience bright, and brighter grew,
  And cheered the way!

Whether to east or westward borne
(Or flushed wi' joy, or wae-forlorn),
Ye hailed the fragrant breath o' morn 135
  Frae orange flower,
Or cassia bud, or logwood thorn,
  Or guava bower:

Or frae the mist-capped mountain blue
Inhaled the spicy gales that flew, 140
Rich frae pimento's groves that grew
  In deep'ning green,
Crowned wi' their flowers o' milk-white hue
  In dazzling sheen!

Whether at midnoon panting laid, 145
Ye wooed coy zephyr's transient aid
Under the banyan's pillared shade,
  On plain or hill,
Or plantain green, that rustling played
  Across the rill: 150

Or 'neath the tam'rind's shelt'ring gloom,
Drank coolness wafted in perfume,
Fresh frae the shaddack's golden bloom,
  As flutt'ring gay
Hummed saft the bird o' peerless plume, 155
  Frae spray to spray!

122 Carib *see note*
124 ken *know*
141 pimento *see note*
153 shaddack *grapefruit*
155 bird *humming bird*

Whether at eve, wi' raptured breast,
The shelving palm-girt beach ye prest,
And ee'd, entranced, the purpling west
  Bepictured o'er, 160
As ocean murm'ring gently kissed
  The whitening shore:

Whether at twilight's parting day
Ye held your solemn musing way,
Whar through the gloom in myriad ray 165
  The fire-flies gleam;
And 'thwart the grove, in harmless play,
  The light'nings stream!

Or, by the moon's bright radiance led,
Roamed late the guinea-verdured glade, 170
Where towered the giant ceiba's shade;
  And, loftier still,
The cabbage rears its regal head
  Owre palm-crowned hill.

Still following close, still whisp'ring near, 175
The muse aye caught your list'ning ear;
'Mid tempest's rage and thunder's rair
  Aye cheering sang:
Touched by her hand (unchilled by fear)
  The harp-strings rang. 180

Returned at last frae varied clime,
Whar youth and hope lang tint their time,
Ance mair to Strevlin's height sublime
  We winged our way;
Ance mair attuned the rural rhyme 185
  On Aichil brae.

'Twas then my native strains ye leared,
For passion spake while fancy cheered;

159 ee'd *eyed*
170 guinea-verdured *see note*
171 ceiba *see note*
173 cabbage *see note*
177 rair *roar*
180 harp-strings *see note*
187 strains *see note* leared *learned*

A while wi' flaunting airs ye flared
  And thought to shine; 190
But nature, judging nature sneered,
  And ca'd it – fine!

Stung wi' the taunt, ye back recoiled,
Pensive ye mused; I marked, and smiled;
Daund'ring depressed 'mang knows flowered wild, 195
  My aten reed
Ye faund ae bonny morning mild
  'Tween Ayr and Tweed.

'Tween past'ral Tweed and wand'ring Ayr,
Whar unbusked nature blooms sae fair! 200
And mony a wild note saft and clear
  Sings sweet by turns,
Tuned by my winsome Allan's ear
  And fav'rite Burns.

Trembling wi' joy ye touched the reed, 205
Doubtfu' ye sighed, and hang your head;
Fearfu' ye sang till some agreed
  The notes war true;
Whan grown mair bauld, ye gae a screed
  That pleased nae few. 210

By Forth's green links bedecked wi' flowers,
By Clyde's clear stream and beechen bowers;
Heartsome and healthfu' flew the hours
  In simple sang,
While Lossit's braes and Eden's towers 215
  The notes prolang!

Thae times are gane! Ah, welladay!
For health has flown wi' spirits gay;

191 nature *see note*
195 daund'ring *strolling* knows *hills*
196 aten *oaten*
197 faund *found*
198 Ayr, Tweed *see note*
200 unbusked *unadorned*
203 Allan *Ramsay*
209 gae *gave* screed *tune*
210 pleased nae few *see note*
211 Forth *see note*
212 Clyde *see note*
213 heartsome *cheerful*
215 Lossit, Eden *see note*
217 thae *those*

Youth, too, has fled, and cauld decay
  Comes creeping on: 220
October's sun cheers na like May
  That brightly shone!

Yet autumn's gloom, though threat'ning bleak,
Has joys, gin folk calm joys wad seek;
Friendship and worth then social cleek 225
  And twine thegither,
And gree and crack by ingle cheek
  Just like twin-brither.

'Tis then (youth's vain vagaries past,
That please a while, but fash at last), 230
Serious, our ee we backward cast
  On bygane frays,
And, marvelling, mourn the thriftless waste
  O' former days!

Then, too, wi' prudence on our side, 235
And moral reas'ning for our guide,
Calmly we view the restless tide
  O' warldly care,
And cull, wi' academic pride,
  The flow'rs o' lare. 240

And while, wi' sure and steady pace,
Coy science' secret paths we trace,
And catch fair nature's beauteous face
  In varied view,
Ardent, though auld, we join the chase, 245
  And pleased pursue.

'Tis sae through life's short circling year,
The seasons change, and, changing, cheer;
Journeying we jog, unawed by fear:
  Hope plays her part! 250
Forward we look, though in the rear
  Death shakes the dart.

224 gin *if*
225 cleek *link arms*
227 gree *concur* crack *chat*
ingle *fireside*
230 fash *annoy*
240 lare *learning*

Catch then the dream, nor count it vain;
Hope's dream's the sweetest balm o' pain:
Heaven's unseen joys may yet remain, 255
  And yet draw near ye:
Meanwhile, ye see, I hear your mane,
  And flee to cheer ye.

Ane too's at hand, to wham ye fled
Frae Britain's cauld, frae misery's bed; 260
Owre seas tempestuous shivering sped
  To friendship's flame;
Whar kindling warm, in sun-beams clad,
  She hails her Graham.

Wi' him (let health but favouring smile) 265
Ance mair ye'll greet fair Albion's isle!
In some calm nook life's cares beguile
  Atween us twa:
Feed the faint lamp wi' friendship's oil –
  Then slip awa!' 270

The flatterer ceased, and smiled adieu,
Just waved her hand, and mild withdrew!
Cheered wi' the picture (fause or true)
  I checked despair,
And frae that moment made a vow 275
  To mourn nae mair.

258 flee *fly*
264 Graham *see note*
266 Albion *Britain*
270 awa' *away*
273 fause *false*
276 nae mair *no more*

MICHAEL BRUCE (1746–67)

Weaving Spiritualised

A web I hear thou hast begun,
And know'st not when it may be done:
So death uncertain see ye fear,
For ever distant, ever near.

See'st thou the shuttle quickly pass? 5
Think mortal life is as the grass,
An empty cloud, a morning dream,
A bubble rising on the stream.

The knife still ready to cut off
Excrescent knots that mar the stuff, 10
To stern affliction's rod compare;
'Tis for thy good, so learn to bear.

Too full a quill oft checks the speed
Of shuttle flying by the reed:
So riches oft keep back the soul, 15
That else would hasten to its goal.

Thine eye the web runs keenly o'er
For things amiss, unseen before:
Thus scan thy life, mend what's amiss,
Next day correct the faults of this. 20

For when the web is at an end,
'Tis then too late a fault to mend:
Let thought of this awaken dread –
Repentance dwells not with the dead.

6 grass *see note*

Ossian's Hymn to the Sun

O thou whose beams the sea-girt earth array,
King of the sky, and father of the day!
O sun, what fountain, hid from human eyes,
Supplies thy circle round the radiant skies,
For ever burning and for ever bright 5
With heaven's pure fire, and everlasting light?
What awful beauty in thy face appears!
Immortal youth, beyond the power of years!
When gloomy darkness to thy reign resigns,
And from the gates of morn thy glory shines, 10
The conscious stars are put to sudden flight,
And all the planets hide their heads in night;
The queen of heaven forsakes th'etheral plain,
To sink inglorious in the western main.
The clouds refulgent deck thy golden throne, 15
High in the heavens, immortal and alone!
Who can abide the brightness of thy face,
Or who attend thee in thy rapid race?
The mountain oaks, like their own leaves, decay;
Themselves the mountains wear with age away; 20
The boundless main, that rolls from land to land,
Lessens at times, and leaves a waste of sand;
The silver moon, refulgent lamp of night,
Is lost in heaven, and emptied of her light:
But thou for ever shalt endure the same, 25
Thy light eternal, and unspent thy flame.

When tempests with their train impend on high,
Darken the day, and load the labouring sky;
When heaven's wide convex glows with lightnings dire,
All ether flaming and all earth on fire; 30
When loud and long the deep-mouthed thunder rolls,
And peals on peals redoubled rend the poles;
If from the opening clouds thy form appears,
Her wonted charm the face of nature wears;
Thy beauteous orb restores departed day, 35
Looks from the sky, and laughs the storm away.

ROBERT FERGUSSON (1750–74)

Auld Reikie, a poem

Auld Reikie, wale o' ilka town
That Scotland kens beneath the moon;
Where couthy chiels at e'ening meet
Their bizzing craigs and mous to weet;
And blythly gar auld Care gae bye 5
Wi' blinkit and wi' bleering eye:
O'er lang frae thee the muse has been
Sae frisky on the simmer's green,
Whan flowers and gowans wont to glent
In bonny blinks upo' the bent; 10
But now the leaves a yellow dye,
Peeled frae the branches, quickly fly;
And now frae nouther bush nor brier
The spreckled mavis greets your ear;
Nor bonny blackbird skims and roves 15
To seek his love in yonder groves.
  Then, Reikie, welcome! Thou canst charm
Unfleggit by the year's alarm;
Not Boreas that sae snelly blows,
Dare here pap in his angry nose: 20
Thanks to our dads, whase biggin stands
A shelter to surrounding lands.
  Now Morn, with bonny purpie-smiles,
Kisses the air-cock o' St Giles;
Rakin their ein, the servant lasses 25
Early begin their lies and clashes;
Ilk tells her friend of saddest distress,
That still she brooks frae scouling mistress;

3 couthy chiels *agreeable chaps*
4 bizzing craigs *buzzing throats* weet *wet*
6 bleering *bleary*
9 gowans *daisies* glent *gleam*
10 bent *open field*
14 spreckled mavis *speckled song-thrush*
18 unfleggit *unfrightened*
19 Boreas *north wind* snelly *keenly*
20 pap *pop*
21 biggin *building*
22 lands *tenements*
23 purpie *purple*
24 air-cock *weather-cock*
26 clashes *gossip*

And wi' her joe in turnpike stair
She'd rather snuff the stinking air, 30
As be subjected to her tongue,
When justly censured in the wrong.
On stair wi' tub, or pat in hand,
The barefoot housemaids looe to stand,
That antrin fock may ken how snell 35
Auld Reikie will at morning smell:
Then, with an inundation big as
The burn that 'neath the Nore Loch brig is,
They kindly shower Edina's roses,
To quicken and regale our noses. 40
Now some for this, wi' satire's leesh,
Ha'e gi'en auld Edinburgh a creesh:
But without souring nocht is sweet;
The morning smells that hail our street,
Prepare, and gently lead the way 45
To simmer canty, braw and gay:
Edina's sons mair eithly share,
Her spices and her dainties rare,
Then he that's never yet been called
Aff frae his plaidie or his fauld. 50
Now stairhead critics, senseless fools,
Censure their aim, and pride their rules,
In Luckenbooths, wi' glouring eye,
Their neighbours sma'est faults descry:
If ony loun should dander there, 55
Of awkward gait, and foreign air,
They trace his steps, till they can tell
His pedigree as weel's himsell.
Whan Phoebus blinks wi' warmer ray
And schools at noonday get the play, 60
Then business, weighty business comes;
The trader glours; he doubts, he hums:
The lawyers eke to Cross repair,
Their wigs to shaw, and toss an air;
While busy agent closely plies, 65

29 joe *sweetheart*
35 antrin fock *strangers*
snell *pungent*
38 Nore Loch *see note*
39 Edina's roses *see note*
41 leesh *lash*
42 creesh *beating*
50 plaidie *shepherd's plaid*
53 Luckenbooths *High Street shops*
55 dander *stroll*
59 Phoebus *the sun*
63 eke *also* Cross *see note*

And a' his kittle cases tries.
  Now Night, that's cunzied chief for fun,
Is wi' her usual rites begun;
Through ilka gate the torches blaze,
And globes send out their blinking rays. 70
The usefu' cadie plies in street,
To bide the profits o' his feet;
For by thir lads Auld Reikie's fock
Ken but a sample, o' the stock
O' thieves, that nightly wad oppress, 75
And make baith goods and gear the less.
Near him the lazy chairman stands,
And wats na how to turn his hands,
Till some daft birky, ranting fu',
Has matters somewhere else to do; 80
The chairman willing, gi'es his light
To deeds o' darkness and o' night:
  It's never sax pence for a lift
That gars thir lads wi' fu'ness rift;
For they wi' better gear are paid, 85
And whores and culls support their trade.
  Near some lamp-post, wi' dowy face,
Wi' heavy ein, and sour grimace,
Stands she that beauty lang had kend,
Whoredom her trade, and vice her end. 90
But see whare now she wuns her bread
By that which nature ne'er decreed;
And sings sad music to the lugs,
'Mang burachs o' damned whores and rogues.
Whane'er we reputation loss – 95
Fair chastity's transparent gloss! –
Redemption seenil kens the name,
But a's black misery and shame.
  Frae joyous tavern, reeling drunk,
Wi' fiery phizz, and ein half sunk, 100
Behad the bruiser, fae to a'

67 cunzied *coined*
71 cadie *errand-boy*
73 thir *those*
78 wats *knows*
79 birky *fellow*
84 rift *belch*
86 culls *dupes*
87 dowy *sad*
94 burachs *crowds*
95 loss *lose*
97 seenil *seldom*
100 phizz *face*
101 behad *behold*

That in the reek o' gardies fa':
Close by his side, a feckless race
O' macaronies shew their face,
And think they're free frae skaith or harm, 105
While pith befriends their leader's arm:
Yet fearfu' aften o' their maught,
They quatt the glory o' the faught
To this same warrior wha led
Thae heroes to bright honour's bed; 110
And aft the hack o' honour shines
In bruiser's face wi' broken lines:
Of them sad tales he tells anon,
Whan ramble and whan fighting's done;
And, like Hectorian, ne'er impairs 115
The brag and glory o' his sairs.
Whan feet in dirty gutters plash,
And fock to wale their fitstaps fash;
At night the macaroni drunk,
In pools or gutters aftimes sunk: 120
Hegh, what a fright he now appears,
Whan he his corpse dejected rears!
Look at that head, and think if there
The pomet slaistered up his hair!
The cheeks observe, where now could shine 125
The scancing glories o' carmine?
Ah, legs, in vain the silk-worm there
Displayed to view her eidant care;
For stink, instead of perfumes, grow,
And clarty odours fragrant flow. 130
Now some to porter, some to punch,
Some to their wife, and some their wench,
Retire, while noisy ten-hours drum
Gars a' your trades gae dand'ring home.
Now mony a club, jocose and free, 135

102 reek *reach* gardies *raised fists*
104 macaronies *fops, dandies*
106 pith *strength*
107 maught *strength*
108 quatt *quit* faught *fight*
110 thae *those*
111 hack *mark*
115 Hectorian *like Hector, the Trojan hero*
118 fitstaps *footsteps*
124 pomet *pomade* slaistered *smeared*
126 scancing *shining*
128 eidant *diligent*
130 clarty *dirty*
133 ten hours drum *ten o' clock signal*

Gie a' to merriment and glee,
Wi' sang and glass, they fley the pow'r
O' care that wad harass the hour:
For wine and Bacchus still bear down
Our thrawart fortune's wildest frown: 140
It maks you stark, and bauld and brave,
Ev'n whan descending to the grave.
  Now some, in Pandemonium's shade
Resume the gormandizing trade;
Whare eager looks, and glancing ein, 145
Forespeak a heart and stamack keen.
Gang on, my lads; it's lang sin syne
We kent auld Epicurus' line;
Save you, the board wad cease to rise,
Bedight wi' daintiths to the skies; 150
And salamanders cease to swill
The comforts of a burning gill.
  But chief, o Cape, we crave thy aid,
To get our cares and poortith laid:
Sincerity, and genius true, 155
Of knights have ever been the due:
Mirth, music, porter deepest dyed,
Are never here to worth denied;
And Health, o' happiness the queen,
Blinks bonny, wi' her smile serene. 160
  Though joy maist part Auld Reikie owns,
Eftsoons she kens sad sorrows frowns;
What group is yon sae dismal grim,
Wi' horrid aspect, cleeding dim?
Says Death, 'They're mine, a dowy crew, 165
To me they'll quickly pay their last adieu.'
  How come mankind, whan lacking woe,
In saulie's face their heart to show,
As if they were a clock, to tell

137 fley *frighten away*
139 Bacchus *god of wine*
140 thrawart *adverse*
141 stark *strong*
143 Pandemonium *a club of diners*
146 stamack *stomach*
147 sin syne *since then*
148 Epicurus *Greek philosopher*
150 bedight *arrayed* daintiths *dainties*
151 salamanders *perhaps a drinking club*
153 Cape *the club Fergusson belonged*
154 poortith *poverty*
164 cleeding *clothing*
165 dowy *sad*
168 saulie *hired mourner*

That grief in them had rung her bell? 170
Then, what is man? Why a' this phraze?
Life's spunk decayed, nae mair can blaze.
Let sober grief alone declare
Our fond anxiety and care:
Nor let the undertakers be 175
The only waefu' friends we see.
  Come on, my muse, and then rehearse
The gloomiest theme in a' your verse:
In morning, whan ane keeks about,
Fu' blyth and free frae ail, nae doubt 180
He lippens not to be misled
Amang the regions of the dead:
But straight a painted corp he sees,
Lang streekit 'neath its canopies.
Soon, soon will this his mirth control, 185
And send damnation to his soul:
Or when the dead-deal (awful shape!)
Makes frighted mankind girn and gape,
Reflection then his reason sours,
For the neist dead-deal may be ours. 190
Whan Sybil led the Trojan down
To haggard Pluto's dreary town,
Shapes war nor thae, I freely ween
Could never meet the soldier's ein.
  If kail sae green, or herbs delight, 195
Edina's street attracts the sight;
Not Covent Garden, clad sae braw,
Mair fouth o' herbs can eithly shaw:
For mony a yeard is here sair sought,
That kail and cabbage may be bought; 200
And healthfu' salad to regale,
Whan pampered wi' a heavy meal.
Glour up the street in simmer morn,
The birks sae green, and sweet brier-thorn,

171 phraze *fancy talk*
172 spunk *spark*
179 keeks *looks*
181 lippens *trusts*
184 streekit *stretched*
187 dead-deal *laying-out board*
188 girn *grimace*
191 Sybil, Trojan *see note*
192 Pluto *god of the underworld*
193 thae *those* ween *think*
197 Covent Garden *a London market*
198 fouth *abundance*
199 yeard *garden*
204 birks *birches*

Wi' sprangit flow'rs that scent the gale, 205
Ca' far awa' the morning smell,
Wi' which our ladies' flow'r-pat's filled,
And every noxious vapour killed.
O Nature, canty, blyth and free,
Whare is there keeking-glass like thee? 210
Is there on earth that can compare
Wi' Mary's shape, and Mary's air,
Save the empurpled speck, that grows
In the saft faulds of yonder rose?
How bonny seems the virgin breast, 215
Whan by the lilies here carest,
And leaves the mind in doubt to tell
Which maist in sweets and hue excel?
 Gillespie's snuff should prime the nose
Of her that to the market goes, 220
If they wad like to shun the smells
That buoy up frae markest cells,
Whare wames o' paunches sav'ry scent
To nostrils gi'e great discontent.
Now wha in Albion could expect 225
O' cleanliness sic great neglect?
Nae Hottentot that daily lairs
'Mang tripe, or ither clarty wares,
Hath ever yet conceived, or seen
Beyond the line, sic scenes unclean. 230
 On Sunday here, an altered scene
O' men and manners meets our ein:
Ane wad maist trow some people chose
To change their faces wi' their clo'es,
And fain wad gar ilk neighbour think 235
They thirst for goodness, as for drink:
But there's an unco dearth o' grace,
That has nae mansion but the face,
And never can obtain a part
In benmost corner of the heart. 240
Why should religion make us sad,

205 sprangit *in various colours*
206 ca' *drive*
210 keeking-glass *mirror*
219 Gillespie *see note*
222 markest *murkiest*
223 wames *bellies* paunches *bowels*
225 Albion *Britain*
227 Hottentot *see note* lairs *lies*
228 clarty *dirty*
240 benmost *innermost*

If good frae virtue's to be had?
Na, rather gleefu' turn your face;
Forsake hypocrisy, grimace;
And never have it understood 245
You fleg mankind frae being good.
In afternoon, a' brawly buskit,
The joes and lasses loe to frisk it:
Some tak a great delight to place
The modest bongrace o'er the face; 250
Though you may see, if so inclined,
The turning o' the leg behind.
Now Comely Garden, and the Park,
Refresh them, after forenoon's wark;
Newhaven, Leith or Canonmills, 255
Supply them in their Sunday's gills;
Whare writers aften spend their pence,
To stock their heads wi' drink and sense.
While dand'ring cits delight to stray
To Castlehill, or public way, 260
Whare they nae other purpose mean,
Than that fool cause o' being seen;
Let me to Arthur's Seat pursue,
Whare bonny pastures meet the view;
And mony a wild-lorn scene accrues, 265
Befitting Willie Shakespeare's muse:
If fancy there would join the thrang,
The desert rocks and hills amang,
To echoes we should lilt and play,
And gie to mirth the lee-lang day. 270
Or should some cankered biting show'r
The day and a' her sweets deflower,
To Holyrood-house let me stray,
And gie to musing a' the day;
Lamenting what auld Scotland knew 275
Bien days for ever frae her view:
O Hamilton, for shame! The muse

246 fleg *frighten*
247 buskit *adorned*
248 joes *sweethearts*
250 bongrace *straw bonnet*
253 Comely Garden, the Park *see note*
255 Newhaven, Leith or Canonmills *see note*
259 dand'ring cits *strolling citizens*
265 wild-lorn *desolate*
267 thrang *throng*
270 lee-lang *live-long*
273 Holyrood-house *see note*
276 bien *prosperous*
277 Hamilton *see note*

Would pay to thee her couthy vows,
Gin ye wad tent the humble strain
And gie's our dignity again: 280
For o, waes me, the thistle springs
In domicile of ancient kings,
Without a patriot to regrete
Our palace, and our ancient state.
  Blest place, whare debtors daily run, 285
To rid themselves frae jail and dun;
Here, though sequestered frae the din
That rings Auld Reikie's waas within,
Yet they may tread the sunny braes,
And brook Apollo's cheery rays; 290
Glour frae St Anthon's grassy hight,
O'er vales in simmer claise bedight,
Nor ever hing their head, I ween,
Wi' jealous fear o' being seen.
May I, whanever duns come nigh, 295
And shake my garret wi' their cry,
Scour here wi' haste, protection get,
To screen mysell frae them and debt;
To breathe the bliss of open sky,
And Simon Fraser's bolts defy. 300
  Now gin a lown should ha'e his clase
In thread-bare autumn o' their days,
St Mary, brokers' guardian saint,
Will satisfy ilk ail and want;
For mony a hungry writer, there 305
Dives down at night, wi' cleading bare,
And quickly rises to the view
A gentleman, perfyte and new.
Ye rich fock, look no wi' disdain
Upo' this ancient brokage lane! 310
For naked poets are supplied,
With what you to their wants denied.
  Peace to thy shade, thou wale o' men,

278 couthy *friendly*
279 tent *heed*
283 regrete *lament*
285 debtors *see note*
288 waas *walls*
290 Apollo *the sun*
291 St Anthon *see note*
295 duns *bailiffs*
297 scour *rush*
300 Simon Fraser *see note*
303 St Mary *see note*
308 perfyte *perfect*

Drummond, relief to poortith's pain:
To thee the greatest bliss we owe; 315
And tribute's tear shall grateful flow:
The sick are cured, the hungry fed,
And dreams of comfort tend their bed:
As lang as Forth weets Lothian's shore,
As lang's on Fife her billows roar, 320
Sae lang shall ilk whase country's dear,
To thy remembrance gie a tear.
By thee Auld Reikie thrave, and grew
Delightfu' to her childer's view:
Nae mair shall Glasgow striplings threap 325
Their city's beauty and its shape,
While our new city spreads around
Her bonny wings on fairy ground.
  But provosts now that ne'er afford
The sma'est dignity to lord, 330
Ne'er care though every scheme gae wild
That Drummond's sacred hand has culled:
The spacious brig neglected lies,
Though plagued wi' pamphlets, dunned wi' cries;
They heed not though destruction come 335
To gulp us in her gaunting womb.
O shame, that safety canna claim
Protection from a provost's name,
But hidden danger lies behind
To torture and to fleg the mind; 340
I may as weel bid Arthur's Seat
To Berwick Law make gleg retreat,
As think that either will or art
Shall get the gate to win their heart;
For politics are a' their mark, 345
Bribes latent, and corruption dark:
If they can eithly turn the pence,
Wi' city's good they will dispense;
Nor care though a' her sons were laired
Ten fathom i' the auld kirk-yard. 350

314 Drummond *see note*
319 weets *wets*
320–21 Forth, Lothian, Fife *see note*
323 thrave *throve*
324 childer's *children's*
325 threap *assert*
333 brig *see note*
336 gaunting *yawning*
340 fleg *frighten*
342 Berwick Law *see note*
  gleg *swift*
349 laired *buried*

To sing yet meikle does remain,
Undecent for a modest strain;
And since the poet's daily bread is
The favour of the muse or ladies,
He downa like to gie offence 355
To delicacy's bonny sense;
Therefore the stews remain unsung,
And bawds in silence drop their tongue.
Reikie, farewell! I ne'er could part
Wi' thee but wi' a dowy heart; 360
Aft frae the Fifan coast I've seen,
Thee tow'ring on thy summit green;
So glowr the saints when first is given
A fav'rite keek o' glore and heaven;
On earth nae mair they bend their ein, 365
But quick assume angelic mien;
So I on Fife wad glowr no more,
But galloped to Edina's shore.

355 downa *cannot*
360 dowy *sad*
364 keek *sight* glore *glory*
366 mien *appearance*

The Daft-Days

Now mirk December's dowie face
Glours owr the rigs wi' sour grimace,
While, through his minimum of space,
  The bleer-eyed sun,
Wi' blinkin light and stealing pace, 5
  His race doth run.

From naked groves nae birdie sings,
To shepherd's pipe nae hillock rings,
The breeze nae od'rous flavour brings
  From Borean cave, 10
And dwyning nature droops her wings,
  Wi' visage grave.

Mankind but scanty pleasure glean
Frae snawy hill or barren plain,
Whan Winter, 'midst his nipping train, 15
  Wi' frozen spear,
Sends drift owr a' his bleak domain,
  And guides the weir.

Auld Reikie! thou'rt the canty hole,
A bield for mony caldrife soul, 20
Wha snugly at thine ingle loll,
  Baith warm and couth;
While round they gar the bicker roll
  To weet their mouth.

When merry Yule-day comes, I trow, 25
You'll scantlins find a hungry mou;
Sma' are our cares, our stamacks fou
  O' gusty gear,
And kickshaws, strangers to our view,
  Sin fairn-year. 30

1 mirk *dark* dowie *sad*
10 Borean *northern*
11 dwyning *wasting*
17 drift *wind-driven snow*
18 weir *war*
20 bield *shelter* caldrife *cold*
22 couth *snug*
23 bicker *drinking vessel*
24 weet *wet*
26 scantlins *scarcely*
28 gusty *tasty*
29 kickshaws *delicacies*
30 fairn-year *last year*

Ye browster wives, now busk ye bra,
And fling your sorrows far awa';
Then come and gies the tither blaw
  Of reaming ale,
Mair precious than the well of Spa, 35
  Our hearts to heal.

Then, though at odds wi' a' the warl',
Amang oursells we'll never quarrel;
Though Discord gie a cankered snarl
  To spoil our glee, 40
As lang's there's pith into the barrel
  We'll drink and 'gree.

Fiddlers, your pins in temper fix,
And roset weel your fiddle-sticks,
And banish vile Italian tricks 45
  From out your quorum,
Nor fortes wi' pianos mix,
  Gie's 'Tulloch Gorum'.

For nought can cheer the heart sae weil
As can a canty Highland reel, 50
It even vivifies the heel
  To skip and dance:
Lifeless is he wha canna feel
  Its influence.

Let mirth abound, let social cheer 55
Invest the dawning of the year;
Let blithesome innocence appear
  To crown our joy,
Nor envy wi' sarcastic sneer
  Our bliss destroy. 60

31 browster *brewer* busk *dress*
33 tither *the other*
34 reaming *foaming*
35 Spa *spa-town in Belgium*
37 warl' *world*
41 pith *power*
44 roset *rosin*
48 'Tulloch Gorum' *a fiddle tune*

And thou, great god of Aqua Vitæ!
Wha sways the empire of this city,
When fou we're sometimes capernoity,
  Be thou prepared
To hedge us frae that black banditti, 65
  The City-Guard.

61 Aqua Vitae *water of life (spirits)* 66 City-Guard *see note*
63 capernoity *quarrelsome*

Hallow-Fair

At Hallowmas, whan nights grow lang,
  And starnies shine fu' clear,
Whan fock, the nippin cald to bang,
  Their winter hap-warms wear,
Near Edinbrough a fair there hads, 5
  I wat there's nane whase name is,
For strappin dames and sturdy lads,
  And cap and stoup, mair famous
    Than it that day.

Upo' the tap o' ilka lum 10
  The sun began to keek,
And bad the trig-made maidens come
  A sightly joe to seek
At Hallow-fair, whare browsters rare
  Keep gude ale on the gantries, 15
And dinna scrimp ye o' a skair
  O' kebbucks frae their pantries,
    Fu' saut that day.

Here country John in bonnet blue,
  An' eke his Sunday's claise on, 20
Rins after Meg wi' rokelay new,
  An' sappy kisses lays on;
She'll tauntin say, 'Ye silly coof!
  Be o' your gab mair spairin';
He'll tak the hint, and criesh her loof 25
  Wi' what will buy her fairin,
    To chow that day.

2 starnies *stars*
3 bang *overcome*
4 hap-warms *warm wraps*
8 cap *cup* stoup *flagon*
10 lum *chimney*
11 keek *look*
12 trig *neat*
13 joe *sweetheart*
14 browsters *ale-wives*
15 gantries *wooden barrel stands*
16 skair *share*
17 kebbucks *cheeses*
21 rokelay *short cloak*
22 sappy *sloppy*
23 coof *fool*
25 creish *gease* loof *palm*
26 fairin *present from a fair*
27 chow *chew*

Here chapmen billies tak their stand,
  An' shaw their bonny wallies;
Wow, but they lie fu' gleg aff hand 30
  To trick the silly fallows:
Heh, sirs, what cairds and tinklers come,
  An' ne'er-do-weel horse-coupers,
An' spae-wives fenzying to be dumb,
  Wi' a' siclike landloupers, 35
    To thrive that day.

Here Sawny cries, frae Aberdeen;
  'Come ye to me fa need:
The brawest shanks that e'er were seen
  I'll sell ye cheap an' guid. 40
I wyt they are as protty hose
  As come frae weyr or leem:
Here tak a rug, and shaw's your pose:
  Forseeth, my ain's but teem
    An' light this day.' 45

Ye wives, as ye gang through the fair,
  O mak your bargains hooly!
O' a' thir wylie lowns beware,
  Or fegs, they will ye spulzie.
For fairn-year Meg Thamson got, 50
  Frae thir mischievous villains,
A scawed bit o' a penny note,
  That lost a score o' shillins
    To her that day.

The dinlin drums alarm our ears, 55
  The serjeant screechs fu' loud,

28 billies *fellows*
29 wallies *fancy goods*
30 gleg *keen*
32 cairds and tinklers *tinkers*
33 horse-coupers *horse-dealers*
35 spae-wives fenzying *fortune-tellers pretending* landloupers *vagabonds*
37 Sawney *see note*
38 fa *who*
39 shanks *stockings*
41 wyt *think* protty *pretty*
42 weyr or leem *needle or loom*
43 rug *bargain* pose *money*
44 forseeth *forsooth* teem *empty*
47 hooly *carefully*
48 lowns *fellows*
49 fegs *faith* spulzie *plunder*
50 fairn-year *last year*
52 scawed *scruffy*
55 dinlin *resounding*
56 screechs *shrieks*

'A' gentlemen and volunteers
  That wish your country gude,
Come here to me, and I sall gie
  Twa guineas and a crown, 60
A bowl o' punch, that like the sea
  Will soum a lang dragoon
    Wi' ease this day.'

Without the cuissers prance and nicker,
  An' our the ley-rig scud; 65
In tents the carles bend the bicker,
  An' rant an' roar like wud.
Then there's sic yellowchin and din,
  Wi' wives and wee-anes gablin,
That ane might true they were a-kin 70
  To a' the tongues at Babylon,
    Confused that day.

Whan Phoebus ligs in Thetis' lap,
  Auld Reikie gies them shelter,
Whare cadgily they kiss the cap, 75
  An' ca't round helter-skelter.
Jock Bell gaed furth to play his freaks,
  Great cause he had to rue it,
For frae a stark Lochaber aix
  He gat a clamihewit, 80
    Fu' sair that night.

'Ohon!' quo' he, 'I'd rather be
  By sword or bagnet stickit,
Than hae my crown or body wi'
  Sic deadly weapons nicket.' 85
Wi' that he gat anither straik
  Mair weighty than before,

62 soum *float*
64 cuissers *stallions*
65 our the ley-rig *over the field*
66 carles bend the bicker *fellows drink hard*
67 wud *mad*
68 yellowchin *yelling*
69 wee-anes *children*
73 Phoebus *sun-god* ligs *lies* Thetis *sea-nymph*
75 cadgily *cheerfully*
77 furth *forth* freaks *tricks*
79 stark Lochaber aix *strong hooked axe*
80 clamihewit *beating*
82 ohon *alas*
83 bagnet *bayonet*
86 straik *stroke*

That garred his feckless body aik,
An' spew the reikin gore,
Fu' red that night. 90

He peching on the cawsey lay,
O' kicks and cuffs weel saired;
A Highland aith the serjeant gae,
'She maun pe see our guard.'
Out spak the weirlike corporal, 95
'Pring in ta drunken sot.'
They trailed him ben, an' by my saul,
He paid his drunken groat
For that neist day.

Good fock, as ye come frae the fair, 100
Bide yont frae this black squad;
There's nae sic savages elsewhere
Allowed to wear cockade.
Than the strong lion's hungry maw,
Or tusk o' Russian bear, 105
Frae their wanruly fellin paw
Mair cause ye hae to fear
Your death that day.

A wee soup drink dis unco weel
To had the heart aboon; 110
It's good as lang's a canny chiel
Can stand steeve in his shoon.
But gin a birkie's owr weel saired,
It gars him aften stammer
To pleys that bring him to the guard, 115
An' eke the Council-chawmir,
Wi' shame that day.

88 feckless *feeble* aik *ache*
91 peching *panting* cawsey *street*
93 aith *oath*
94 pe *be*
95 weirlike *warlike*
96 pring in ta *bring in the*
97 ben *inside* saul *soul*
101 bide yont *stay away*
106 wanruly fellin paw *unruly fierce gesture*
109 soup *sup* dis *does*
111 chiel *fellow*
112 steeve *firm*
113 birkie *fellow* saired *full of drink*
115 pleys *quarrels*
117 eke *also* chawmir *chamber*

Leith Races

In July month, ae bonny morn,
  Whan Nature's rokelay green
Was spread o'er ilka rigg o' corn
  To charm our roving een;
Glouring about I saw a quean, 5
  The fairest 'neath the lift;
Her een ware o' the siller sheen,
  Her skin like snawy drift,
    Sae white that day.

Quod she, 'I ferly unco sair, 10
  That ye sud musand gae,
Ye wha hae sung o' Hallow-fair,
  Her winter's pranks and play:
Whan on Leith-Sands the racers rare,
  Wi' jocky louns are met, 15
Their orro pennies there to ware,
  And drown themsel's in debt
    Fu' deep that day.'

'An' wha are ye, my winsome dear,
  That takes the gate sae early? 20
Whare do ye win, gin ane may spier,
  For I right meikle ferly,
That sic braw buskit laughing lass
  Thir bonny blinks should gi'e,
An' loup like Hebe o'er the grass, 25
  As wanton and as free
    Frae dule this day.'

2 rokelay *cloak*
3 rigg *strip of farmland*
5 glouring *staring* quean *girl*
6 lift *sky*
8 snawy *snowy*
10 ferly *marvel*
11 sud musand *should musing*
15 louns *fellows*
16 orro *spare* ware *spend*
21 win *live*
23 buskit *dressed*
25 loup *leap* Hebe *goddess of youth*
27 dule *sadness*

'I dwall amang the caller springs
  That weet the Land o' Cakes,
And aften tune my canty strings 30
  At bridals and late-wakes:
They ca' me Mirth; I ne'er was kend
  To grumble or look sour,
But blyth wad be a lift to lend,
  Gif ye wad sey my pow'r 35
    An' pith this day.'

'A bargain be't, and, by my feggs,
  Gif ye will be my mate,
Wi' you I'll screw the cheery pegs,
  Ye shanna find me blate; 40
We'll reel an' ramble through the sands,
  And jeer wi' a' we meet;
Nor hip the daft and gleesome bands
  That fill Edina's street
    Sae thrang this day.' 45

Ere servant maids had wont to rise
  To seeth the breakfast kettle,
Ilk dame her brawest ribbons tries,
  To put her on her mettle,
Wi' wiles some silly chiel to trap, 50
  (And troth he's fain to get her),
But she'll craw kniefly in his crap,
  Whan, wow! he canna flit her
    Frae hame that day.

Now, mony a scawed and bare-arsed lown 55
  Rise early to their wark,
Enough to fley a muckle town,
  Wi' dinsome squeel and bark.

29 weet *wet* Land o' Cakes *Scotland*
31 late-wakes *pre-burial vigil*
35 sey *test*
36 pith *mettle*
37 feggs *faith*
39 pegs *fiddle tuning pegs*
40 shanna *shall not* blate *bashful*
43 hip *omit*
45 thrang *busy*
47 seeth *boil*
50 chiel *fellow*
51 fain *eager*
52 craw kniefly in his crap *vigorously henpeck him*
55 scawed *scabby* lown *fellow*
57 fley *scare*

'Here is the true an' faithfu' list
  O' noblemen and horses; 60
Their eild, their weight, their height, their grist,
  That rin for plates or purses
    Fu' fleet this day.'

To whisky plooks that brunt for wooks
  On town-guard soldiers faces, 65
Their barber bauld his whittle crooks,
  An' scrapes them for the races:
Their stumps erst used to filipegs,
  Are dight in spaterdashes,
Whase barkent hides scarce fend their legs 70
  Frae weet, and weary plashes
    O' dirt that day.

'Come, hafe a care,' the captain cries,
  'On guns your bagnets thraw;
Now mind your manual exercise, 75
  An' marsh down raw by raw.'
And as they march he'll glowr about,
  Tent a' their cuts and scars:
'Mang them fell mony a gausy snout
  Has gusht in birth-day wars, 80
    Wi' blude that day.

Her nanesel maun be carefu' now,
  Nor maun she pe misleard,
Sin baxter lads hae sealed a vow
  To skelp and clout the guard: 85
I'm sure Auld Reikie kens o' nane
  That would be sorry at it,
Though they should dearly pay the kane,
  An' get their tails weel sautit
    And sair thir days. 90

61 eild *age* grist *girth*
64 plooks *pimples* brunt *burned* wooks *weeks*
66 whittle *knife*
68 erst *first* filipegs *kilts*
69 dight *dressed*
70 barkent *tanned*
73 hafe *have*
74 bagnets thraw *bayonets fix*
76 raw *row*
78 tent *observe*
79 fell *very* gausy *imposing*
80 birth-day wars *see note*
82 her nanesel *he himself*
83 she pe misleard *he be mistaken*
84 baxter *baker*
85 skelp *hit*
88 kane *penalty*

The tinkler billies i' the Bow
  Are now less eidant clinking,
As lang's their pith or siller dow,
  They're daffin', and they're drinking.
Bedown Leith Walk what burrochs reel 95
  Of ilka trade and station,
That gar their wives an' childer feel
  Toom weyms for their libation
    O' drink thir days.

The browster wives thegither harl 100
  A' trash that they can fa' on;
They rake the grounds o' ilka barrel,
  To profit by the lawen:
For weel wat they a skin leal het
  For drinking needs nae hire; 105
At drumbly gear they take nae pet;
  Foul water slockens fire
    And drouth thir days.

They say, ill ale has been the deid
  O' mony a beirdly lown; 110
Then dinna gape like gleds wi' greed
  To sweel hail bickers down;
Gin Lord send mony ane the morn,
  They'll ban fu' sair the time
That e'er they toutit aff the horn 115
  Which wambles through their weym
    Wi' pain that day.

91 tinkler billies *tinker fellows*
  Bow *see note*
92 eidant *diligent*
93 dow *can*
94 daffin *having fun*
95 Leith Walk *see note* burrochs *crowds*
97 childer *children*
98 toom weyms *empty bellies*
100 browster *brewer* thegither harl *together scrape*
103 lawen *tavern bill*
104 leal het *really hot*
106 drumbly gear *cloudy liquor*
  pet *offence*
107 slockens *quenches*
108 drouth *thirst*
110 beirdly lown *burly fellow*
111 gleds *kites*
112 sweel hail bickers *swill whole mugs*
114 ban *curse*
115 toutit aff the horn *drained the cup*
116 wambles *rumbles*

The Buchan bodies through the beach
  Their bunch of findrums cry,
An' skirl out baul', in norland speech, 120
  'Gueed speldings, fa will buy.'
An', by my saul, they're nae wrang gear
  To gust a stirrah's mow;
Weel stawed wi' them, he'll never spear
  The price o' being fu' 125
    Wi' drink that day.

Now wyly wights at rowly powl,
  An' flingin' o' the dice,
Here brake the banes o' mony a soul
  Wi' fa's upo' the ice: 130
At first the gate seems fair an' straught,
  So they had fairly till her;
But wow, in spite o' a' their maught,
  They're rookit o' their siller
    An' goud that day. 135

Around whare'er ye fling your een,
  The haiks like wind are scourin';
Some chaises honest folk contain,
  An' some hae mony a whore in;
Wi' rose and lily, red and white, 140
  They gie themselves sic fit airs,
Like Dian, they will seem perfite;
  But its nae goud that glitters
    Wi' them thir days.

The Lyon here, wi' open paw, 145
  May cleek in mony hunder,
Wha geck at Scotland and her law,
  His wyly talons under;

118 Buchan *see note*
119 findrums *smoked haddocks*
120 skirl *shriek* norland *northern*
121 gueed speldings *good split haddock* fa *who*
122 saul *soul*
123 gust *gratify* stirrah *fellow*
124 stawed *stuffed*
126 rowly powl *roly-poly, skittles*
131 straught *straight*
133 maught *might*
137 haiks *hackney carriages*
142 Dian *goddess of chastity* perfyte *perfect*
145 Lyon *see note*
146 cleek *hook*
147 geck *mock*

For ken, though Jamie's laws are auld
  (Thanks to the wise recorder), 150
His Lyon yet roars loud and bawld,
  To had the Whigs in order
    Sae prime this day.

To town-guard drum of clangor clear,
  Baith men and steeds are raingit; 155
Some liveries red or yellow wear,
  And some are tartan spraingit:
And now the red, the blue e'en-now,
  Bids fairest for the market;
But, ere the sport be done, I trow 160
  Their skins are gayly yarkit
    And peeled thir days.

Siclike in Robinhood debates,
  Whan twa chiels hae a pingle;
E'en-now some couli gets his aits, 165
  An' dirt wi' words they mingle,
Till up loups he, wi' diction fu',
  There's lang and dreech contesting;
For now they're near the point in view;
  Now ten miles frae the question 170
    In hand that night.

The races o'er, they hale the dools,
  Wi' drink o' a' kin-kind;
Great feck gae hirpling hame like fools,
  The cripple lead the blind. 175
May ne'er the canker o' the drink
  E'er make our spirits thrawart,
'Case we git wharewitha' to wink
  Wi' een as blue's a blawart
    Wi' straiks thir days! 180

149 Jamie *see note*
155 raingit *lined up*
157 spraingit *in many colours*
161 yarkit *battered*
163 Robinhood *a debating club*
164 chiels *fellows* pingle *quarrel*
165 couli *fellow* aits *oats*
167 loups *leaps*
168 dreech *dreary*
172 hale the dools *go all out*
173 kin-kind *kinds*
174 feck *part* hirpling *hobbling*
177 thrawart *twisted*
179 blawart *bluebell*
180 straiks *strokes*

The Rising of the Session

To a' men living be it kend,
The Session now is at an end:
Writers, your finger-nebbs unbend,
  And quatt the pen,
Till Time wi' lyart pow shall send 5
  Blythe June again.

Tired o' the law, and a' its phrases,
The wylie writers, rich as Croesus,
Hurl frae the town in hackney chaises,
  For country cheer: 10
The powny that in spring-time grazes,
  Thrives a' the year.

Ye lawyers, bid fareweel to lies,
Fareweel to din, fareweel to fees,
The canny hours o' rest may please 15
  Instead o' siller:
Hained multer hads the mill at ease,
  And finds the miller.

Blyth they may be wha wanton play
In fortune's bonny blinkin ray, 20
Fu' weel can they ding dool away
  Wi' comrades couthy,
And never dree a hungert day,
  Or e'ening drouthy.

Ohon, the day for him that's laid, 25
In dowie poortith's caldrife shade,

3 writers *lawyers* nebbs *tips*
4 quatt *quit*
5 lyart pow *grey-haired head*
6 phrases *rhetoric*
7 Croesus *fabulously rich king of Lydia*
11 powny *riding horse*
17 hained multer *hoarded multure*
18 finds *supports*
21 ding dool *beat sorrow*
22 couthy *agreeable*
23 dree *endure*
24 drouthy *thirsty*
25 ohon *alas*
26 dowie poortith *sad poverty* caldrife *cold*

Ablins owr honest for his trade,
He racks his wits,
How he may get his buick weel clad,
And fill his guts. 30

The farmer's sons, as yap as sparrows,
Are glad, I trow, to flee the barras,
And whistle to the plough and harrows
At barley seed:
What writer wadna gang as far as 35
He could for bread.

After their yokin, I wat weel
They'll stoo the kebbuck to the heel;
Eith can the plough-stilts gar a chiel
Be unco vogie, 40
Clean to lick aff his crowdy-meal,
And scart his cogie.

Now mony a fallow's dung adrift
To a' the blasts beneath the lift,
And though their stamack's aft in tift 45
In vacance time,
Yet seenil do they ken the rift
O' stappit weym.

Now gin a notar should be wanted,
You'll find the pillars gayly planted; 50
For little thing protests are granted
Upo' a bill,
And weightiest matters covenanted
For haf a gill.

29 buick *body*
31 yap *eager*
32 barras *barrows*
37 yokin *work*
38 stoo *slice* kebbuck *cheese*
39 eith *easily* stilt *shaft* chiel *fellow*
40 vogie *glad*
41 crowdy-meal *milk-porridge*
42 scart *scrape* cogie *bowl*
43 dung *driven*
44 lift *sky*
45 tift *in order*
47 seenil *seldom* rift *belch*
48 stappit *gorged*
49 notar *notary*
50 pillars *arcade frequented by lawyers*
51 protests *see note*

Nae body takes a morning dribb 55
O' Holland gin frae Robin Gibb;
And though a dram to Rob's mair sib
Than is his wife,
He maun take time to daut his rib
Till siller's rife. 60

This vacance is a heavy doom
On Indian Peter's coffee-room,
For a' his china pigs are toom;
Nor do we see
In wine the sucker biskets soom 65
As light's a flee.

But stop, my muse, nor make a main,
Pate disna fend on that alane;
He can fell twa dogs wi' ae bane,
While ither fock 70
Maun rest themselves content wi' ane,
Nor farer trock.

Ye change-house keepers never grumble,
Though you a while your bickers whumble,
Be unco patientfu' and humble, 75
Nor make a din,
Though gude joot binna kend to rumble
Your weym within.

You needna grudge to draw your breath
For little mair than haf a reath, 80
Than, gin we a' be spared frae death,
We'll gladly prie
Fresh noggans o' your reaming graith
Wi' blythsome glee.

55 dribb *drop*
56 Robin Gibb *see note*
57 sib *related*
59 daut *caress*
rib *wife (Adam's rib)*
60 rife *plentiful*
62 Indian Peter *see note*
63 pigs *pitchers*
65 sucker *sugar* soom *swim*
72 farer trock *farther trade*
74 bickers whumble *beakers invert*
77 joot *drink* binna *be not*
80 reath *quarter (three months)*
82 prie *taste*
83 reaming graith *foaming liquor*

The King's Birth-Day in Edinburgh

Oh! qualis hurly-burly fuit, si forte vidisses.
Polemo-Middinia.

I sing the day sae aften sung,
Wi' which our lugs hae yearly rung,
In whase loud praise the Muse has dung
  A' kind o' print;
But wow, the limmer's fairly flung; 5
  There's naething in't.

I'm fain to think the joys the same
In London town as here at hame,
Whare fock of ilka age and name,
  Baith blind and cripple, 10
Forgather aft – oh fy for shame! –
  To drink and tipple.

O Muse, be kind, and dinna fash us
To flee awa' beyont Parnassus,
Nor seek for Helicon to wash us, 15
  That heath'nish spring;
Wi' Highland whisky scour our hawses,
  And gar us sing.

Begin then, dame, ye've drunk your fill,
You wouldna hae the tither gill? 20
You'll trust me, mair would do you ill,
  And ding you doitet;
Troth 'twould be sair agains my will
  To hae the wyte o't.

2 lugs *ears*
3 dung *worn out*
5 limmer *loose woman*
  flung *cheated*
7 fain *eager*
13 fash *trouble*
14 Parnassus *mountain sacred to the Muses*
15 Helicon *source of poetic inspiration*
17 hawses *throats*
22 ding *beat* doitet *crazy*
24 wyte *blame*

Sing then, how, on the fourth of June, 25
Our bells screed aff a loyal tune,
Our ancient castle shoots at noon,
  Wi' flag-staff buskit,
Frae which the soldier blades come down
  To cock their musket. 30

Oh willawins, Mons Meg, for you,
'Twas firing cracked thy muckle mou;
What black mishanter gart ye spew
  Baith gut and ga'?
I fear they banged thy belly fu' 35
  Against the law.

Right seldom am I gi'en to bannin,
But, by my saul, ye was a cannon,
Could hit a man, had he been stannin
  In shire o' Fife, 40
Sax long Scots miles ayont Clackmannan,
  And tak his life.

The hills in terror would cry out,
And echo to thy dinsome rout;
The herds would gather in their nowt, 45
  That glowred wi' wonder,
Haflins afraid to bide thereout
  To hear thy thunder.

Sing likewise, Muse, how blue-gown bodies,
Like scar-craws new ta'en down frae woodies, 50
Come here to cast their clouted duddies,
  And get their pay:
Than them, what magistrate mair proud is
  On king's birth-day?

26 screed *play loudly*
28 buskit *dressed*
31 willawins *alas*
  Mons Meg *see note*
33 mishanter *misfortune*
34 ga' *gall*
35 banged *stuffed*
37 bannin *cursing*
28 saul *soul*
41 Clackmannan *see note*
45 nowt *cattle*
49 blue-gown bodies *licensed beggars*
50 woodies *gallow's ropes*
51 clouted duddies *patched rags*

On this great day the City Guard, 55
In military art well leared,
Wi' powdered pow and shaven beard,
  Gang through their functions,
By hostile rabble seldom spared
  Of clarty unctions. 60

O soldiers, for your ain dear sakes,
For Scotland's, alias Land of Cakes,
Gie not her bairns sic deadly pakes,
  Nor be sae rude,
Wi' firelock or Lochaber aix, 65
  As spill their blude.

Now round and round the serpents whiz,
Wi' hissing wrath and angry phiz;
Sometimes they catch a gentle gizz,
  Alake the day! 70
And singe, wi' hair-devouring bizz,
  Its curls away.

Should th'owner patiently keek round,
To view the nature of his wound,
Dead pussie, dragled through the pond, 75
  Takes him a lounder,
Which lays his honour on the ground
  As flat's a flounder.

The Muse maun also now implore
Auld wives to steek ilk hole and bore; 80
If Baudrins slip but to the door,
  I fear, I fear,
She'll no lang shank upon all-four
  This time o' year.

57 pow *head*
60 clarty *dirty*
63 pakes *blows*
65 Lochaber aix *hooked axe*
66 blude *blood*
67 serpents *fireworks*
69 gizz *wig*
73 keek *look*
76 lounder *heavy blow*
80 steek *close*
81 Baudrins *cat's name*

Next day each hero tells his news 85
O' crackit crowns and broken brows,
And deeds that here forbid the Muse
  Her theme to swell,
Or time mair precious abuse
  Their crimes to tell. 90

She'll rather to the fields resort,
Whare music gars the day seem short,
Whare doggies play, and lambies sport
  On gowany braes,
Whare peerless Fancy hads her court, 95
  And tunes her lays.

94 gowany *daisy-covered*

Epilogue, spoken by Mr Wilson, at the Theatre Royal, in the Character of an Edinburgh Buck

Ye who oft finish care in Lethe's cup,
Who love to swear, and roar, and keep it up,
List to a brother's voice, whose sole delight
Is sleep all day, and riot all the night.
  Last night, when potent draughts of mellow wine 5
Did sober reason into wit refine:
When lusty Bacchus had contrived to drain
The sullen vapours from our shallow brain,
We sallied forth (for valour's dazzling sun
Up to his bright meridian had run); 10
And, like renowned Quixote and his squire,
Spoils and adventures were our sole desire.
  First we approached a seeming sober dame,
Preceded by a lanthorn's pallid flame,
Borne by a liveried puppy's servile hand, 15
The slave obsequious of her stern command.
'Curse on those cits,' said I, 'who dare disgrace
Our streets at midnight with a sober face;
Let never tallow-chandler give them light,
To guide them through the dangers of the night.' 20
The valet's cane we snatched, and, demme! I
Made the frail lanthorn on the pavement lie.
The Guard, still watchful of the lieges' harm,
With slow-paced motion stalked at the alarm.
'Guard, seize the rogues!' the angry madam cried, 25
And all the guard with 'Seize ta rogue!' replied.
  As in a war, there's nothing judged so right
As a concerted and prudential flight;
So we from Guard and scandal to be freed,
Left them the field and burial of their dead. 30
  Next we approached the bounds of George's Square,
Blest place! No watch, no constables come there.

1 Lethe *river of forgetfulness*
7 Bacchus *god of wine*
9 sun *see note*
11 Quixote *see note*
17 cits *citizens*
21 demme *damn me*
23 Guard *City Guard*
25 ta *the (mock Highland pronunciation)*
31 George's Square *see note*

Now had they borrowed Argus' eyes who saw us,
All was made dark and desolate as chaos;
Lamps tumbled after lamps, and lost their lustres, 35
Like Doomsday, when the stars shall fall in clusters.
Let fancy paint what dazzling glory grew
From crystal gems, when Phoebus came in view;
Each shattered orb ten thousand fragments strews,
And a new sun in ev'ry fragment shews. 40
  Hear then, my bucks, how drunken fate decreed us
For a nocturnal visit to the Meadows,
And how we, val'rous champions, durst engage –
O deed unequalled! – both the Bridge and Cage,
The rage of perilous winters which had stood, 45
This 'gainst the wind, and that against the flood;
But what nor wind, nor flood, nor heav'n could bend e'er,
We tumbled down, my bucks, and made surrender.
  What are your far famed warriors to us,
'Bout whom historians make such mighty fuss? 50
Posterity may think it was uncommon
That Troy should be pillaged for a woman;
But ours your ten years' sieges will excel,
And justly be esteemed the nonpareil.
Our cause is slighter than a dame's betrothing, 55
For all these mighty feats have sprung from nothing.

33 Argus *multi-eyed god*
38 Phoebus *the sun god*
42 Meadows *see note*
44 Bridge and Cage *see note*
52 Troy *see note*

Braid Claith

Ye wha are fain to hae your name
Wrote in the bonny book of fame,
Let merit nae pretension claim
  To laureled wreath,
But hap ye weel, baith back and wame, 5
  In gude Braid Claith.

He that some ells o' this may fa,
An' slae-black hat on pow like snaw,
Bids bauld to bear the gree awa',
  Wi' a' this graith, 10
Whan bienly clad wi' shell fu' braw
  O' gude Braid Claith.

Waesuck for him wha has na fek o't!
For he's a gowk they're sure to geck at,
A chiel that ne'er will be respekit 15
  While he draws breath,
Till his four quarters are bedeckit
  Wi' gude Braid Claith.

On Sabbath-days the barber spark,
Whan he has done wi' scrapin wark, 20
Wi' siller broachie in his sark,
  Gangs trigly, faith!
Or to the Meadow, or the Park,
  In gude Braid Claith.

Weel might ye trow, to see them there, 25
That they to shave your haffits bare,
Or curl an' sleek a pickle hair,

1 fain *eager*
5 hap *wrap* wame *belly*
6 claith *cloth*
7 fa *obtain*
8 slae *sloe* pow *head*
9 gree *first place*
10 graith *outfit*
11 bienly *prosperously*
13 waesuck *alas* fek *part*
14 gowk *fool* geck *mock*
15 chiel *fellow* respekit *respected*
21 broachie *brooch* sark *shirt*
22 trigly *smartly*
23 Meadow, Park *see note*
26 haffits *side-locks of hair*
27 pickle *a little, small amount*

Would be right laith,
When pacing wi' a gawsy air
In gude Braid Claith. 30

If ony mettled stirrah green
For favour frae a lady's ein,
He maunna care for being seen
Before he sheath
His body in a scabbard clean 35
O' gude Braid Claith.

For, gin he come wi' coat thread-bare,
A feg for him she winna care,
But crook her bonny mou' fu' sair,
And scald him baith. 40
Wooers should ay their travel spare
Without Braid Claith.

Braid Claith lends fock an unco heese,
Makes mony kail-worms butterflies,
Gies mony a doctor his degrees 45
For little skaith:
In short, you may be what you please
Wi' gude Braid Claith.

For thof ye had as wise a snout on
As Shakespeare or Sir Isaac Newton, 50
Your judgment fouk would hae a doubt on,
I'll tak my aith,
Till they could see ye wi' a suit on
O' gude Braid Claith.

28 laith *loath*
29 gawsy *imposing*
31 mettled stirrah *spirited fellow*
green *yearn*
38 feg *fig*
39 crook *curl*
40 scald *scold*
43 heese *lift*
49 thof *though*
50 Sir Isaac Newton *see note*
52 aith *oath*

Caller Oysters

Happy the man who, free from care and strife,
In silken or in leathern purse retains
A splendid shilling. He nor hears with pain
New oysters cried, nor sighs for cheerful ale.
Phillips

Of a' the waters that can hobble
A fishin yole or salmon coble,
And can reward the fisher's trouble,
  Or south or north,
There's nane sae spacious and sae noble   5
  As Firth o' Forth.

In her the skate and codlin sail,
The eil fou souple wags her tail,
Wi' herrin, fleuk, and mackarel,
  And whitens dainty: 10
Their spindle-shanks the labsters trail,
  Wi' partans plenty.

Auld Reikie's sons blyth faces wear;
September's merry month is near,
That brings in Neptune's caller cheer,   15
  New oysters fresh;
The halesomest and nicest gear
  Of fish or flesh.

O! then we needna gie a plack
For dand'ring mountebank or quack,   20
Wha o' their drogs sae bauldly crack,
  And spred sic notions,
As gar their feckless patient tak
  Their stinkin potions.

1 hobble *rock*
2 yole *yawl* coble *boat*
8 eil *eel* souple *supple*
9 fleuk *flounder*
10 whitens *whitings*
11 labsters *lobsters*
12 partans *edible crabs*
15 Neptune *god of the sea*
19 plack *small coin*
20 dand'ring *strolling*
21 drogs *drugs* crack *brag*
23 feckless *feeble*

Come prie, frail man! for gin thou art sick, 25
The oyster is a rare cathartic,
As ever doctor patient gart lick
To cure his ails;
Whether you hae the head or heart-ake,
It ay prevails. 30

Ye tipplers, open a' your poses,
Ye wha are faushed wi' plouky noses,
Fling owr your craig sufficient doses,
You'll thole a hunder,
To fleg awa' your simmer roses, 35
And naething under.

Whan big as burns the gutters rin,
Gin ye hae catcht a droukit skin,
To Luckie Middlemist's loup in,
And sit fu snug 40
Oe'r oysters and a dram o' gin,
Or haddock lug.

When auld Saunt Giles, at aught o'clock,
Gars merchant lowns their chopies lock,
There we adjourn wi' hearty fock 45
To birle our boddles,
And get wharewi' to crack our joke,
And clear our noddles.

Whan Phoebus did his windocks steek,
How aften at that ingle cheek 50
Did I my frosty fingers beek,
And taste gude fare?
I trow there was nae hame to seek
Whan steghin there.

25 prie *taste*
31 poses *savings*
32 faushed *troubled* plouky *pimply*
33 craig *throat*
34 thole *endure*
35 fleg *scare* simmer roses *skin rash*
38 droukit *soaked*
39 Luckie Middlemist *see note*
42 lug *fillet*
43 Saunt Giles *see note*
44 chopies *shops*
46 birle *twirl* boddles *small coins*
49 Phoebus *the sun* windocks steek *windows close*
51 beek *warm*
54 steghing *stuffing*

While glakit fools, o'er rife o' cash, 55
Pamper their weyms wi' fousom trash,
I think a chiel may gayly pass;
He's no ill boden
That gusts his gabb wi' oyster sauce,
And hen weel soden. 60

At Musselbrough, and eke Newhaven,
The fisher-wives will get top livin,
Whan lads gang out on Sunday's even
To treat their joes,
And tak of fat pandours a prieven, 65
Or mussel brose:

Than sometimes ere they flit their doup,
They'll ablins a' their siller coup
For liquor clear frae cutty stoup,
To weet their wizen, 70
And swallow o'er a dainty soup,
For fear they gizzen.

A' ye wha canna stand sae sicker,
Whan twice you've toomed the big-arsed bicker,
Mix caller oysters wi' your liquor, 75
And I'm your debtor,
If greedy priest or drouthy vicar
Will thole it better.

55 glakit *silly* rife *supplied*
56 weyms *stomachs*
fousom *loathsome*
57 chiel *fellow*
58 boden *provided*
59 gusts his gab *delights his palate*
60 soden *boiled*
61 Musselbrough *see note*
64 joes *sweethearts*
65 pandours *large oysters*
prieven *sample*
66 brose *porridge*
67 doup *bottom*
68 coup *drink away*
69 cutty stoup *small drinking vessel*
70 weet *wet* wizen *gullet*
72 gizzen *shrivel*
73 sicker *steady*
74 bicker *beaker*
77 drouthy *thirsty*

Mutual Complaint of Plainstanes and Causey, in their Mother-tongue

Since Merlin laid Auld Reikie's causey,
And made her o' his wark right saucy,
The spacious street and plainstanes
Were never kend to crack but anes,
Whilk happened on the hinder night, 5
Whan Fraser's ulie tint its light,
Of Highland sentries nane were waukin,
To hear thir cronies glibly taukin;
For them this wonder might hae rotten,
And, like night robb'ry, been forgotten, 10
Had na' a cadie, wi' his lanthorn,
Been gleg enough to hear them bant'rin,
Wha came to me neist morning early,
To gi'e me tidings o' this ferly.
Ye taunting lowns trow this nae joke, 15
For anes the ass of Balaam spoke,
Better than lawyers do, forsooth,
For it spake naething but the truth:
Whether they follow its example,
You'll ken best whan you hear the sample. 20

PLAINSTANES:
My friend, thir hunder years and mair,
We've been forfoughen late and air,
In sunshine, and in weety weather,
Our thrawart lot we bure thegither.
I never growled, but was content 25
Whan ilk ane had an equal stent,
But now to flyte I'se e'en be bauld,
Whan I'm wi' sic a grievance thralled.

1 Merlin *see note* causey *street*
3 plainstanes *pavement*
4 crack *talk*
6 Fraser's ulie *see note* tint *lost*
7 waukin *on watch, awake*
11 cadie *messenger boy*
12 gleg *keen*
14 ferly *wonder*
15 lowns *fellows*
16 Balaam *see note*
22 forfoughen *exhausted*
23 weety *wet*
24 thrawart *adverse* bure *bore*
26 stent *portion*
27 flyte *complain*

How haps it, say, that mealy bakers,
Hair-kaimers, crieshy gezy-makers, 30
Should a' get leave to waste their powders
Upon my beaux' and ladies' shoulders?
My travellers are fleyed to deid
Wi' creels wanchancy, heaped wi' bread,
Frae whilk hing down uncanny nicksticks, 35
That aften gie the maidens sic licks,
As make them blyth to skreen their faces
Wi' hats and muckle maun bon-graces,
And cheat the lads that fain wad see
The glances o' a pauky eie, 40
Or gie their loves a wylie wink,
That erst might lend their hearts a clink.
Speak, was I made to dree the laidin
Of Gaelic chairman heavy treadin,
Wha in my tender buke bore holes 45
Wi' waefu' tackets i' the soles
O' broags, whilk on my body tramp,
And wound like death at ilka clamp.

CAUSEY:
Weil crackit, friend! It aft hads true,
Wi' naething fock make maist ado: 50
Weel ken ye, though ye doughtna tell,
I pay the sairest kain mysell;
Owr me ilk day big waggons rumble,
And a' my fabric birze and jumble;
Owr me the muckle horses gallop, 55
Enought to rug my very saul up;
And coachmen never trow they're sinning,
While down the street his wheels are spinning,
Like thee, do I not bide the brunt

30 kaimers *combers* crieshy gezy-makers *greasy wig-makers*
33 fleyed to deid *scared to death*
34 creels wanchancy *baskets dangerous*
35 nicksticks *tally sticks*
36 licks *blows*
38 muckle maun bon-graces *great big straw hats*
42 erst *first* clink *jolt*
43 dree *endure* laidin *loading*
44 chairman *sedan-chair bearers*
45 buke *body*
46 tackets *hobnails*
47 broags *shoes*
48 clamp *stamp*
51 doughtna *will not*
52 kain *penalty*
54 birze *bruise*
56 rug *rip* saul *soul*

Of Highland chairman's heavy dunt? 60
Yet I hae never thought o' breathing
Complaint, or making din for naething.

PLAINSTANES:
Had sae, and lat me get a word in,
Your back's best fitted for the burden;
And I can eithly tell you why, 65
Ye're doughtier by far than I;
For whin-stanes, howkit frae the craigs,
May thole the prancing feet of nags,
Nor ever fear uncanny hotches
Frae clumsy carts or hackney-coaches, 70
While I, a weak and feckless creature,
Am moulded by a safter nature.
Wi' mason's chisel dighted neat,
To gar me look baith clean and feat,
I scarce can bear a sairer thump 75
Than comes frae sole of shoe or pump.
I grant, indeed, that, now and than,
Yield to a patten's pith I maun;
But pattens, though they're aften plenty,
Are ay laid down wi' feet fou tenty, 80
And strokes frae ladies, though they're teasing,
I freely maun avow are pleasing.
For what use was I made, I wonder,
It was na tamely to chap under
The weight of ilka codroch chiel, 85
That does my skin to targits peel;
But gin I guess aright, my trade is
To fend frae skaith the bonny ladies,
To keep the bairnies free frae harms
Whan airing in their nurses' arms, 90
To be a safe and canny bield

65 eithly *easily*
67 whin-stanes *hard road stone*
howkit *dug* craigs *cliffs*
68 thole *endure*
69 hotches *jolts*
71 feckless *feeble*
73 dighted *dressed*
74 feat *neat*
78 patten *iron-soled overshoe*
pith *force*
80 tenty *careful*
84 chap *knock*
85 codroch chiel *low-class fellow*
86 targits *tatters*
88 skaith *harm*
91 bield *shelter*

For growing youth or drooping eild.
Take then frae me the heavy load
Of burden-bearers heavy shod,
Or, by my troth, the gude auld town shall 95
Hae this affair before their Council.

CAUSEY:
I dinna care a single jot,
Though summoned by a shelly-coat,
Sae leally I'll propone defences,
As get ye flung for my expenses; 100
Your libel I'll impugn *verbatim*,
And hae a *magnum damnum datum*;
For though frae Arthur's Seat I sprang,
And am in constitution strang,
Wad it no fret the hardest stane 105
Beneath the Luckenbooths to grane?
Though magistrates the Cross discard,
It makes na whan they leave the Guard,
A lumbersome and stinkin bigging,
That rides the sairest on my rigging. 110
Poor me owr meikle do ye blame,
For tradesmen tramping on your wame,
Yet a' your advocates and braw fock
Come still to me 'twixt ane and twa clock,
And never yet were kend to range 115
At Charlie's statue or Exchange.
Then tak your beaux and macaronies,
Gie me trades-fock and country Johnies;
The deil's in't gin ye dinna sign
Your sentiments conjunct wi' mine. 120

PLAINSTANES:
Gin we twa could be as auld-farrant
As gar the Council gie a warrant,

92 eild *age*
98 shelly-coat *sheriff's officer*
99 leally *loyally* propone *put forward*
102 *magnum damnum datum see note*
106 Luckenbooths *High Street shops*
108 it makes na *it matters not*
Guard *see note*
109 bigging *building*
110 rigging *back*
116 Charlie's statue, Exchange *see note*
117 macaronies *dandies*
121 auld-farrant *ingenious*

Ilk lown rebellious to tak,
Wha walks not in the proper track,
And o' three shilling Scottish suck him; 125
Or in the water-hole sair douk him;
This might assist the poor's collection,
And gie baith parties satisfaction.

CAUSEY:
But first, I think it will be good
To bring it to the Robinhood, 130
Whare we shall hae the question stated,
And keen and crabbitly debated,
Whether the provost and the baillies,
For the towns' good whase daily toil is,
Should listen to our joint petitions, 135
And see obtempered the conditions.

PLAINSTANES:
Content am I. But east the gate is
The sun, wha taks his leave of Thetis,
And comes to wauken honest fock,
That gang to wark at sax o'clock; 140
It sets us to be dumb a while,
And let our words gie place to toil.

122 lown *fellow*
126 douk *duck*
130 Robinhood *a debating club*
132 crabbitly *crossly*
133 baillies *city magistrates*
136 obtempered *obeyed*
138 Thetis *a sea-nymph*

The Ghaists: A Kirk-yard Eclogue

Did you not say, on good Ann's day
And vow and did protest, Sir
That when Hanover should come o'er.
We surely should be blest, Sir?
'An Auld Sang Made New Again'

Whare the braid planes in dowy murmurs wave
Their ancient taps out o'er the cald, cald grave,
Whare Geordie Girdwood, mony a lang-spun day,
Houkit for gentlest banes the humblest clay,
Twa sheeted ghaists, sae grizzly and sae wan, 5
'Mang lanely tombs their douff discourse began.

WATSON:
Cauld blaws the nippin north wi' angry sough,
And showers his hailstanes frae the Castle Cleugh
O'er the Greyfriars, whare, at mirkest hour,
Bogles and spectres wont to tak their tour, 10
Harlin' the pows and shanks to hidden cairns,
Amang the hamlocks wild, and sun-burnt fearns,
But nane the night save you and I hae come
Frae the dern mansions of the midnight tomb,
Now whan the dawning's near, whan cock maun craw, 15
And wi' his angry bougil gar's withdraw,
Ayont the kirk we'll stap, and there tak bield,
While the black hours our nightly freedom yield.

HERRIOT:
I'm weel content; but binna cassen down,
Nor trow the cock will ca' ye hame o'er soon, 20
For though the eastern lift betakens day,

1 dowy *doleful*
3 Geordie Girdwood *see note*
4 houkit *dug*
6 douff *sad*
7 sough *sigh*
8 cleugh *cliff*
9 mirkest *darkest*
10 bogles *ghosts*
11 harlin' *dragging* pows *heads*
12 hamlocks *hemlocks*
13 the night *tonight*
14 dern *secret*
16 bougil *cock-crow*
17 stap *step* bield *shelter*
19 binna cassen *be not cast*
21 lift betakens *sky betokens*

Changing her rokelay black for mantle grey,
Nae weirlike bird our knell of parting rings,
Nor sheds the caller moisture frae his wings.
Nature has changed her course; the birds o' day 25
Dozin' in silence on the bending spray,
While owlets round the craigs at noon-tide flee,
And bludey bawks sit singand on the tree.
Ah, Caledon, the land I yence held dear,
Sair mane mak I for thy destruction near; 30
And thou, Edina, anes my dear abode,
Whan royal Jamie swayed the sovereign rod,
In thae blest days, weel did I think bestowed,
To blaw thy poortith by wi' heaps o' gowd;
To mak thee sonsy seem wi' mony a gift, 35
And gar thy stately turrets speel the lift:
In vain did Danish Jones, wi' gimcrack pains,
In Gothic sculpture fret the pliant stanes:
In vain did he affix my statue here,
Brawly to busk wi' flow'rs ilk coming year; 40
My tow'rs are sunk, my lands are barren now,
My fame, my honour, like my flow'rs maun dow.

WATSON:
Sure Major Weir, or some sic warlock wight,
Has flung beguilin' glamour o'er your sight;
Or else some kittle cantrup thrown, I ween, 45
Has bound in mirlygoes my ain twa ein,
If ever aught frae sense could be believed
(And seenil hae my senses been deceived),
This moment, o'er the tap of Adam's tomb,
Fu' easy can I see your chiefest dome: 50
Nae corbie fleein' there, nor croupin' craws,
Seem to forspeak the ruin of thy haws,

22 rokelay *cloak*
23 weirlike *warlike*
27 craigs *cliffs*
28 bludey bawks *bloody bats*
32 royal Jamie *see note*
34 poortith *poverty*
35 sonsy *cheerful*
36 speel the lift *climb the sky*
37 Danish Jones *see note*
40 busk wi' flow'rs *see note*
42 dow *wither*
43 Major Weir *see note*
44 glamour *enchantment*
45 cantrup *spell*
46 mirlygoes *dizziness*
48 seenil *seldom*
49 Adam's tomb *see note*
51 corbie *raven* croupin' craws *croaking crows*
52 forspeak *predict* haws *halls*

But a' your tow'rs in wonted order stand,
Steeve as the rocks that hem our native land.

HERRIOT:
Think na I vent my well-a-day in vain, 55
Kent ye the cause, ye sure wad join my mane.
Black be the day that e'er to England's ground
Scotland was eikit by the Union's bond;
For mony a menzie of destructive ills
The country now maun brook frae mortmain bills, 60
That void our test'ments, and can freely gie
Sic will and scoup to the ordained trustee,
That he may tir our stateliest riggins bare,
Nor acres, houses, woods, nor fishins spare,
Till he can lend the stoitering state a lift 65
Wi' gowd in gowpins as a grassum gift;
In lieu o' whilk, we maun be weel content
To tyne the capital at three per cent.
A doughty sum indeed, whan now-a-days
They raise provisions as the stents they raise, 70
Yoke hard the poor, and lat the rich chiels be,
Pampered at ease by ither's industry.
Hale interest for my fund can scantly now
Cleed a' my callants backs, and stap their mou'.
How maun their weyms wi' sairest hunger slack, 75
Their duds in targets flaff upo' their back,
Whan they are doomed to keep a lasting Lent,
Starving for England's weel at three per cent.

WATSON:
Auld Reikie than may bless the gowden times,
Whan honesty and poortith baith are crimes; 80
She little kend, whan you and I endowed
Our hospitals for back-gaun burghers gude,
That e'er our siller or our lands should bring

53 steeve *firm*
58 eikit *added* Union *see note*
59 menzie *crowd*
60 mortmain bills *see note to poem*
62 scoup *scope*
63 tir *strip* riggins *roofs*
65 stoitering *staggering*
66 gowpins *handfuls* grassum gift *see note*
70 stents *taxes*
74 callants *young men*
75 weyms *stomachs*
76 duds *rags* targets *shreds* flaff *flutter*
82 back-gaun *needy*

A gude bien living to a back-gaun king,
Wha, thanks to ministry, is grown sae wise, 85
He douna chew the bitter cud of vice;
For gin, frae Castlehill to Netherbow,
Wad honest houses bawdy-houses grow,
The crown wad never spier the price o' sin,
Nor hinder younkers to the de'il to rin, 90
But gif some mortal grien for pious fame,
And leave the poor man's pray'r to sane his name,
His gear maun a' be scattered by the claws
O' ruthless, ravenous, and harpy laws.
Yet, should I think, although the bill tak place, 95
The Council winna lack sae meikle grace
As lat our heritage at wanworth gang,
Or the succeeding generations wrang
O' braw bien maintenance and walth o' lear,
Whilk else had drappit to their children's skair; 100
For mony a deep, and mony a rare engyne
Ha'e sprung frae Herriot's wark, and sprung frae mine.

HERRIOT:
I find, my friend, that ye but little ken,
There's einow on the earth a set o' men,
Wha, if they get their private pouches lined, 105
Gie na a winnelstrae for a' mankind;
They'll sell their country, flay their conscience bare,
To gar the weigh-bauk turn a single hair.
The government need only bait the line
Wi' the prevailing flee, the gowden coin, 110
Then our executors, and wise trustees,
Will sell them fishes in forbidden seas,
Upo' their dwining country girn in sport,
Laugh in their sleeve, and get a place at court.

84 bien *comfortable*
86 douna *will not*
87 Castlehill to Netherbow *see note*
90 younkers *youngsters*
91 grien *yearn*
92 sane *bless*
97 wanworth *low price*
99 walth *wealth*
100 skair *share*
101 engyne *genius*
104 einow *even now*
106 winnelstrae *straw*
108 weigh-bauk *balance*
113 dwining *wasting away*
girn *grin*

WATSON:
'Ere that day come, I'll 'mang our spirits pick 115
Some ghaist that trokes and conjures wi' Auld Nick,
To gar the wind wi' rougher rumbles blaw,
And weightier thuds than ever mortal saw:
Fire-flaught and hail, wi' tenfald fury's fires,
Shall lay yird-laigh Edina's airy spires: 120
Tweed shall rin rowtin' down his banks out o'er,
Till Scotland's out o' reach o' England's pow'r;
Upo' the briny Borean jaws to float,
And mourn in dowy soughs her dowy lot.

HERRIOT:
Yonder's the tomb of wise Mackenzie famed, 125
Whase laws rebellious bigotry reclaimed,
Freed the hail land frae Covenanting fools,
Wha erst ha'e fashed us wi' unnumbered dools;
Till night we'll tak the swaird aboon our pows,
And than, whan she her ebon chariot rows, 130
We'll travel to the vaut wi' stealing stap,
And wauk Mackenzie frae his quiet nap:
Tell him our ails, that he, wi' wonted skill,
May fleg the schemers o' the mortmain-bill.

116 trokes *barters* Auld Nick *the Devil*
119 fire-flaucht *lightning*
120 yird-laigh *earth-low*
121 Tweed *see note* rowtin' *rumbling*
123 Borean jaws *northern waves*
124 dowy *doleful*
125 Mackenzie *see note*
128 fashed *troubled* dools *griefs*
129 swaird *sward* pows *heads*
130 rows *rolls*
131 vaut *vault*
134 fleg *scare off*

Elegy, on the Death of Mr David Gregory, late Professor of Mathematics in the University of St Andrews

Now mourn, ye college masters a'!
And frae your ein a tear lat fa',
Famed Gregory death has taen awa'
  Without remeid;
The skaith ye've met wi's nae that sma', 5
  Sin Gregory's dead.

The students too will miss him sair,
To school them weel his eident care,
Now they may mourn for ever mair,
  They hae great need; 10
They'll hip the maist fek o' their lear,
  Sin Gregory's dead.

He could, by Euclid, prove lang sine
A ganging point composed a line;
By numbers too he could divine, 15
  Whan he did read,
That three times three just made up nine;
  But now he's dead.

In algebra weel skilled he was,
An' kent fu' well proportion's laws; 20
He could make clear baith B's and A's
  Wi' his lang head;
Rin owr surd roots, but cracks or flaws;
  But now he's dead.

Weel versed was he in architecture, 25
An' kent the nature o' the sector,
Upon baith globes he weel could lecture,
  An' gar's tak heed;

2 lat *let*
4 remeid *remedy*
5 skaith *harm*
8 eident *diligent*
11 hip *miss* fek *part*
13 Euclid *the Greek geometer*
27 baith globes *the terrestrial and the celestial*

Of geometry he was the Hector;
  But now he's dead. 30

Sae weel's he'd fley the students a',
Whan they war skelpin at the ba',
They took leg bail and ran awa',
  Wi' pith and speid;
We winna get a sport sae braw 35
  Sin Gregory's dead.

Great 'casion hae we a' to weep,
An' cleed our skins in mourning deep,
For Gregory Death will fairly keep
  To take his nap; 40
He'll till the Resurrection sleep
  As sound's a tap.

29 Hector *the greatest Trojan hero*
31 fley *frighten away*
32 skelpin *striking*
33 took leg bail *ran away*
34 pith *energy*
42 tap *top*

Elegy on John Hogg, late Porter to the University of St Andrews

Death, what's ado? the de'il be licket,
Or wi' your stang, you ne'er had pricket,
Or our auld Alma Mater tricket
  O' poor John Hogg,
And trailed him ben through your mark wicket 5
  As dead's a log.

Now ilka glaikit scholar lown
May dander wae wi' duddy gown;
Kate Kennedy to dowy crune
  May mourn and clink, 10
And steeples o' Saint Andrew's town
  To yird may sink.

Sin' Pauly Tam, wi' cankered snout,
First held the students in about,
To wear their claes as black as soot 15
  They ne'er had reason,
Till death John's haffit ga'e a clout
  Sae out o' season.

Whan regents met at common schools,
He taught auld Tam to hale the dules, 20
And eidant to row right the bowls
  Like ony emmack;
He kept us a' within the rules
  Strict academic.

Heh, wha will tell the students now 25
To meet the Pauly cheek for chow,

1 licket *struck*
2 stang *sting*
3 Alma Mater *see note*
5 ben *inside* mark *murky*
7 glaikit *silly* lown *fellow*
8 dander *saunter* duddy *ragged*
9 Kate Kennedy *see note*
  dowy crune *doleful croon*
12 yird *earth*
13 Pauly Tam *see note*
17 haffit *side-lock*
19 regents *see note*
20 hale the dules *go all out*
21 eidant *diligent* row *roll*
22 emmack *ant*
26 chow *jaw*

Whan he, like frightsome wirrikow,
  Had wont to rail,
And set our stamacks in a low,
  Or we turned tail. 30

Ah, Johnny, aften did I grumble
Frae cozy bed fu' ear' to tumble;
Whan art and part I'd been in some ill,
  Troth I was sweer,
His words they brodit like a wumill 35
  Frae ear to ear.

Whan I had been fu' laith to rise,
John than begude to moralize:
'The tither nap, the sluggard cries,
  And turns him round; 40
Sae spake auld Solomon the wise,
  Divine profound!'

Nae dominie, or wise Mess John,
Was better leared in Solomon;
He cited proverbs one by one 45
  Ilk vice to tame;
He garred ilk sinner sigh an' groan,
  And fear Hell's flame.

'I hae nae meikle skill,' quo' he,
'In what you ca' philosophy; 50
It tells that baith the earth and sea
  Rin round about;
Either the Bible tells a lie,
  Or you're a' out.

Its i' the psalms o' David writ, 55
That this wide warld ne'er should flit,
But on the waters coshly sit
  Fu' steeve and lasting' –

27 wirrikow *scarecrow*
29 stamacks *stomachs* low *flame*
34 sweer *reluctant*
35 brodit *pierced* wumill *gimlet*
37 laith *loath*
38 begude *began*
41 Solomon *see note*
43 dominie *teacher*
  Mess John *minister*
55 psalms *see note*
57 coshly *snugly*
58 steeve *firm*

An' was na he a head o' wit
At sic contesting! 60

On einings cauld wi' glee we'd trudge
To heat our shins in Johnny's lodge;
The de'il ane thought his bum to budge
Wi' siller on us:
To claw het pints we'd never grudge 65
O' *molationis*.

Say ye, red gowns, that aften here
Hae toasted bakes to Katie's beer,
Gin e'er thir days hae had their peer,
Sae blyth, sae daft; 70
You'll ne'er again in life's career
Sit ha'f sae saft.

Wi' haffit locks, sae smooth and sleek,
John looked like ony ancient Greek;
He was a Nazarene a' the week, 75
And doughtna tell out
A bawbee Scots to straik his cheek
Till Sunday fell out.

For John ay lo'ed to turn the pence,
Thought poortith was a great offence: 80
'What recks though ye ken mood and tense?
A hungry weyme
For gowd wad wi' them baith dispense
At ony time.

Ye ken what ails maun ay befall 85
The chiel that will be prodigal;
Whan wasted to the very spaul
He turns his tusk,
For want o' comfort to his saul
O' hungry husk.' 90

65 claw *clutch* het *hot*
66 *molationis spirits distilled from molasses*
67 red gowns *see note*
75 Nazarene *see note*
76 doughtna *would not*
77 bawbee *halfpenny* straik *comb*
80 poortith *poverty*
81 recks *matters*
82 weyme *stomach*
86 chiel *fellow* prodigal *see note*
87 spaul *shoulder*
89 saul *soul*

Ye royit lowns, just do as he'd do;
For mony braw green shaw and meadow
He's left to cheer his dowy widow,
  His winsome Kate,
That to him proved a canny she-dow, 95
  Baith ear' and late.

91 royit lowns *wild lads*
93 dowy *doleful*
95 she-dow *she-dove*

An Eclogue, to the Memory of Dr William Wilkie, late Professor of Natural Philosophy in the University of St Andrews

GEORDIE:
Blaw saft, my reed, and kindly to my maen,
Weel may ye thole a saft and dowie strain;
Nae mair to you shall shepherds in a ring,
Wi' blythness skip, or lasses lilt an' sing;
Sic sorrow now maun sadden ilka eie, 5
An' ilka waefu' shepherd grieve wi' me.

DAVIE:
Wharefor begin a sad an' dowie strain,
Or banish lilting frae the Fifan plain?
Though simmer's gane, an' we nae langer view
The blades o' claver wat wi' pearls o' dew. 10
Cauld winter's bleakest blasts we'll eithly cowr,
Our eldin's driven, an' our har'st is owr;
Our rucks fu' thick are stackit i' the yard,
For the Yule-feast a sautit mart's prepared;
The ingle-nook supplies the simmer fields, 15
An' aft as mony gleefu' maments yields.
Swyth, man, fling a' your sleepy springs awa',
An' on your canty whistle gie's a blaw:
Blythness, I trow, maun lighten ilka eie,
An' ilka canty callant sing like me. 20

GEORDIE:
Na, na, a canty spring wad now impart
Just threefald sorrow to my heavy heart.
Thof to the weet my ripened aits had fawn,
Or shake-winds owr my rigs wi' pith had blawn,

1 maen *moan*
2 thole *suffer* dowie *doleful*
8 Fifan *in Fife*
10 claver *clover* wat *wet*
11 cowr *recover from*
12 eldin *fuel* driven *piled* har'st *harvest*
13 rucks *ricks*
14 sautit mart *beef salted for winter*
16 maments *moments*
17 swyth *quickly* springs *tunes*
20 callant *young man*
23 thof *though* weet *wet* aits *oats* fawn *fallen*
24 shake-winds *winds that shake ripe ears off corn* rigs *fields* pith *force*

To this I could hae said, 'I carena by', 25
Nor fund occasion now my cheeks to dry.
Crosses like thae, or lake o' warld's gear,
Are naething whan we tyne a friend that's dear.
Ah, waes me for you, Willy! Mony a day
Did I wi' you on yon broom-thackit brae 30
Hound aff my sheep, an' lat them careless gang
To harken to your cheery tale or sang;
Sangs that for ay, on Caledonia's strand,
Shall fit the foremost 'mang her tunefu' band.
I dreamt yestreen his deadly wraith I saw 35
Gang by my ein as white's the driven snaw;
My colley, Ringie, youfed an' yowled a' night,
Coured an' crap near me in an unco fright,
I wakened fleyed, an' shook baith lith an' limb;
A cauldness took me, an' my sight grew dim; 40
I kent that it forspak approachin wae
When my poor doggie was disturbit sae.
Nae sooner did the day begin to dawn,
Than I beyont the know fu' speedy ran,
Whare I was keppit wi' the heavy tale 45
That sets ilk dowie sangster to bewail.

DAVIE:
An' wha on Fifan bents can weel refuse
To gie the tear o' tribute to his muse?
Fareweel ilk cheery spring, ilk canty note,
Be daffin an' ilk idle play forgot; 50
Bring ilka herd the mournfu', mournfu' boughs,
Rosemary sad, and ever dreary yews;
Thae lat be steepit i' the saut, saut tear,
To weet wi' hallowed draps his sacred bier,
Whase sangs will ay in Scotland be revered, 55
While slow-gawn owsen turn the flow'ry swaird;
While bonny lambies lick the dews of spring,
While gaudsmen whistle, or while birdies sing,

27 lake *lack*
30 thackit *thatched*
35 yestreen *last night*
37 colley *sheepdog* youfed *barked*
38 coured *cowered* crap *crept*
39 fleyed *afraid* lith *joint*
44 know *knoll, hill*
45 keppit *met*
47 bents *fields*
50 daffin *fun*
56 owsen *oxen* swaird *sward*
58 gaudsmen *ploughman*

GEORDIE:
'Twas na for weel-timed verse or sangs alane,
He bore the bell frae ilka shepherd swain. 60
Nature to him had gi'en a kindly lore,
Deep a' her mystic ferlies to explore:
For a' her secret working he could gie
Reasons that wi' her principles agree.
Ye saw yoursell how weel his mailin thrave, 65
Ay better faughed an' snodit than the lave;
Lang had the thristles an' the dockans been
In use to wag their taps upo' the green,
Whare now his bonny riggs delight the view,
An' thrivin hedges drink the caller dew. 70

DAVIE:
They tell me, Geordie, he had sic a gift
That scarce a starnie blinkit frae the lift,
But he would some auld warld name for't find,
As gart him keep it freshly in his mind:
For this some ca'd him an uncanny wight; 75
The clash gaed round, he had the second sight,
A tale that never failed to be the pride
Of grannies spinnin at the ingle side.

GEORDIE:
But now he's gane, an' Fame that, whan alive,
Seenil lats ony o' her vot'ries thrive, 80
Will frae his shinin name a' motes withdraw,
And on her loudest trump his praises blaw.
Lang may his sacred banes untroubled rest!
Lang may his truff in gowans gay be drest!
Scholars and bards unheard of yet shall come, 85
And stamp memorials on his grassy tomb,
Which in yon ancient kirk-yard shall remain,
Famed as the urn that hads the Mantuan swain.

60 bore the bell *took the prize*
62 ferlies *marvels*
65 mailin *farm* thrave *thrived*
66 faughed *harrowed* snodit *put in order*
67 dockans *dock plants* thristles *thistles*
72 starnie *star* lift *sky*
75 wight *man*
76 clash *talk* second sight *psychic powers*
80 seenil lats *seldom lets*
83 banes *bones*
84 truff *turf, grave* gowans *daisies*
88 Mantuan swain *Virgil, the Roman poet*

To Dr Samuel Johnson: Food for a New Edition of his Dictionary

Let Wilkes and Churchill rage no more,
Tho' scarce provision, learning's good;
What can these hungry's next implore,
Even Samuel Johnson loves our food.
Rodondo.

Great Pedagogue, whose literanian lore,
With syllable and syllable conjoined
To transmutate and varify, has learned
The whole revolving scientific names
That in the alphabetic columns lie, 5
Far from the knowledge of mortalic shapes,
As we, who never can peroculate
The miracles by thee miraculised,
The Muse silential long, with mouth apert
Would give vibration to stagnatic tongue, 10
And loud encomiate thy puissant name,
Eulogiated from the green decline
Of Thames's banks to Scoticanian shores,
Where Loch-lomondian liquids undulise.
To meminate thy name in after times, 15
The mighty Mayor of each regalian town
Shall consignate thy work to parchment fair
In roll burgharian, and their tables all
Shall fumigate with fumigation strong:
Scotland, from perpendicularian hills, 20
Shall emigrate her fair muttonian store,
Which late had there in pedestration walked,
And o'er her airy heights perambulised.
Oh, blackest execrations on thy head,
Edina shameless! Though he came within 25
The bounds of your notation, though you knew
His honorific name, you noted not,
But basely suffered him to chariotise
Far from your tow'rs, with smoke that nubilate,
Nor drank one amicitial swelling cup 30
To welcome him convivial. Baillies all,
With rage inflated, catenations tear,

31 Baillies *see note*

Nor ever after be you vinculised,
Since you that sociability denied
To him whose potent lexiphanian stile 35
Words can prolongate, and inswell his page
With what in others to a line's confined.
  Welcome, thou verbal potentate and prince,
To hills and valleys, where emerging oats
From earth assurge our pauperty to bay, 40
And bless thy name, thy dictionarian skill,
Which there definitive will still remain,
And oft be speculised by taper blue,
While youth studentious turn thy folio page.
  Have you as yet, in per'patetic mood, 45
Regarded with the texture of the eye
The cave cavernic, where fraternal bard,
Churchill, depicted pauperated swains
With thraldom and black want, reducted sore,
Where Nature, colorised, so coarsely fades, 50
And puts her russet par'phernalia on?
Have you as yet the way explorified,
To let lignarian chalice, swelled with oats,
Thy orifice approach? Have you as yet,
With skin fresh rubified by scarlet spheres, 55
Applied brimstonic unction to your hide,
To terrify the salamandrian fire
That from involuntary digits asks
The strong allaceration? Or can you swill
The usquebalian flames of whisky blue 60
In fermentation strong? Have you applied
The kilt aerian to your Anglian thighs,
And with renunciation assignised
Your breeches in Londona to be worn?
Can you, in frigor of Highlandian sky, 65
On heathy summits take nocturnal rest?
It cannot be – you may as well desire
An alderman leave plum-puddenian store,
And scratch the tegument from pottage-dish,
As bid thy countrymen, and thee conjoined, 70
Forsake stomachic joys. Then hie you home,
And be a malcontent, that naked hinds,
On lentils fed, can make your kingdom quake,
And tremulate Old England libertised.

39 oats *see note*
48 Churchill *see note*
60 usquebalian *see note*
68 plum-puddenian *see note*

To the Principal and Professors of the University of St Andrews, on their superb treat to Dr Samuel Johnson

St Andrews town may look right gawsy,
Nae grass will grow upon her cawsey,
Nor wa'-flow'rs of a yellow dye,
Glour dowy o'er her ruins high,
Sin Sammy's head weel pang'd wi' lear 5
Has seen the Alma Mater there:
Regents, my winsome billy boys!
'Bout him you've made an unco noise;
Nae doubt for him your bells wad clink,
To find him upon Eden's brink, 10
An' a' things nicely set in order,
Wad kep him on the Fifan border:
I'se warrant now frae France an' Spain,
Baith cooks and scullions mony ane
Wad gar the pats an' kettles tingle 15
Around the college kitchen ingle,
To fleg frae a' your craigs the roup,
Wi' reeking het and crieshy soup;
And snails and puddocks mony hunder
Wad beeking lie the hearth-stane under, 20
Wi' roast and boil'd, an' a' kin kind,
To heat the body, cool the mind.
  But hear me, lads, gin I'd been there,
How I wad trimmed the bill o' fare!
For ne'er sic surly wight as he 25
Had met wi' sic respect frae me.
Mind ye what Sam, the lying loun,
Has in his *Dictionar* laid down?

1 gawsy *pleased*
2 cawsey *street*
4 dowy *dolefully*
5 sin *since* pang'd *crammed*
7 regents *university teachers*
10 Eden *river near St Andrews*
12 kep *meet*
15 pats *pots*
17 fleg *scare* craigs *throats*
  roup *hoarseness*
18 reeking het *steaming hot*
  crieshy *greasy*
19 puddocks *frogs*
20 beeking *warming*
21 a' kin kind *all kinds*
27 loun *fellow*

That aits in England are a feast
To cow an' horse, an' siccan beast, 30
While in Scots ground this growth was common
To gust the gab o' man an' woman.
Tak tent, ye regents, then, an' hear
My list o' gudely hamel gear,
Sic as ha'e often raxed the wyme 35
O' blyther fallows mony time;
Mair hardy, souple, steive an' swank,
Than ever stood on Sammy's shank.
Imprimis, then, a haggis fat,
Weel tottled in a seything pat, 40
Wi' spice and ingans weel ca'd through,
Had helped to gust the stirrah's mow,
And placed itsel in truncher clean
Before the gilpy's glowrin een.
Secundo, then a gude sheep's head 45
Whase hide was singit, never flead,
And four black trotters cled wi' girsle,
Bedown his throat had learned to hirsle.
What think ye neist, o' gude fat brose
To clag his ribs? A dainty dose! 50
And white and bloody puddins routh,
To gar the Doctor skirl 'O drouth!'
Whan he could never houp to merit
A cordial o' reaming claret,
But thraw his nose, and brize and pegh 55
O'er the contents o' sma' ale quegh:
Then let his wisdom girn an' snarl
O' er a weel-toastit girdle farl,

29 aits *see note*
32 gust the gab *delight the palate*
33 tent *heed*
34 hamel *homely*
35 raxed the wyme *stretched the stomach*
37 steive and swank *firm and strong*
39 *imprimis in the first place*
40 tottled *simmered* seything *boiling*
41 ingans *onions* ca'd *mixed*
42 stirrah *fellow*
43 truncher *trencher*
44 gilpy *rascal*
45 *secundo secondly*
46 singit *singed* flead *skinned*
47 girsle *gristle*
48 hirsle *rustle*
49 brose *porridge*
50 clag *clog*
51 routh *plenty*
52 skirl *shriek* drouth *thirst*
53 houp *hope*
54 reaming *foaming*
55 thraw *twist* brize *squeeze* pegh *pant*
56 quegh *drinking-cup*
57 girn *grimace*
58 girdle farl *oatcake*

An' learn, that, maugre o' his wame,
Ill bairns are ay best heard at hame. 60
Drummond, lang syne, o' Hawthornden,
The wyliest an' best o' men,
Has gi'en you dishes ane or mae,
That wad ha' gard his grinders play,
Not to roast beef, old England's life, 65
But to the auld East Nook of Fife,
Whare Creilian crafts could weel ha'e gi'en
Scate-rumples to ha'e cleared his een;
Then neist, whan Sammy's heart was faintin,
He'd langed for scate to mak him wanton. 70
Ah, willawins, for Scotland now,
Whan she maun stap ilk birky's mow
Wi' eistacks, grown as 'tware in pet
In foreign land, or green-house het,
When cog o' brose an' cutty spoon 75
Is a' our cottar childer's boon,
Wha thro' the week, till Sunday's speal,
Toil for pease-clods an' gude lang kail.
Devall then, sirs, and never send
For daintiths to regale a friend, 80
Or, like a torch at baith ends burning,
Your house'll soon grow mirk and mourning.
What's this I hear some cynic say?
'Robin, ye loun, it's nae fair play;
Is there nae ither subject rife 85
To clap your thumb upon but Fife?
Gi'e o'er, young man, you'll meet your corning,
Than caption war, or charge o' horning;

59 maugre *despite* wame *stomach*
61 Drummond *see note*
65–66 roast beef, East Nook of Fife *see note*
67 Creilian crafts *boats from Crail, south of St Andrews*
68 scate-rumples *skate-tails*
71 willawins *alas*
72 stap *stuff* birky *fellow*
73 eistacks *rare dainties* in pet *like pets*
74 het *hot*
75 cog *bowl* cutty spoon *small horn spoon*
76 cottar childer *peasant children*
77 speal *time of rest*
78 pease-clods *rolls made of pease-meal* lang kail *uncut colewort*
79 devall *desist*
82 mirk *dark*
85 rife *available*
87 corning *fill*
88 caption *arrest for debt* horning *bankruptcy*

Some cankered surly sour-mowed carline
Bred near the abbey o' Dumfarline, 90
Your shoulders yet may gi'e a lounder,
An' be of verse the mal-confounder.'
  Come on, ye blades! But ere ye tulzie,
Or hack our flesh wi' sword or gulzie,
Ne'er shaw your teeth, nor look like stink, 95
Nor o'er an empty bicker blink:
What weets the wizen an' the wyme,
Will mend your prose and heal my rhyme.

89 carline *old woman*
90 Dumfarline *see note*
91 lounder *heavy blow*
93 tulzie *fight*
94 gulzie *knife*
96 bicker *drinking-cup*
97 weets *wets* wizen *gullet*
wyme *stomach*

Elegy, on the Death of Scots Music

Mark it, Cæsario; it is old and plain,
The spinsters and the knitters in the sun
And the free maids that weave their thread with bones
Do use to chant it.
Shakespeare's Twelfth Night.

On Scotia's plains, in days of yore,
When lads and lasses tartan wore,
Saft Music rang on ilka shore,
In hamely weed;
But harmony is now no more, 5
And music dead.

Round her the feathered choir would wing,
Sae bonnily she wont to sing,
And sleely wake the sleeping string,
Their sang to lead, 10
Sweet as the zephyrs of the spring;
But now she's dead.

Mourn, ilka nymph and ilka swain,
Ilk sunny hill and dowie glen;
Let weeping streams and naiads drain 15
Their fountain head;
Let echo swell the dolefu' strain,
Since music's dead.

Whan the saft vernal breezes ca'
The grey-haired winter's fogs awa', 20
Naebody than is heard to blaw,
Near hill or mead,
On chaunter, or on aiten straw,
Since music's dead.

3 saft *soft* rang *reigned*
9 sleely *slyly*
10 sang *song*
14 dowie *sad*
15 naiads *water nymphs*
19 ca' *drive*
23 chaunter *chanter* aiten *oaten*

Nae lasses now, on simmer days, 25
Will lilt at bleaching of their claes;
Nae herds on Yarrow's bonny braes,
Or banks of Tweed,
Delight to chant their hameil lays,
Since music's dead. 30

At glomin now the bagpipe's dumb,
Whan weary owsen hameward come;
Sae sweetly as it wont to bum,
And pibrachs skreed;
We never hear its warlike hum; 35
For music's dead.

Macgibbon's gane – ah, waes my heart!
The man in music maist expert,
Wha could sweet melody impart,
And tune the reed, 40
Wi' sic a slee and pawky art;
But now he's dead.

Ilk carline now may grunt and grane,
Ilk bonny lassie make great mane,
Since he's awa', I trow there's nane 45
Can fill his stead;
The blythest sangster on the plain!
Alake, he's dead!

Now foreign sonnets bear the gree,
And crabbit queer variety 50
Of sound fresh sprung frae Italy,
A bastard breed!
Unlike that saft-tongued melody
Which now lies dead.

27 herds *shepherds*
Yarrow *Borders river*
29 hameil *homely*
31 glomin *dusk*
32 owsen *oxen*
33 bum *hum*
34 pibrachs skreed *pipe-musics shriek*
37 Macgibbon *see note*
41 slee *sly*
43 carline *old woman*
47 sangster *songster*
49 gree *first place*
50 crabbit *crabbed*

Could lav'rocks at the dawning day, 55
Could linties chirming frae the spray,
Or toddling burns that smoothly play
 O'er gowden bed,
Compare wi' 'Birks of Invermay'?
 But now they're dead. 60

O Scotland! that could yence afford
To bang the pith of Roman sword,
Winna your sons, wi' joint accord,
 To battle speed,
And fight till Music be restored, 65
 Which now lies dead?

55 lav'rocks *larks*
56 linties chirming *linnets chirping*
 spray *twig*
57 toddling *rippling*
59 'Birks of Invermay' *see note*
61 yence *once*
62 bang *overcame* pith *strength*
 Roman *see note*

The Sow of Feeling

Well! I protest there's no such thing as dealing
With these starch'd poets – with these Men of Feeling!
Epilogue to *The Prince of Tunis*

Malignant planets! do ye still combine
Against this wayward, dreary life of mine!
Has pitiless oppression – cruel case! –
Gained sole possession of the human race?
By cruel hands has every virtue bled, 5
And innocence from men to vultures fled?
  Thrice happy, had I lived in Jewish time,
When swallowing pork or pig was doomed a crime;
My husband long had blest my longing arms,
Long, long had known love's sympathetic charms! 10
My children too, a little suckling race,
With all their father growing in their face,
From their prolific dam had ne'er been torn,
Nor to the bloody stalls of butchers borne.
  Ah, Luxury, to you my being owes 15
Its load of misery – its load of woes!
With heavy heart, I saunter all the day,
Gruntle and murmur all my hours away!
In vain I try to summon old desire,
For favourite sports – for wallowing in the mire: 20
Thoughts of my husband, of my children slain,
Turn all my wonted pleasure into pain!
How oft did we, in Phoebus' warming ray,
Bask on the humid softness of the clay?
Oft did his lusty head defend my tail 25
From the rude whispers of the angry gale;
While nose-refreshing puddles streamed around,
And floating odours hailed the dung-clad ground.
  Near by a rustic mill's enchanting clack,
Where plenteous bushels load the peasant's back, 30
In straw-crowned hovel, there to life we came,
One boar our father and one sow our dam:
While tender infants on the mother's breast,
A flame divine on either shone confessed;
In riper hours love's more than ardent blaze, 35

Enkindled all his passion, all his praise!
No deadly, sinful passion fired his soul,
Virtue o'er all his actions gained control!
That cherub which attracts the female heart,
And makes them soonest with their beauty part, 40
Attracted mine: I gave him all my love,
In the recesses of a verdant grove:
'Twas there I listened to his warmest vows,
Amidst the pendant melancholy boughs;
'Twas there my trusty lover shook for me 45
A show'r of acorns from the oaken tree;
And from the teeming earth, with joy, ploughed out
The roots salubrious with his hardy snout.
  But Happiness, a floating meteor thou,
That still inconstant art to man and sow, 50
Left us in gloomiest horrors to reside,
Near by the deep-dyed sanguinary tide,
Where whetting steel prepares the butch'ring knives,
With greater ease to take the harmless lives
Of cows, and calves, and sheep, and hog, who fear 55
The bite of bull-dogs, that incessant tear
Their flesh, and keenly suck the blood-distilling ear!
  At length the day, th'eventful day drew near,
Detested cause of many a briny tear!
I'll weep till sorrow shall my eye-lids drain, 60
A tender husband, and a brother slain!
Alas, the lovely languor of his eye,
When the base murd'rers bore him captive by!
His mournful voice, the music of his groans,
Had melted any hearts – but hearts of stones! 65
O, had some angel at that instant come,
Giv'n me four nimble fingers and a thumb,
The blood-stained blade I'd turned upon his foe,
And sudden sent him to the shades below –
Where, or Pythagoras' opinion jests, 70
Beasts are made butchers, butchers changed to beasts.
  In early times the law had wise decreed,
For human food but reptiles few should bleed;
But monstrous man, still erring from the laws,
The curse of heaven on his banquet draws! 75
Already has he drained the marshes dry

70 Pythagoras *see note*

For frogs, new emblems of his luxury;
And soon the toad and lizard will come home,
Pure victims to the hungry glutton's womb:
Cats, rats, and mice, their destiny may mourn, 80
In time their carcases on spits must turn;
They may rejoice to-day – while I resign
Life, to be numbered 'mongst the feeling swine.

Ode to the Gowdspink

Frae fields whare Spring her sweets has blawn
Wi' caller verdure o'er the lawn,
The gowdspink comes in new attire,
The brawest 'mang the whistling choir,
That, ere the sun can clear his ein, 5
Wi' glib notes sane the simmer's green.
  Sure Nature herried mony a tree,
For spraings and bonny spats to thee:
Nae mair the rainbow can impart
Sic glowing ferlies o' her art, 10
Whase pencil wrought its freaks at will
On thee the sey-piece o' her skill.
Nae mair through straths in simmer dight
We seek the rose to bless our sight;
Or bid the bonny wa'flowers sprout 15
On yonder ruin's lofty snout.
Thy shining garments far outstrip
The cherries upo' Hebe's lip,
And fool the tints that Nature chose
To busk and paint the crimson rose. 20
  'Mang man, wae's-heart, we aften find
The brawest drest want peace of mind,
While he that gangs wi' ragged coat
Is weil contentit wi' his lot.
Whan wand wi' gluey birdlime's set, 25
To steal far aff your dautit mate,
Blyth wad ye change your cleething gay
In lieu of lav'rock's sober grey.
In vain through woods you sair may ban
Th'envious treachery of man, 30
That, wi' your gowden glister ta'en,
Still hunts you on the simmer's plain,
And traps you 'mang the sudden fa's

3 gowdspink *goldfinch*
6 glib *fluent* sane *bless*
7 herried *plundered*
8 spraings *stripes* spats *spots*
10 ferlies *marvels*
12 sey-piece *test-piece*
13 straths *valleys* dight *dressed*
18 Hebe *goddess of youth*
20 busk *adorn*
26 dautit *adored*
28 lav'rock *lark*
29 ban *curse*

O' winter's dreary dreepin' snaws.
Now steekit frae the gowany field, 35
Frae ilka fav'rite houff and bield,
But mergh, alas, to disengage
Your bonny bouck frae fettering cage,
Your free-born bosom beats in vain
For darling liberty again. 40
In window hung, how aft we see
Thee keek around at warblers free,
That carol saft, and sweetly sing
Wi' a' the blythness of the spring?
Like Tantalus they hing you here 45
To spy the glories o' the year;
And though you're at the burnie's brink,
They douna suffer you to drink.
  Ah, Liberty, thou bonny dame,
How wildly wanton is thy stream, 50
Round whilk the birdies a' rejoice,
An' hail you wi' a gratefu' voice!
The gowdspink chatters joyous here,
And courts wi' gleesome sangs his peer:
The mavis frae the new-bloomed thorn 55
Begins his lauds at earest morn;
And herd lowns louping o'er the grass,
Needs far less fleetching till his lass,
Than paughty damsels bred at courts,
Wha thraw their mou's, and take the dorts: 60
But, reft of thee, fient flee we care
For a' that life ahint can spare.
The gowdspink, that sae lang has kend
Thy happy sweets (his wonted friend),
Her sad confinement ill can brook 65
In some dark chamber's dowy nook:
Though Mary's hand his nebb supplies,

35 steekit *shut* gowany *daisy-covered*
36 houff *haunt* bield *shelter*
37 mergh *marrow*
38 bouck *body*
42 keek *look*
45 Tantalus *see note*
48 douna *will not*
55 mavis *song thrush*
56 earest *earliest*
57 lowns louping *lads jumping*
58 fleetching *flattery* till *to*
59 paughty *proud*
60 thraw *twist* dorts *sulks*
61 fient flee *scarce a fly*
62 ahint *behind*
66 dowy *sad*
67 nebb *beak*

Unkend to hunger's painfu' cries,
Ev'n beauty canna cheer the heart
Frae life, frae liberty apart; 70
For now we tyne its wonted lay,
Sae lightsome sweet, sae blythly gay.
  Thus Fortune aft a curse can gie,
To wyle us far frae liberty:
Then tent her syren smiles wha list, 75
I'll ne'er envy your girnal's grist;
For whan fair freedom smiles nae mair,
Care I for life? Shame fa' the hair;
A field o'ergrown wi' rankest stubble,
The essence of a paltry bubble. 80

75 tent *attend*
76 girnal's grist *meal-chest's size*
78 shame fa' *not for as much as*
80 bubble *cheat*

On Seeing a Butterfly in the Street

Daft gowk, in macaroni dress,
Are ye come here to shew your face,
Bowden wi' pride o' simmer gloss,
To cast a dash at Reikie's Cross;
And glowr at mony twa-legged creature, 5
Flees braw by art, though worms by nature?
  Like country laird in city cleeding,
Ye're come to town to lear' good breeding;
To bring ilk darling toast and fashion,
In vogue amang the flee creation, 10
That they, like buskit Belles and Beaus,
May crook their mou' fu' sour at those
Whase weird is still to creep, alas!
Unnoticed 'mang the humble grass;
While you, wi' wings new buskit trim, 15
Can far frae yird and reptiles skim;
Newfangle grown wi' new-got form,
You soar aboon your mither worm.
  Kind Nature lent but for a day
Her wings to make ye sprush and gay; 20
In her habuliments a while
Ye may your former sel' beguile,
And ding awa' the vexing thought
Of hourly dwining into nought,
By beenging to your foppish brithers, 25
Black corbies dressed in peacock's feathers;
Like thee they dander here an' there,
Whan simmer's blinks are warm an' fair,
An' loo to snuff the healthy balm
Whan ev'nin' spreads her wing sae calm; 30
But whan she girns an' glowrs sae dowr

1 gowk *fool*   macaroni *foppish*
3 bowden *swollen*
6 flees *flies*
7 cleeding *clothing*
11 buskit *adorned*
12 crook *twist*
13 weird *fate*
16 yird *earth*
20 sprush *spruce*
23 ding *beat*
24 dwining *wasting*
25 beenging *fawning*
26 corbies *ravens*
27 dander *saunter*
29 snuff *sniff*
31 girns *snarls*   dowr *stern*

Frae Borean houff in angry show'r,
Like thee they scoug frae street or field,
An' hap them in a lyther bield;
For they war' never made to dree 35
The adverse gloom o' Fortune's eie,
Nor ever pried life's pining woes,
Nor pu'd the prickles wi' the rose.
Poor butterfly, thy case I mourn,
To green kail-yeard and fruits return: 40
How could you troke the mavis' note
For 'Penny pies all piping hot'?
Can lintie's music be compared
Wi' gruntles frae the City Guard?
Or can our flow'rs at ten hours bell 45
The gowan or the spink excel.
Now should our sclates wi' hailstanes ring,
What cabbage fald wad screen your wing?
Say, fluttering fairy, wer't thy hap
To light beneath braw Nany's cap, 50
Wad she, proud butterfly of May,
In pity lat you skaithless stay?
The fury's glancing frae her ein
Wad rug your wings o' siller sheen,
That, wae for thee, far, far outvy 55
Her Paris artist's finest dye;
Then a' your bonny spraings wad fall,
An' you a worm be left to crawl.
To sic mishanter rins the laird
Wha quats his ha'-house an' kail-yard, 60
Grows politician, scours to court,
Whare he's the laughing-stock and sport
Of ministers, wha jeer an' jibe,
And heeze his hopes wi' thought o' bribe,

32 Borean houff *north wind's haunt*
33 scoug *skulk*
34 hap *cover* lyther bield *snugger shelter*
35 dree *endure*
37 pried *tasted*
38 pu'd *pulled*
40 kail-yeard *cabbage-garden*
41 troke *exchange* mavis *thrush*
43 lintie *linnet*
44 gruntles *grunts*
46 gowan *daisy* spink *chaffinch*
47 sclates *slates*
48 fald *fold*
54 rug *tear*
57 spraings *colours*
59 mishanter *misfortune*
61 scours *rushes*
64 heeze *lift*

Till in the end they flae him bare, 65
Leave him to poortith, and to care.
Their fleetching words o'er late he sees,
He trudges hame, repines and dies.
  Sic be their fa' wha dirk thir-ben
In blackest business no their ain; 70
And may they scad their lips fu' leal,
That dip their spoons in ither's kail.

66 poortith *poverty*
67 fleetching *flattering*
69 dirk thir-ben *slink deep inside*
71 scad *scald* leal *thoroughly*

The Farmer's Ingle

Et multo in primis hilarans convivia Baccho
Ante focum, si frigus erit.
Virgil, Buc.

Whan gloming grey out o'er the welkin keeks,
  Whan Batie ca's his owsen to the byre,
Whan Thrasher John, sair dung, his barn-door steeks,
  And lusty lasses at the dighting tire:
What bangs fu' leal the e'enings coming cauld, 5
  And gars snaw-tappit winter freeze in vain;
Gars dowie mortals look baith blyth and bauld,
  Nor fleyed wi' a' the poortith o' the plain;
  Begin, my Muse, and chant in hamely strain.

Frae the big stack, weel winnow't on the hill, 10
  Wi' divets theekit frae the weet and drift,
Sods, peats, and heath'ry trufs the chimley fill,
  And gar their thick'ning smeek salute the lift;
The gudeman, new come hame, is blyth to find,
  Whan he out o'er the halland flings his een, 15
That ilka turn is handled to his mind,
  That a' his housie looks sae cosh and clean;
  For cleanly house looes he, though e'er sae mean.

Weel kens the gudewife that the pleughs require
  A heartsome meltith, and refreshing synd 20
O' nappy liquor, o'er a bleezing fire:
  Sair wark and poortith douna weel be joined.
Wi' buttered bannocks now the girdle reeks,

1 gloming *dusk* welkin keeks *sky looks*
2 owsen *oxen*
3 dung *fatigued* steeks *shuts*
4 dighting *sifting grain*
5 bangs *overcomes* leal *thoroughly*
7 dowie *sad*
8 fleyed *frightened* poortith *poverty*
11 theekit *thatched* weet *wet*
12 trufs *turfs*
13 smeek *smoke*
15 halland *inner screen between door and fireplace*
17 cosh *cosy*
19 pleughs *ploughmen*
20 meltith *meal* synd *drink*
21 nappy *strong ale* bleezing *blazing*
22 douna *cannot*
23 bannocks *oatmeal cakes* girdle *hot plate*

I' the far nook the bowie briskly reams;
The readied kail stand by the chimley cheeks, 25
And had the riggin het wi' welcome steams,
Whilk than the daintiest kitchen nicer seems.

Frae this lat gentler gabs a lesson lear;
Wad they to labouring lend an eidant hand,
They'd rax fell strang upo' the simplest fare, 30
Nor find their stamacks ever at a stand.
Fu' hale and healthy wad they pass the day,
At night in calmest slumbers doze fu' sound,
Nor doctor need their weary life to spae,
Nor drogs their noddle and their sense confound, 35
Till death slip sleely on, and gi'e the hindmost wound.

On siccan food has mony a doughty deed
By Caledonia's ancestors been done;
By this did mony wight fu' weirlike bleed
In brulzies frae the dawn to set o' sun: 40
'Twas this that braced their gardies, stiff and strang,
That bent the deidly yew in ancient days,
Laid Denmark's daring sons on yird alang,
Garred Scottish thristles bang the Roman bays;
For near our crest their heads they doughtna raise. 45

The couthy cracks begin whan supper's o'er,
The cheering bicker gars them glibly gash
O' simmer's showery blinks and winters sour,
Whase floods did erst their mailin's produce hash:
'Bout kirk and market eke their tales gae on, 50
How Jock wooed Jenny here to be his bride,
And there how Marion, for a bastard son,

24 bowie *keg* reams *foams*
26 riggin *roof* het *hot*
29 eidant *busy*
30 rax *grow* fell *very*
34 spae *predict*
35 drogs *drugs*
36 sleely *slyly*
39 wight *man* weirlike *warlike*
40 brulzies *brawls*
41 gardies *fists*
42 deidly *deadly*
43 Denmark's daring sons *see note* yird *earth*
44 bang *surpass* bays *laurels*
45 doughtna *dare not*
46 couthy cracks *cosy chat*
47 bicker *cup* gash *talkative*
49 erst *first* mailins *rented farms* hash *spoil*
50 eke *also*

Upo' the cutty-stool was forced to ride,
The waefu' scald o' our Mess John to bide.

The fient a chiep's amang the bairnies now; 55
For a' their anger's wi' their hunger gane:
Ay maun the childer, wi' a fastin mou',
Grumble and greet, and make an unco mane,
In rangles round before the ingle's low:
Frae gudame's mouth auld warld tale they hear, 60
O' warlocks louping round the wirrikow,
O' gaists that win in glen and kirk-yard drear,
Whilk touzles a' their tap, and gars them shak wi' fear.

For weel she trows that fiends and fairies be
Sent frae the de'il to fleetch us to our ill; 65
That ky hae tint their milk wi' evil eie,
And corn been scowdered on the glowing kill.
O mock na this, my friends, but rather mourn,
Ye in life's brawest spring wi' reason clear,
Wi' eild our idle fancies a' return, 70
And dim our dolefu' days wi' bairnly fear;
The mind's ay cradled whan the grave is near.

Yet thrift, industrious, bides her latest days,
Though age her sair dowed front wi' runcles wave,
Yet frae the russet lap the spindle plays, 75
Her e'enin stent reels she as weel's the lave.
On some feast-day, the wee-things buskit braw
Shall heeze her heart up wi' a silent joy,
Fu' cadgie that her head was up and saw
Her ain spun cleething on a darling oy, 80
Careless though death should make the feast her foy.

53 cutty-stool *repentance stool in church*
54 scald *scold* Mess John *name for a minister*
55 fient a *scarce a*
59 low *flame*
60 gudame *grandmother*
61 wirrikow *devil*
62 gaists *ghosts* win *dwell*
63 touzles *ruffles*
65 fleetch *flatter*
66 tint *lost*
67 scowdered *toasted* kill *kiln*
70 eild *old age*
74 dowed *withered* runcles *wrinkles*
76 stent *stint*
77 buskit *dressed*
78 heeze *lift*
79 cadgie *cheerful*
80 oy *grandchild*
81 foy *farewell feast*

In its auld lerroch yet the deas remains,
  Whare the gudeman aft streeks him at his ease,
A warm and canny lean for weary banes
  O' lab'rers doiled upo' the wintry leas: 85
Round him will badrins and the colly come,
  To wag their tail, and cast a thankfu' eie
To him wha kindly flings them mony a crumb
  O' kebbock whanged, and dainty fadge to prie;
  This a' the boon they crave, and a' the fee. 90

Frae him the lads their morning counsel tak,
  What stacks he wants to thrash, what rigs to till;
How big a birn maun lie on Bassie's back,
  For meal and multure to the thirling mill.
Neist the gudewife her hireling damsels bids 95
  Glowr through the byre, and see the hawkies bound,
Take tent case Crummy tak her wonted tids,
  And ca' the leglin's treasure on the ground,
  Whilk spills a kebbuck nice, or yellow pound.

Then a' the house for sleep begin to grien, 100
  Their joints to slack frae industry a while;
The leaden God fa's heavy on their ein,
  And hafflins steeks them frae their daily toil:
The cruizy too can only blink and bleer,
  The restit ingle's done the maist it dow; 105
Tacksman and cottar eke to bed maun steer,
  Upo' the cod to clear their drumly pow,
  Till waukened by the dawning's ruddy glow.

82 lerroch *place* deas *settle-bed*
83 streeks *stretches*
85 doiled *wearied*
86 badrins *cat* colly *sheep dog*
89 kebbock whanged *cheese sliced* fadge *barley loaf* prie *taste*
92 thrash *thresh* rigs *field sections*
93 birn *burden* Bassie *horse's name*
94 thirling mill *mill a tenant is obliged to use*
96 glowr *stare* hawkies *cows*
97 Crummy *cow's name* tids *bad mood*
98 leglin *milk-pail*
99 kebbuck *cheese* pound *of butter*
100 grien *yearn*
102 leaden God *sleep*
103 hafflins steeks *half shuts*
104 cruizy *oil lamp* bleer *shine dimly*
105 restit *damped down* dow *can*
106 tacksman *tenant farmer* cottar *farm labourer* steer *go*
107 cod *pillow* drumly pow *murky head*

Peace to the husbandman and a' his tribe,
  Whase care fells a' our wants frae year to year; 110
Lang may his sock and couter turn the glebe,
  And bauks o' corn bend down wi' laded ear.
May Scotia's simmers ay look gay and green,
  Her yellow har'sts frae scowry blasts decreed;
May a' her tenants sit fu' snug and bien, 115
  Frae the hard grip of ails and poortith freed,
  And a lang lasting train o' peaceful hours succeed.

110 fells *supplies*
111 sock *ploughshare* couter *iron tip of ploughshare*
112 bauks *ridges* laded *loaded*
114 har'sts *harvests* scowry *showery*
115 bien *comfortable*
116 poortith *poverty*

ANNE LINDSAY (1750–1825)

Auld Robin Gray

When the sheep are in the fauld, and the ky a' hame,
And a' the weary warld to rest are gane,
The waes o' my heart fa' in showers frae my e'e,
While my gudeman lies sound by me.

Young Jamie lo'ed me weel, and sought me for his bride; 5
But saving a croun he had naething else beside:
To make the croun a pund, young Jamie gaed to sea;
And the croun and the pund were baith for me.

He hadna been awa' a week but only twa,
When my father brak his arm, and the cow was stown awa; 10
My mither she fell sick, and my Jamie at the sea –
And auld Robin Gray cam a-courtin' me.

My father couldna wark, and my mither couldna spin;
I toiled day and night, but their bread I couldna win;
Auld Rob maintained them baith, and wi' tears in his e'e 15
Said, 'Jeanie, for their sakes, will ye marry me?'

My heart it said nay, I looked for Jamie back;
But the wind it blew high, and the ship it was a wrack;
His ship it was a wrack – why didna Jamie dee?
Or why do I live to cry 'wae's me'? 20

My father urgit sair: my mither didna speak,
But she looked in my face till my heart was like to break:
They gi'ed him my hand, but my heart was at the sea;
Sae auld Robin Gray, he was gudeman to me.

I hadna been a wife a week but only four, 25
When, mournfu' as I sat on the stane at the door,
I saw my Jamie's wraith, for I couldna think it he –
Till he said, 'I'm come hame to marry thee.'

1 fauld *fold*
4 gudeman *husband*
6 croun *crown, five shillings*
7 pund *pound*
10 brak *broke* stown *stolen*

Oh, sair did we greet, and muckle did we say;
We took but ae kiss, and I bade him gang away: 30
I wish that I were dead, but I'm no like to dee;
And why was I born to say 'wae's me'?

I gang like a ghaist, and I carena to spin;
I daurna think on Jamie, for that wad be a sin;
But I'll do my best a gude wife to be, 35
For auld Robin Gray, he is kind to me.

34 daurna *dare not*

JOHN TAIT (c.1750–1817)

The Banks of the Dee

'Twas summer, and softly the breezes were blowing,
  And sweetly the nightingale sang from the tree.
At the foot of a rock, where the river was flowing,
  I sat myself down on the banks of the Dee.
Flow on, lovely Dee, flow on, thou sweet river 5
Thy banks' purest stream shall be dear to me ever;
For there I first gained the affection and favour
  Of Jamie, the glory and pride of the Dee.

But now he's gone from me, and left me thus mourning,
  To quell the proud rebels, for valiant is he; 10
And ah, there's no hope of his speedy returning,
  To wander again on the banks of the Dee.
He's gone, hapless youth, o'er the rude roaring billows,
The kindest, the sweetest, of all the gay fellows,
And left me to wander 'mongst these once loved willows, 15
  The loneliest lass on the banks of the Dee.

But time and my prayers may perhaps yet restore him,
  Blest peace may restore my dear lover to me;
And when he returns, with such care I'll watch o'er him,
  He never shall leave the sweet banks of the Dee. 20
The Dee then shall flow, all its beauties displaying
The lambs on its banks shall again be seen playing
While I, with my Jamie, am carelessly straying
  And tasting again all the sweets of the Dee.

4 Dee *see note* 10 rebels *see note*

ELIZABETH HAMILTON (1758–1816)

My Ain Fireside

Oh, I hae seen great anes and sat in great ha's,
'Mang lords and fine ladies a' covered wi' braws,
At feasts made for princes, wi' princes I've been,
When the grand shine o' splendour has dazzled my e'en;
But a sight sae delightfu' I trow I ne'er spied, 5
As the bonny blythe blink o' my ain fireside.
My ain fireside, my ain fireside,
Oh, cheery's the blink o' my ain fireside.
  My ain fireside, my ain fireside,
Oh, there's naught to compare wi' ane's ain fireside. 10

Ance mair, Gude be praised, round my ain heartsome ingle,
Wi' the friends o' my youth I cordially mingle.
Nae forms to compel me to seem wae or glad,
I may laugh when I'm merry, and sigh when I'm sad;
Nae falsehood to dread, and nae malice to fear, 15
But truth to delight me, and friendship to cheer.
Of a' roads to happiness ever were tried,
There's nane half so sure as ane's ain fireside.
  My ain fireside, my ain fireside,
Oh, there's naught to compare wi' ane's ain fireside. 20

When I draw in my stool on my cosy hearthstane,
My heart loups sae light I scarce ken't for my ain;
Care's down on the wind, it is clean out o' sight,
Past troubles they seem but as dreams o' the night.
I hear but kend voices, kend faces I see, 25
And mark saft affection glent fond frae ilk e'e.
Nae fleechings o' flattery, nae boastings o' pride,
'Tis heart speaks to heart at ane's ain fireside.
  My ain fireside, my ain fireside,
Oh, there's naught to compare wi' ane's ain fireside. 30

2 braws *fine clothes*
11 heartsome *cheerful*
22 loups *leaps*
25 kend *known, familiar*
26 glent *gleam*
27 fleechings *cajolings*

JOANNA BAILLIE (1762–1851)

Wooed and Married and A'

The bride she is winsome and bonny,
Her hair it is snooded sae sleek,
And faithfu' and kind is her Johnny,
Yet fast fa' the tears on her cheek.
New pearlins are cause of her sorrow, 5
New pearlins and plenishing too,
The bride that has a' to borrow,
Has e'en right mickle ado,
  Wooed and married and a'!
  Wooed and married and a'! 10
  Is na' she very weel aff
  To be wooed and married at a'?

Her mither then hastily spak,
'The lassie is glaikit wi' pride;
In my pouch I had never a plack 15
On the day when I was a bride.
E'en tak' to your wheel, and be clever,
And draw out your thread in the sun;
The gear that is gifted, it never
Will last like the gear that is won. 20
  Wooed and married and a'!
  Wi' havins and tocher sae sma'!
  I think ye are very weel aff,
  To be wooed and married at a'!'

'Toot, toot!' quo' her grey-headed faither, 25
'She's less o' a bride than a bairn,
She's ta'en like a cout frae the heather,
Wi' sense and discretion to learn.
Half-husband, I trow, and half-daddy,

2 snooded *held by a ribbon*
6 pearlins *lace*
  plenishing *trousseau*
14 glaikit *silly*
15 plack *small coin*
17 wheel *spinning wheel*
22 havins *possessions* tocher *dowry*
27 cout *colt, adolescent*

As humour inconstantly leans, 30
The chiel maun be patient and steady,
That yokes wi' a mate in her teens.
  A kerchief sae douce and sae neat,
  O'er her locks that the winds used to blaw!
  I'm baith like to laugh and to greet, 35
  When I think o' her married at a'!'

Then out spak' the wily bridegroom,
Weel waled were his wordies, I ween,
'I'm rich, though my coffer be toom,
Wi' the blinks o' your bonny blue een. 40
I'm prouder o' thee by my side,
Though thy ruffles or ribbons be few,
Than if Kate o' the Croft were my bride,
Wi' purfles and pearlins enow.
  Dear and dearest of ony! 45
  Ye're wooed and buikit and a'!
  And do ye think scorn o' your Johnny,
  And grieve to be married at a'?'

She turned, and she blushed, and she smiled,
And she looket sae bashfully down; 50
The pride o' her heart was beguiled,
And she played wi' the sleeves o' her gown;
She twirled the tag o' her lace,
And she nippet her bodice sae blue,
Syne blinket sae sweet in his face, 55
And aff like a maukin she flew.
  Wooed and married and a'!
  Wi' Johnny to roose her and a'!
  She thinks hersel very weel aff,
  To be wooed and married at a'! 60

33 kerchief *see note* douce *prudent*
38 waled *chosen* ween *know*
44 purfles *trimmings* enow *enough*
46 buiket *registered*
54 nippet *drew in*
56 maukin *hare*
58 roose *praise*

Fy, Let Us A' to the Wedding

Fy, let us a' to the wedding,
  For they will be lilting there;
For Jock's to be married to Maggy,
  The lass wi' the gowden hair.
And there will be jibing and jeering, 5
  And glancing of bonny dark een,
Loud laughing and smooth-gabbit speering
  O' questions baith pawky and keen.

And there will be Bessy the beauty,
  Wha raises her cock-up sae hie, 10
And giggles at preachings and duty,
  Guid grant that she gang na' ajee!
And there will be auld Geordie Taunser,
  Wha coft a young wife wi' his gowd;
She'll flaunt wi' a silk gown upon her, 15
  But wow, he looks dowie and cowed.

And brown Tibby Fouler the heiress
  Will perk at the tap o' the ha',
Encircled wi' suitors, wha's care is
  To catch up her gloves when they fa', 20
Repeat a' her jokes as they're cleckit,
  And haver and glower in her face,
When tocherless mays are negleckit –
  A crying and scandalous case.

And Mysie, wha's clavering aunty 25
  Wad match her wi' Laurie the laird,
And learns the young fule to be vaunty,
  But neither to spin nor to caird.

7 gabbit *mouthed*
8 pawky *crafty, humorous*
10 cock-up *pad of false hair*
12 guid *good (God)* ajee *to one side, off the straight*
14 coft *bought*
16 dowie *doleful, sad*
17 perk *perch*
21 cleckit *given birth, brought out*
22 haver *talk nonsense*
23 tocherless *dowryless* mays *maidens*
25 clavering *gossiping*
27 vaunty *vain*
28 caird *card wool*

And Andrew, whase granny is yearning
  To see him a clerical blade, 30
Was sent to the college for learning,
  And cam' back a coof as he gaed.

And there will be auld Widow Martin,
  That ca's hersel thritty and twa!
And thraw-gabbit Madge wha for certain 35
  Was jilted by Hab o' the Shaw.
And Elspy the sewster sae genty,
  A pattern of havens and sense,
Will straik on her mittens sae dainty,
  And crack wi' Mess John i' the spence. 40

And Angus, the seer o' ferlies,
  That sits on the stane at his door,
And tells about bogles, and mair lies
  Than tongue ever utter'd before.
And there will be Bauldy the boaster, 45
  Sae ready wi' hands and wi' tongue;
Proud Paty and silly Sam Foster,
  Wha quarrel wi' auld and wi' young:

And Hugh the town-writer, I'm thinking,
  That trades in his lawyerly skill, 50
Will egg on the fighting and drinking
  To bring after grist to his mill:
And Maggy – na, na, we'll be civil,
  And let the wee bridie a-be;
A vilipend tongue is the devil, 55
  And ne'er was encouraged by me.

Then fy, let us a' to the wedding,
  For they will be lilting there,
Frae mony a far-distant ha'ding,
  The fun and the feasting to share. 60

32 coof *fool*
35 thraw *twisted*
37 sewster *seamstress* genty *neat, genteel*
38 havens *manners*
39 straik *stroke*
40 crack *gossip* spence *sitting-room*
41 ferlies *wonders*
49 writer *lawyer*
55 vilipend *spiteful*
59 ha'ding *holding*

For they will get sheep's head, and haggis,
  And browst o' the barley-mow;
E'en he that comes latest, and lag is,
  May feast upon dainties enow.

Veal florentines in the o'en baken, 65
  Weel plenish'd wi' raisins and fat,
Beef, mutton, and chuckies, a' taken
  Het reeking frae spit and frae pat:
And glasses (I trow 'tis na' said ill)
  To drink the young couple good luck, 70
Weel fill'd wi' a braw beechen ladle
  Frae punch-bowl as big as Dumbuck.

And then will come dancing and daffing,
  And reelin and crossin o' hans,
Till even auld Lucky is laughing, 75
  As back by the aumry she stans.
Sic bobbing and flinging and whirling,
  While fiddlers are making their din;
And pipers are droning and skirling,
  As loud as the roar o' the lin. 80

Then fy, let us a' to the wedding,
  For they will be lilting there,
For Jock's to be married to Maggy,
  The lass wi' the gowden hair.

62 browst *brew* mow *heap of grain*
64 enow *enough*
65 o'en *oven*
67 chuckies *chickens*
68 reeking *smoking*
72 Dumbuck *see note*
73 daffing *fun, folly*
76 aumry *cupboard*
80 lin *waterfall*

Notes

ANONYMOUS

Blythsome Bridal

This song has sometimes been attributed to Francis Sempill (1616–82), the son of Robert Sempill (1595–1665), the author of 'The Life and Death of the Piper of Kilbarchan [Habbie Simpson]'. It was included in David Herd's *Ancient and Modern Scottish Songs* (1776), vol. 2, p. 24, and was often imitated (see Allan Ramsay's 'Marrow Ballad', p. 23, and Joanna Baillie's 'Fy, Let Us A' to the Wedding', p. 297). See A.H. MacLaine, *The Christis Kirk Tradition* (Glasgow 1996), pp. 50–3.

24 stool: the stool of repentance, a seat in a prominent place in a church, usually in front of the pulpit, on which offenders, especially against chastity, sat, or sometimes stood, to be rebuked by the minister in front of the congregation.

32 Mons Meg: a huge fifteenth-century cannon, probably cast at Mons in Flanders. In the seventeenth century the barrel was cracked when firing a salute from the walls of Edinburgh Castle. It was taken from the castle in 1754 but returned in 1824. Its muzzle is just about wide enough for someone to climb in.

Maggie Lauder

This poem has, like the previous one, been attributed to Francis Sempill. It also appears in David Herd's collection (vol. 2, p. 72). It later inspired the comic epic *Anster Fair* (1812) by William Tennant (1784–1848).

36 Habby Simpson: a reference to the subject of Robert Sempill's mock elegy (see note to 'Blythsome Bridal' above).

39 Anster: the local pronunciation of Anstruther (the first vowel in Anster is long, as in 'aim'), an East Fife fishing village on the Firth of Forth, famous for its annual fair.

Tarry Woo

Another song from Herd's collection (vol. 2, p. 100). Scottish sheep were usually covered in tar to protect them from the weather.

This is No my Ain House
David Herd prints a version of this song (vol. 2, p. 105) which is a simple love song; this version, however, neatly combines images of eviction and an exile's longing for home with a political message, since the word 'whiggin' in the last line clearly refers to the triumph of the Protestant parliamentarians over the Stewart king James VII and II, forced to abdicate in 1688 in favour of his daughter Mary and her Dutch husband, William of Orange. The 'house' in the song thus becomes a royal one, and the song a Jacobite protest.

Whistle O'er the Lave O't
Also in Herd's collection, vol. 2, p. 208.

GRIZEL BAILLIE (1665–1746)
She was the daughter of Sir Patrick Hume of Marchmont, who at one time had to hide from his political enemies in the family vault in Polwarth churchyard; Grizel used to steal food for him and sneak out at night with it, despite her fear of ghosts. Later she dug a hole for him to hide in under a bed in the house. The whole family fled to Holland before returning in 1692, after the deposition of James VII and II. Grizel Baillie's daughter left a memoir of her, extracts from which, along with some of her own writings, can be found in Dorothy McMillan's *The Scotswoman At Home and Abroad* (Glasgow, 1999). 'Werena my Heart Light I Wad Die' was included in Allan Ramsay's *The Tea-Table Miscellany*.

ALEXANDER ROBERTSON OF STRUAN (1668–1749)
Robertson became the thirteenth chief of his clan in 1688 and immediately became involved in Jacobite resistance to William III, for which he was exiled to France, returning to Scotland in the reign of Queen Anne at the beginning of the next century. He lived handsomely, and beyond his means, with his sister Margaret on his Atholl estates until the 1715 Jacobite rising, after which he was again exiled to France. Pardoned by George I in 1723, he returned to Scotland. He was too old in 1745 to fight for Prince Charles, but after the Jacobite defeat he was attainted once again, although not exiled. He left a number of poems in English, many of a libertine nature, though also frequently misogynistic.

WILLIAM HAMILTON OF GILBERTFIELD (1670–1751)
Hamilton retired from the army at an early age and lived most of his life as a country gentleman on his estate near Cambuslang, not far from Glasgow. In 1722 he published a version of Blind Hary's fifteenth-century epic poem on William Wallace which became more

popular than the original. He conducted a verse correspondence with Allan Ramsay (see page 51).

The Last Dying Words of Bonnie Heck
First published in James Watson's *Choice Collection of Comic and Serious Scots Poems*, 1706.

14 Kilrenny: a village in Fife, a mile or so north-west of Anstruther (see notes to 'Maggie Lauder' above).
31 Kings-muir and Kelly-law: Kingsmuir is a few miles north of Anstruther, on the road to St Andrews; Kellie Law is a steep hill a few miles to the west.
38 Ardry: there is a farm called Airdrie in the vicinity of the other places mentioned in the poem.
68 East-Neuk: the part of Fife which extends towards the North Sea between the firths of Forth and Tay.

ALLAN RAMSAY (1685–1758)
Ramsay was born in or around 1685 at Leadhills in Lanarkshire. His father died when he was very young and after his mother, who had remarried, died in 1700, Ramsay went to Edinburgh and was apprenticed to a wigmaker. In that trade he set up shop in the capital, but at the same time he immersed himself in the literary life of the city. His poems circulated in broadsheet form until 1721, when he published about eighty of them in a volume which established his fame as a poet. Increasingly his shop became a bookseller's, and eventually a lending library. Ramsay had access to the Bannatyne Manuscript, a sixteenth-century collection of verse, from which he republished many old Scots poems in *The Ever Green* (1724), altering and adding to them as he saw fit. About the same time he also published the first volume of *The Tea-Table Miscellany*, a collection of Scottish songs, both old and new, including some of his own. A second collection of his poems appeared in 1728 and in the following year he added numerous songs to his pastoral drama *The Gentle Shepherd*, which had been published in 1725, to turn it into a very successful ballad opera. In 1736 he tried to set up a theatre in Edinburgh but after a long struggle was forced to abandon the project because of the hostility of the Church. He retired from his shop in 1740 and lived in his own house in Edinburgh until his death in 1758. His son, also called Allan, became a successful portrait painter. Ramsay's best verse, in its easy tone, its urbane moralising and its imitation of the classics, especially the Roman poet Horace, brings the Augustan mode into Scots verse, but as well as his city poems he also wrote freshly about the country, establishing a version of pastoral which seemed closer to the reality of rural life. In this he was helped by his knowledge of traditional songs, and his

facility in imitating them. Above all, and because of his interest in the earlier poetry of Scotland, Ramsay created the idea of a Scottish poetic tradition to which modern poets could belong and contribute. His sense of himself as a poet, and one belonging to a community of poets, living and dead, shaped the image of the modern Scottish poet.

An thou were my ain thing
From the first volume of *The Tea-Table Miscellany* (1723).

The Lass of Peattie's Mill
From *Scots Songs* (1718).

26 Hopeton's high mountains: 'Thirty three miles south west of Edinburgh, where the Right Honourable the Earl of Hopeton's mines of gold and lead are.' (Ramsay's note: his father, John Ramsay, had been superintendent of the lead mines.)

Polwart on the Green
From *Scots Songs* (1720). Polwarth in Berwickshire was where marriages were celebrated with dances around the hawthorn trees on the green.

A Song: Lochaber No More
From the second volume of *The Tea-Table Miscellany* (1726), an early example of a poem of exile from Scotland. Lochaber is a region in the south-west Highlands of Scotland.

Up in the air
From *Scots Songs* (1720).

The Marrow Ballad
Not published in Ramsay's lifetime. The General Assembly of the Church of Scotland in 1720 condemned the Calvinistic doctrines of Edward Fisher's book *The Marrow of Modern Divinity* (1646), provoking a long controversy. Ramsay's song makes fun of the extreme Presbyterians who supported 'Marrow' doctrines, the kind of people who also opposed his attempt to start a theatre in Edinburgh. It is an imitation of 'Blythsome Bridal' (p. 3).

4 Erskine and Mair: Ebenezer Erskine (1680–1754) and Ralph Erskine (1685–1752), together with Thomas Mair (1701–68), seceded from the Church of Scotland in 1732 over the issue of patronage (see note to line 40 below) and set up their own church. Michael Bruce (see page 319) was a member.

28 them that have the oaths tane: that is, clergy of the Established Church, who have sworn loyalty to the government; extreme Presbyterians rejected such compromise with the state.

38 Bishops of Baal: Presbyterians reject church government by bishops; since bishops of the Church of England are members of the House of Lords, extreme Presbyterians also oppose the authority of Parliament. Baal was a false god rejected by the Israelites in the Old Testament.

40 right call: an allusion to the conflict over church patronage. Congregations insisted they, not their landlords, had the right to appoint or 'call' a new minister to a vacant church; landlords sometimes resorted to desperate measures, including forced entry to churches, to insert their candidates in the pulpit in the face of popular opposition.

Lucky Spence's Last Advice (1718)

34 Saxty pounds Scots: the pound Scots was worth one twelfth of the English pound sterling.

Elegy on Lucky Wood in the Canongate, May 1717

First published in 1718.

1 Cannigate: Canongate, now part of Edinburgh, but originally a separate burgh between the city and Holyrood in the east. The two burghs were linked by the Netherbow Port (see Ramsay's note to line 60).

Elegy on Maggy Johnston, who died Anno 1711

First published in 1718.

The Life and Acts of, or An Elegy on Patie Birnie (1721)

1721. Below the epigraph Ramsay quotes lines 49–50 of 'The Life and Death of the Piper of Kilbarchan' by Sir Robert Sempill of Beltrees (1595–1660), an early mock elegy in Scots.

Epigraph, line 1: Kinghorn: a small port on the south coast of Fife where ferries across the Firth of Forth from Leith landed.

51 note: Horace, Odes Book 3, 11, lines 3–4: 'and you, shell, trained to resound with seven strings'.

Elegy on John Cowper Kirk-Treasurer's Man, Anno 1714

First published in 1718, along with the elegies on Lucky Wood and Maggy Johnston.

47 Guard: the City Guardhouse in the High Street, where those arrested by the Guard were imprisoned.

To the Right Honourable, The Town-Council of Edinburgh, the Address of Allan Ramsay (1719)

The elaborate stanza form is usually named after *The Cherry and the*

Slae, a poem by Alexander Montgomerie (c. 1556–1610); Ramsay's use of it is evidence of his interest in older Scots poetry, but the poem itself is about his own poetical reputation. Ramsay alleged that his poem 'Richy and Sandy', an elegy on the death of the English writer Joseph Addison (1672–1719), had been pirated by an Edinburgh printer and a version full of errors published in London. Here he appeals to the Town Council for the right to licence publication of his own poems. This was granted.

Familiar Epistles between Lieutenant William Hamilton and Allan Ramsay: Probably first published in 1719.

For information about William Hamilton of Gilbertfield, see page 301.

Epistle I [Hamilton to Ramsay]

19 Ben and Dryden: Ben Jonson (1572–1637), English playwright; John Dryden (1631–1700), English poet and critic.

59 the Hague: a city in the Netherlands, frequently the centre of diplomatic discussions.

Answer I [Ramsay to Hamilton]

3 short hought gilly: 'hought' usually means 'thighed' (from 'hoch', the thigh); the phrase may mean a gill-sized drinking vessel of a certain shape, or 'hought' might be a corruption of 'Hawick', since a Hawick gill was a measure equal to half a pint (making 'short' ironic).

12 Heck: a reference to Hamilton's poem 'The Last Dying Words of Bonnie Heck' (see page 15).

36 Standart Habby: Ramsay names the six-line stanza form he and Hamilton are using after 'The Life and Death of the Piper of Kilbarchan' by Sir Robert Sempill of Beltrees (1595–1660); the piper's name was Habbie Simpson. Standart Habby became a very popular form and was used so extensively by Robert Burns that it is now sometimes called the Burns stanza.

51 Of Rapes, of Buckets, Sarks and Locks: Ramsay is referring to Alexander Pope's poem *The Rape of the Lock* (1712) and 'La Secchia Rapita' ('The Rape of the Bucket', 1622) by Alessandro Tassoni (1595–1635).

55 Gawn Dunkell: Gavin Douglas (1474–1522), bishop of Dunkeld and translator of Vergil's *Aeneid* into Scots. Ramsay took 'Gavin Douglas' as his pseudonym when a member of the Easy Club, for which he wrote most of his early verse.

59 note James the First and Fifth: James I of Scotland (1394–1437) is generally credited with the authorship of *The Kingis Quair* (1423–24); James V (1512–42) was thought in the eighteenth

century to be the author of two ballads, 'The Gaberlunzie Man' and 'The Jolly Beggar', and even of 'Christis Kirk on the Green'.

Epistle II [Hamilton to Ramsay]

5 knight of the Scots thistle: the Order of the Thistle is the Scottish order of chivalry.

49 Rosycrucians: the Rosicrucians were a curiously famous secret society reputed to deal in alchemy and other magic arts.

68 Habby: Habbie Simpson (see note to line 36 of Ramsay's first *Answer* above).

Answer II [Ramsay to Hamilton]

59 Horace: the Roman poet Quintus Horatius Flaccus (65–8 BC).

Answer III [Ramsay to Hamilton]

14 Pharsalia: Pharsalus, where Caesar defeated Pompey in 48 BC.

43 note Ode of Horace: the eleventh ode of Horace's first book advises Leuconoe 'carpe diem', that is, reap the harvest of today.

Epistle to Robert Yarde of Devonshire, Esquire (1724)

Nothing is known of Robert Yarde or his connection with Ramsay.

Epistle to Mr John Gay

First published in 1729, after a possible meeting between Ramsay and John Gay (1685–1732), friend of Pope and Swift, author of many poems, songs and fables, whose most famous work is *The Beggar's Opera* (1728), a ballad opera that influenced *The Gentle Shepherd*.

2 Blowzalind and Bowzybee: Blouzelind and Bowzybee are characters in Gay mock-pastoral poem *The Shepherd's Week* (1714).

7 Pentland height: the Pentland Hills to the south of Edinburgh.

25 Pope, and skilfu' John: Alexander Pope (1688–1744), the leading English poet of his day, and his close friend John Arbuthnot (1667–1735), a Scottish doctor in London.

44 Clarinda: Ramsay's poetic name for the Duchess of Queensberry, Gay's patron.

74 'Trivia': Gay's poem about London published in 1716.

81 Dover cliffs, with samphire crowned: an allusion to Shakespeare's *King Lear*, IV, vi, 15.

82 Thule: the ancient Greek name for an island in the far north, perhaps Shetland.

85 Arthur's height: Arthur's Seat, the small mountain in Edinburgh.

86 Chiviot: the Cheviot Hills, on the border with England.

An Epistle Wrote from Mavisbank, March 1748
Not published in Ramsay's lifetime. Mavisbank, near Lasswade, was a house belonging to Sir John Clerk of Penicuik.

6 mercury: used to treat syphilis, one of whose symptoms is nasal degeneration.
20 *Mercury, Courant: The Caledonian Mercury* and *Edinburgh Evening Courant*, Edinburgh newspapers.
30 Hungary's Imperial Queen: Empress Maria Theresa (1717–80), Archduchess of Austria and Queen of Hungary and Bohemia, whose accession prompted the War of the Austrian Succession (1740–48). The surrounding lines allude to military and diplomatic events in this war.
106 Hermetic wings: Hermes, or Mercury, the messenger of the gods, is usually depicted with winged heels to denote his swiftness.
120 Prior, Gay, and Swift: Matthew Prior (1664–1721), John Gay (1685–1732) and Jonathan Swift (1667–1745), three poets noted for humorous verse in English.
121 Newton: Sir Isaac Newton (1642–1727), the English scientist and cosmologist.
125 Milton, Pope: John Milton (1608–74) and Alexander Pope (1688–1744), English poets.

An Ode to Mr Forbes (1720)
The poem was probably addressed to John Forbes of Newhall and is a loose imitation of Horace's fourth ode of his first book, from which Ramsay quotes the first three words as an epigraph; they may be translated 'Keen winter is breaking up'.

25 Forbes: usually pronounced as two syllables in the eighteenth century.

To R— H— B—, an Ode (1720)
'R—H—B—' could stand for 'Right Honourable Baron', meaning Sir John Clerk of Penicuik, who was a Baron of Exchequer, a Scottish legal title. The poem is a loose imitation of Horace's eighteenth ode of his first book, from which Ramsay quotes the first two lines as an epigraph; they may be translated 'Varus, plant no tree in preference to the sacred vine about the mellow soil of Tibur and the walls of Catilus'.

1 B— : Baron (see note above)

The Vision
From *The Ever Green* (1724): although Ramsay's devices – the attribution to 'a most lernit Clerk', the disguised signature, the 'antique' language – to make this seem an old poem are transparent, it may nevertheless be grouped with other eighteenth-century attempts to

recreate ancient literature, the most famous of which is Macpherson's Ossian. Ramsay's imitation of mediaeval Scots consists mainly of outlandish spellings. No attempt has been made to gloss all of these, since puzzling them out is part of the point of the poem, for eighteenth-century as much as for modern readers. Though the poem is about the plight of Scotland during its war for independence from England in the late thirteenth century, it probably also expresses Ramsay's dismay over the parliamentary union of these countries in 1707; that may be one reason for disguising his authorship. The stanza form is that named after *The Cherry and the Slae* by Alexander Montgomerie (c. 1556–1610).

1 Banquo: a reference to the legendary ancestor of the Stewart dynasty who appears in Shakespeare's *Macbeth*.

5 stane frae Scone: the Stone of Scone (near Perth), sometimes called the Stone of Destiny, a block of sandstone (not marble) used as a coronation seat for Scottish kings since Pictish times until seized by the English and taken to London in 1296, where it was built into the throne used at the crowning of all subsequent English and British monarchs. It was returned to Edinburgh in 1996.

7 Edert: Edward I, King of England (reigned 1272–1307), who would have subjugated Scotland had it not been for the resistance first of Sir William Wallace (1272?–1305) and then of Robert the Bruce (1234–1329), King of Scots as Robert I from 1306.

10 Baliol: John Baliol, King of Scots, 1292–96. He became king after the Scots appealed to Edward I of England to settle the disputed succession to the Scottish throne. Edward used the occasion to assert feudal superiority over the King of Scots.

13 Romans: Ramsay alludes to the fact that the Romans never fully conquered Scotland.

74 'Nemo me impune lacesset': the Scottish motto, often translated 'Wha daur meddle wi' me?'

86 Warden: this was the title used by Wallace when he led the resistance to Edward of England.

103 Langshanks: Edward I, so called because of his height.

129 paction: this word seems more appropriate for the Act of Union, 1707, than events in the thirteenth century.

177 Saxon gold: another contemporary allusion; it was known that some Scots had been paid by the English to vote for the Union of 1707. The following stanza describes some of the fears of opponents of the Union.

201 neir Forthe: the battle of Bannockburn (1314), King Robert Bruce's victory over an English army which ensured Scotland's independence, was fought beside the river Forth near Stirling; but Ramsay may be hinting at another, future battle, to restore a Stewart king in his time.

281 Gothus, Vandall: not clear which nations these represent; long before the thirteenth century the Goths and Vandals had invaded Italy, Spain and North Africa.

298 Heptarchus: England, sometimes called the Heptarchy by historians because there were originally seven Anglo-Saxon kingdoms. Again Ramsay is alluding to recent events, the deposition of the Stewart king, James VII and II, in favour of his daughter in 1688, and the subsequent rule of the Hanoverian dynasty with the accession of George I in 1714, all requiring a changeful approach to matters of allegiance.

337 Bruce: Robert the Bruce (1234–1329), King of Scots as Robert I from 1306.

The Gentle Shepherd

The first scene was published as a pastoral dialogue, 'Patie and Roger', in 1720, and the second scene as 'Jenny and Meggy' in 1723; a full version of the play was first published in 1725, followed by others in 1726 and 1728, until in 1734 there appeared an edition incorporating all the songs Ramsay had added to turn the play into a ballad opera, after the success of John Gay's *The Beggar's Opera* (1728). As the note on scene and time of action at the beginning shows, Ramsay observes the neo-classical unities of place and time, and by linking Bauldy's dealings with Mause closely to the fate of Patie and Peggy, the hero and heroine, he probably thought he had maintained the unity of action, too. Scots as the speech of the shepherds corresponded to the rustic or Doric dialect used in Classical Greek pastoral (Scots is still sometimes referred to as 'the Doric') but the vernacular liveliness of the characters' language, and the firm setting of the action in the Pentland Hills just south-west of Edinburgh, gave an actuality to the play which seemed, at least to Ramsay's contemporaries, to shift his version of pastoral closer to the real life of country people. At any rate, *The Gentle Shepherd* had an enormous influence on the idea of Scotland for nearly two centuries, proving immensely popular, especially as an amateur theatrical (there is some evidence that it was first written for performance at Haddington Grammar School in East Lothian). It seems to have escaped the opposition to stage plays which destroyed Ramsay's later efforts to start an Edinburgh theatre because of its musical nature, and perhaps also because of its conventional morality. Modern readers will be dismayed by the class prejudice of *The Gentle Shepherd*, inherent in its very title, and its complacent acceptance of woman's domestic lot; they will also be disappointed that Bauldy's encounter with Madge pretending to be a ghost is reported not enacted. The double revelation of gentle birth which resolves the plot is only the most prominent conventionality of the plot, though the long pedigree of such devices in comedy probably made

Ramsay pleased to have used them. Nevertheless, the play's dialogue often has charm and vigour and it packs in a surprising amount of information about the lives of old and young in the rural Scotland of its day, so that it is little wonder that it created an image of the Scottish peasantry which powerfully influenced later Scottish literature, from Fergusson's 'The Farmer's Ingle' (p. 286) onwards.

Act I, scene (i):

88 West Port: the western gateway to Edinburgh. 'The sheep market place of Edinburgh' (Ramsay's note).

217 grace-drink: 'The King's Health, begun first by the religious Margaret, Queen of Scots, known by the name of St Margaret. The piety of her design was to oblige the courtiers not to rise from table till the thanksgiving grace was said, well judging, that though some folks have little regard for religion, yet they will be mannerly to their prince' (Ramsay's note).

Act I, scene (ii):

13 Habby's How: on the river North Esk south of Edinburgh near Carlops.

123 bonny lass of Branksome: a song title.

131 The deil gaes o'er John Wobster: things get out of hand (proverb).

Act II, scene (i):

28–29 Montrose, Cromwell, Monk: James Graham, Marquess of Montrose (1612–50), led forces in Scotland loyal to Charles I before his capture and execution a year after Charles's own execution by English Parliamentarians, led by Oliver Cromwell (1599–1658). George Monk (1608–70), one of Cromwell's generals, later mounted an armed rebellion against Parliament which restored Charles II to the throne of England and Scotland in 1660. *The Gentle Shepherd* is therefore set at the time of the restoration of a Stewart king, hinting at Ramsay's own Jacobite sympathies.

30 Rumple: the so-called Rump Parliament, 1648–60, the small group of members left after the forcible exclusion of the rest at the end of the Civil War.

Act II, scene (iii):

13 lucky: this can be a familiar form of address to an elderly woman, or a grandmother, but it is also used to mean a hag or a witch.

Act III, scene (ii):

112 lyon: the heraldic symbol of the Scottish monarch.

Act III, scene (iv):

73 Ben: Ben Jonson (1572–1637), English playwright.

75–76 Hawthrenden, Stirling, Cowley: William Drummond of Hawthornden (1585–1649), Scottish poet; Sir William Alexander, Earl of Stirling (1567?–1640), Scottish courtier and poet; Abraham Cowley (1618–67), English royalist and poet.

Act IV, scene (i):

40 King Bruce: Robert the Bruce (1234–1329), King of Scots as Robert I from 1306. The famous victor over the English at Bannockburn (1314) has become a legendary figure for Madge.

49 s.d. Bauldy singing: in the early editions Bauldy sang only one verse, and the song was unnumbered. Ramsay later expanded his song, but still did not number it like the rest, perhaps because it is not by Ramsay himself, but entirely traditional. Bauldy sings the last verse as the first, and omits the true first verse:

Jocky said to Jenny, Jenny wilt thou do't,
Ne'er a fit, quoth Jenny, for my tocher good,
For my tocher good I winna marry thee:
E'ens ye like, quoth Jocky, ye may let it be.

Act V, scene (i):

23 witch: witchcraft trials were common in seventeenth-century Scotland; the last execution of a witch was in 1722 (five years before the last in England). Sir William expresses the scepticism about the supernatural which was a mark of the eighteenth-century Enlightenment, though it did not prevent Ramsay (and Burns) from exploiting country superstitions for literary effect.

ROBERT CRAWFORD (1695–1733)

Little is known about this poet. His elder brother was a diplomat in France and Robert may have spent some years there. He contributed four songs, including the two given here, to Ramsay's *The Tea-Table Miscellany* and three more to a similar collection, *Orpheus Caledonius* (1725).

The Broom of Cowdenknowes

Based on a traditional song. The hill of Cowdenknowes is near Drygrange, between Melrose and Dryburgh Abbey in the Scottish Borders.

1 Tweed: a river in the Scottish Borders, like those mentioned later: the Leader (line 15), Teviot (line 21) and Yarrow (line 23). The rivers listed in line 13 are further north.

24 Traquair: in the Scottish Borders, overlooking the Tweed near Innerleithen.

The Bush Aboon Traquair

Also based on a traditional song.

ALEXANDER ROSS (1699–1784)
Ross was born in Aberdeenshire and graduated from Marischal College in Aberdeen in 1718. He held various teaching posts until he was appointed the schoolmaster at Lochlee in Glenesk, in the Grampian Mountains, where he remained for the last fifty years of his life. In 1766 he took some of his poems to James Beattie, Professor of Moral Philosophy in Aberdeen, and he assisted the publication of a selection of Ross's work in 1768. This included a few songs and the pastoral narrative 'Helenore, or the Fortunate Shepherdess'. A second edition of this, dedicated to the Duchess of Gordon, appeared in 1778 and Ross enjoyed a modest fame. 'Helenore' was to remain a popular work for over a century. Ross writes in a north-east dialect of Scots often different from the Lowland Scots of Ramsay, Fergusson and Burns. He left a mass of unpublished material, including a companion piece to 'Helenore' and much religious verse. In 1938 the Scottish Text Society published *The Scottish Works of Alexander Ross* edited by Margaret Wattie.

Married and Wooed an' A' (1768)
There is another version of this song, 'Woo'd and Married and A' ', in Herd (vol. 2, p. 115) and elsewhere, which is attributed to Ross. Both versions are based on a popular song, also imitated by Joanna Baillie (see page 295).

64 feauto: according to the *Scottish National Dictionary*, this word derives from the Old French 'feauté', meaning fidelity, short for a faithful husband, so that the line means something like 'as long as you have a husband to drive the wheel' (perhaps with a sexual innuendo, given the references to child-bearing earlier in the stanza). This stanza appears only in the 1768 edition, and has not often been reprinted.

What Ails the Lasses at Me? (1768)
Billet by Jeany Gradden (1768)
An answer to the previous poem.

19 Jenny, Jockie: a reference to the song 'Jocky said to Jenny' (Herd, vol. 2, p. 195); see Ramsay's *The Gentle Shepherd*, Act IV(i).
33 forsta': perhaps 'forestall', in the sense 'anticipate [wrongly]', or 'jump to a [wrong] conclusion'; but some authorities suggest it means 'understand' (compare German 'verstehen').

WILLIAM HAMILTON OF BANGOUR (1704–54)
Hamilton, the second son of a gentleman from an Ayrshire family, was born at Bangour near Dechmont in West Lothian. At the age of twenty he contributed to Ramsay's *The Tea-Table Miscellany*. A

Jacobite, he went into hiding after the battle of Culloden in 1746, and then fled to France. He returned to Scotland in 1749 and inherited the family estates on the death of his elder brother in 1750, but poor health drove him abroad again and he died at Lyons. He left a considerable quantity of verse, almost all in English, including translations from Horace and many other ancient authors.

The Braes of Yarrow
First published in *Orpheus Caledonius* (1725). The first stanza is from a traditional ballad. The Yarrow Water flows through the Scottish Borders west of Selkirk.

DAVID MALLET (1705–65)
Mallet changed his surname from Malloch after he went to London to make his fortune. This attempt to accommodate English tongues and ears has blasted his reputation with later generations. In his time he was a successful writer and dramatist, acquainted with many of the leading English authors of the period. He collaborated with his fellow Scot James Thomson (1700–48) on the masque 'Alfred' (1740). His poems were included in the collection for which Samuel Johnson wrote his *Lives of the Poets* (1779–81).

The Birks of Invermay
A version with eighteen more lines (said to have been added by Alexander Bryce of Kirknewton, 1713–86) was published by Herd (vol. 1, p. 191). Invermay is in the Ochil Hills south-west of Perth.

ALISON RUTHERFORD COCKBURN (1712–94)
Alison Rutherford was the daughter of a Selkirkshire gentleman. She married an advocate, Patrick Cockburn, who died in 1753. She was a member of the intellectual circle in Enlightenment Edinburgh which included the philosopher David Hume (1711–76) and his cousin John Home (1722–1808), the playwright, and she saw Burns when he visited the capital in 1786. She was related to Sir Walter Scott's mother and encouraged her son's early attempts at verse. Dorothy McMillan reprints her autobiography in *The Scotswoman at Home and Abroad* (1999).

The Flowers of the Forest (1765)
Mrs Cockburn's version of this traditional song is said to refer to the financial ruin in one year of seven proprietors in the area of the Scottish Borders known as the Ettrick Forest. Compare Jean Elliot's version of the same song on page 191.

HENRY ERSKINE (1720–65)
Colonel Sir Harry Erskine of Alva had a long army career, including the expedition to L'Orient in 1746 in which the philosopher David Hume also participated.

Highland March
First published in *The Lark* (1765). By the end of the eighteenth century 'In the Garb of Old Gaul' had become a march of the 42nd Highlanders (The Black Watch); it is also the regimental slow march of the Scots Guards (though they are not a kilted regiment). The tune is by John Reid (1721–1807), who founded the Chair of Music at the University of Edinburgh.

5 Gaul: the Roman name for what is now France. Gaul, or 'Gallia' in Latin, was inhabited by Celts, related in customs and language to the Celtic people of the Scottish Highlands, so that it is possible to suppose the Gauls wore kilts; it seems odd to invoke the spirit of Ancient Gaul in the wars against modern France.

7 Romans: Scottish patriots were fond of mentioning the fact that the Romans, though they conquered England, along with many other countries, never subdued the tribes north of the Border.

21 Quebec, Cape Breton: places in Canada captured by the British from the French during the wars for colonies in the eighteenth century. After the failure of the Jacobite Rebellion of 1745 the British government raised several regiments of Highlanders which were successfully used in the wars against France. For a different attitude to Highland soldiers see the references to the Edinburgh City Guard in Robert Fergusson's poems, for example, 'The Daft-Days' and 'Hallow-Fair'.

JOHN SKINNER (1721–1807)
Skinner was an Episcopalian clergyman near Peterhead in Aberdeenshire and as such suffered persecution for his refusal to conform to the established Church of Scotland, and for suspected Jacobitism. Nevertheless he wrote a number of lively songs and a poem in the *Christis Kirk* tradition, 'The Christmass Bawing of Monumusk' (1739: see A.H. MacLaine, *The Christis Kirk Tradition* (Glasgow, 1996), pp. 69–79). He corresponded with Burns but never met him.

Tullochgorum (1776)
Tullochgorm is on the west side of Loch Fyne in Argyll and gave its name to a fiddle tune, to which Skinner was challenged to fit suitable words, partly as a distraction from a political argument after dinner at the house of an excise officer called Montgomerie. Burns called it 'the best Scots song Scotland ever saw'.

5 Whig and Tory: the names of the two main political factions in the eighteenth century. The Whigs were slightly more progressive and approved of the replacement of the Stewart dynasty by the Hanoverians; the Tories stood for traditional rights and privileges, and were suspected of Jacobitism, the wish to restore the exiled Stewarts to the throne.

TOBIAS SMOLLETT (1721–71)
Smollett, like Mallett, left Scotland as a young man. After serving as a doctor in the Royal Navy he embarked on a literary career in London, writing and editing periodicals, histories and reference works, and engaging in political propaganda. He is best remembered now for his novels, especially the last, *Humphry Clinker* (1771), which has scenes set in Scotland. Although he remained a Scottish patriot and became the centre of a circle of London Scots, he rarely returned to Scotland and died in Italy.

Ode to Leven-Water
Published in *Humphry Clinker* (in Matthew Bramble's letter of 28 August). The river Leven flows out of Loch Lomond into the Clyde near Dumbarton; Smollett was born and brought up nearby.

4 Arcadian: Arcadia was the region of Greece traditionally associated with shepherds and pastoral poetry.

WILLIAM WILKIE (1721–72)
Wilkie was of humble origin but managed to go to Edinburgh University and was appointed minister of Ratho in Midlothian. He then became Professor of Natural Philosophy at the University of St Andrews, where he befriended the young Robert Fergusson, who wrote an eclogue in his memory (see page 265). Wilkie had a farm where he experimented with new agricultural methods. In 1757 he published a Homeric epic, *The Epigoniad*, which was enthusiastically praised by his fellow Scots.

The Hare and the Partan
From the *Fables* (1768).

JEAN ELLIOT (1727–1805)
The third daughter of Sir Gilbert Elliot of Minto, Jean Elliot was born in Teviotdale but lived most of her life in Edinburgh. She helped her father avoid capture by the Jacobites when they took the city in the 1745 Rebellion. She never married.

The Flowers of the Forest
Based on an old song (compare Alison Rutherford Cockburn's version, page 182), from which the first and last lines come. Jean Elliot is said to have composed her poem in 1756 after hearing friends talk of the battle of Flodden, 1513, a disastrous defeat in northern England where James IV and many of his nobles were killed.

JAMES BEATTIE (1735–1803)
Beattie became Professor of Moral Philosophy at Marischal College, Aberdeen, and engaged in controversy with David Hume (1711–76), the sceptical Edinburgh philosopher, but he is better remembered for his long poem, *The Minstrel* (1771–74), which describes the development of a poet in a way which anticipates the romanticism of Wordsworth. *The Minstrel*, like most of Beattie's verse, is in English, and he is notorious for having drawn up a list of Scotticisms, words and phrases that a Scottish writer should avoid in writing English. Nevertheless he himself wrote Scots verse, though most of it remains unpublished.

To Mr Alexander Ross
First published in the *Aberdeen Journal* in 1768 and later prefaced to editions of Ross's poems, which Beattie had helped to publish (see note on Alexander Ross above).

8 Habby: a reference to 'The Life and Death of the Piper of Kilbarchan [Habbie Simpson]' by Robert Sempill (1595–1665).

20 Lochlee: the village at the end of Glenesk where Ross was schoolmaster.

40 Forth: the river which flows most of the way across Scotland north of Edinburgh; Beattie is contrasting Ross and himself with the culture of the capital.

75 Gawin Douglas: Gavin Douglas (1474?–1522), bishop of Dunkeld, wrote a number of poems and translated Virgil's *Aeneid* into Scots.

77 King James: James V (see note to Allan Ramsay's Answer I [Ramsay to Hamilton], line 59 note, page 305).

79 Montgomery, Ramsay: Alexander Montgomerie (1556?–1610?) and Allan Ramsay.

80 Dunbar, Scott, Hawthornden: William Dunbar (1465?–1530?), Alexander Scott (c. 1524–84) and William Drummond of Hawthornden (1585–1649).

91 Mearns, Angus: the Mearns is the land between the mountains and the sea between Brechin and Stonehaven in eastern Scotland; Angus is south of this, around Forfar north of Dundee.

93 Cairn-a-Mounth: a peak in the eastern Grampian Mountains by which passes a road south from Aberdeenshire.

ISOBEL PAGAN (1741–1821)
Tibby Pagan was born in New Cumnock. Some say she kept an inn at Muirkirk in Ayrshire, but others that she lived by begging, selling whisky without a licence, and singing. How much of 'Ca' the Yowes to the Knowes' is hers is debatable; the last stanza is said to have been written by Robert Burns.

ALEXANDER, DUKE OF GORDON (1743–1827)
The fourth Duke of Gordon was one of the great landowners in the north-east of Scotland. In the 1770s he rebuilt and extended the town of Huntly, and in 1793 he raised the regiment which became the Gordon Highlanders. He was helped in this by his wife Jane Maxwell, who is said to have kissed each new recruit; she was also regarded by Burns, who met her in Edinburgh, as one of his patrons, and she was the patron of Alexander Ross. The duke established the breed of dogs called Gordon setters.

Cauld Kail in Aberdeen
Based on an old song, of which there are several versions all with the same opening lines.
2 Stra'bogie: Strathbogie, the valley of the river Bogie near Huntly, Aberdeenshire.

HECTOR MACNEILL (1746–1818)
Born at Rosebank near Roslin in Midlothian and educated at Stirling, Macneill sailed from Bristol as a teenager to begin a varied life in the West Indies, mainly in Jamaica. In 1788 he returned to Scotland to seek literary fame, with small success. He produced some poems and songs, in Scots and English, and even a few novels. He continued to visit Jamaica, where a former employer, John Graham of Three Mile River, left him an annuity in 1800. He returned permanently to Edinburgh and became the editor of the *Scots Magazine*. His poems were published by himself at Edinburgh in 1801.

The Scottish Muse (1798)
Macneill later added four stanzas to mark the death of his friend, James Currie, the biographer of Burns. The epigraph is from *Twelfth Night*, Act II, scene iv.
2 pain: 'The author's complaints were such, that, unable either to read or to write above a few minutes without distress, his only amusement was to compose by the help of memory alone . . .' (Macneill's note).
99 Aichil: the Ochil Hills, north-east of Stirling.
110 Elephanta: an island in Bombay harbour famous for its magni-

ficent excavated temple. Macneill adds a note referring to his own published account of the caves of Elephanta, Canary (or Kanheri, see next note) and Ambola.

116 Salsett: an island immediately north of Bombay which contains the extensive caves of Kanheri.

117 hope: 'By an unforeseen change in administration, the author lost a lucrative appointment in India, which in a short time would have yielded an ample fortune' (Macneill's note).

122 Carib: the Caribbean.

141 pimento: pimento or all-spice trees are evergreens much cultivated in Jamaica.

170 guinea-verdured: covered in guinea grass.

171 ceiba: the silk cotton tree.

173 cabbage: 'The palmeto royal, or mountain cabbage, from 150 to 200 feet in height; a tree . . . which, without doubt, is among the most graceful of all the vegetable creation' (Macneill's note).

180 harp-strings: 'The second part of "The Harp" [1789] was composed during the author's first passage home from Jamaica' (Macneill's note).

187 strains: 'The author's first attempts in Scottish poetry were the composing of words to some of our most simple pastoral and Gaelic airs . . .' (Macneill's note).

191 nature: Macneill is undoubtedly referring in these lines to the reception of his early verses; 'nature' must here ironically mean the critics.

198 Ayr, Tweed: rivers in southern Scotland, the first associated with the Ayrshire ploughman, Robert Burns, the second with the Border ballads and songs; Macneill is identifying his muse with these poetic traditions.

210 pleased nae few: 'Alluding to the uncommon sale of "Will and Jean" ["Scotland's Scaith" (1795), a ballad about the evils of whisky] . . .' (Macneill's note).

211 Forth: the river which runs by Stirling and the subject of Macneill's poem 'The Links o' Forth' (1796).

212 Clyde: the river that runs through Glasgow.

215 Lossit, Eden: 'Lossit, in Cantyre [Kintyre], Argyleshire, where some of the songs, from their resemblance to the Gaelic, were particularly relished. They were afterwards set to music, and published in Edinburgh ['Eden's towers']' (Macneill's note; Lossit is on the island of Islay).

264 Graham: 'John Graham, Esq., of Three Mile River, Jamaica, under whose kind and hospitable roof the present poem was composed' (Macneill's note; Graham died shortly after the poem was written).

MICHAEL BRUCE (1746–67)

Born the son of a weaver in Kinnesswood by Loch Leven in Kinross-shire, Bruce went to the University of Edinburgh, leaving without graduating in 1765. He spent some months as a schoolteacher at Gairneybridge, by Loch Leven, and then entered the 'theological hall' in Kinross of the Secession Church, which had broken away from the Church of Scotland over the issue of patronage in 1732. The hall however closed soon after and Bruce took up another teaching post in Forest Mill near Alloa in 1766, but his health broke down and in the following year he returned to Kinnesswood to die. A few months later a young man called John Logan persuaded Bruce's father to give him his son's manuscripts for publication. When the volume at last appeared in 1770 Logan's preface stated that works by other poets had been included, but as authors were not identified in the text it was impossible to be sure which poems were Michael Bruce's. Then in 1781 Logan published a volume of what he called his own verse which included work by Bruce, notably the popular 'Ode to the Cuckoo'. It took over a century to vindicate Michael Bruce's claims (see *Life and Works of Michael Bruce* by Edward Vernon, Perth, 1951). Bruce left a wide range of sacred and secular verse, including translations and paraphrases, almost all in English.

Weaving Spiritualised

Said to have been written to his brother James, when he heard that he had begun to learn weaving.

6 grass: 'all flesh is grass' (Isaiah 40, 6).

Ossian's Hymn to the Sun

This is a versification of part of the last paragraph of James Macpherson's prose-poem 'Carthon', published by him in 1765 as one of his translations from the works of the ancient Highland bard Ossian (see *The Poems of Ossian and Related Works*, edited by Howard Gaskill, Edinburgh, 1996, p. 133). The original text reads as follows:

> O thou that rollest above, round as the shield of my fathers! Whence are thy beams, O sun! thy everlasting light? Thou comest forth, in thy awful beauty, and the stars hide themselves in the sky; the moon, cold and pale, sinks in the western wave. But thou thyself movest alone: who can be a companion of thy course! The oaks of the mountains fall: the mountains themselves decay with years; the ocean shrinks and grows again: the moon herself is lost in heaven; but thou art for ever the same; rejoicing in the brightness of thy course. When the world is dark with tempests; when thunder rolls,

> and lightning flies; thou lookest in thy beauty, from the clouds, and laughest at the storm.

Macpherson added a footnote comparing this passage to Milton's *Paradise Lost*, Book 4, lines 32ff.

ROBERT FERGUSSON (1750–74)

Fergusson was born in Edinburgh in 1750. His family was from Aberdeenshire. He was able to secure a scholarship first to Dundee High School and then to the University of St Andrews in Fife, which he left in 1768 without graduating, a normal practice at the time. Some of Fergusson's early poems, for example, the 'Elegy on David Gregory', may date from his student period, during which his father died. After leaving St Andrews he went to an uncle's farm in Aberdeenshire, possibly to seek employment, but nothing came of this visit except an estrangement from the uncle. Fergusson returned to Edinburgh where he secured a post as a clerk and copyist in the Commissary Records Office, transcribing legal documents at a penny per page. This dull task at least left him time and energy to enter the world of Edinburgh clubs and social life, still flourishing in the Old Town, the high tenements lining the rocky ridge between the castle and Holyrood Palace, though plans were already laid for the New Town to the north, whither those who could afford it would migrate before the end of the century. In 1771 the *Weekly Magazine* published the first of many poems by Fergusson to appear in its pages, at first in English, but, after 'The Daft-Days' in early 1772, more and more in Scots. Fergusson was swiftly recognised as the unofficial laureate of the city and hailed as the successor to Allan Ramsay. By the end of the year he had enough poems written to make a book and in 1773 a volume of his verses, more in English than in Scots, was published by subscription. This was soon followed by the separate publication of his most ambitious poem, *Auld Reikie*, about Edinburgh itself. Throughout 1773 Fergusson's work continued to appear in the *Weekly Magazine*, but he seems to have been prone to bouts of depression and in the following year his mental health deteriorated. Dark religious fears played a part in this, but there was also a serious fall down some stairs, after which Fergusson became so violent that his mother, unable to cope, arranged to have her son committed to the public asylum. There, two months later, in October 1774, Fergusson died, just twenty-four years old. He was buried in an unmarked grave in the Canongate churchyard. When Robert Burns visited Edinburgh in 1786 he was instrumental in marking the grave of a poet he intensely admired with the headstone which still stands there, complete with the epitaph Burns himself wrote. Nevertheless, no poet has suffered more from comparison with Burns than Fergusson. Because so many of his works inspired in theme and style so many of Burns's, Fergusson has too often been seen only as a predecessor of the Ayrshire bard. Of course he is, but this neglects his own distinctive qualities: his dry humour, his ear for dialect and spoken Scots (and English), his command of neo-classical tropes (a product of his university education) and his amused tolerance of the human scene, a city-bred trait. Fergusson also deserves more credit for his use of traditional forms, such as Standart Habbie and the Christis Kirk genre, also, of course, used by Ramsay, and to be taken up by Burns. Fergusson was younger than Keats when he died, and much younger than Burns, and his poems, more of which are in English than in Scots, show the variety and versatility of a young writer testing the range of his talent. Yet the fluency of his rhyming, the poise of his rhetorical stance and the polish of his best work, apparently written at great speed, belie his youth and are extraordinary achievements.

In the following notes identifications of Edinburgh names and features are not repeated from poem to poem; please refer back to notes on previous poems for such information.

Auld Reikie, a poem (1773)
In the first edition the text is followed by the words 'End of Canto I', implying that Fergusson intended to continue the poem in further sections. The first edition text ends with line 328; the final forty lines are taken from an edition of Fergusson's poems published in 1779. For the meaning of the title, see Ramsay's note to the first line of 'Elegy on Maggy Johnston', p. 34.

38 Nore Loch: a muddy stretch of water on the north side of old Edinburgh, progressively drained in the eighteenth century.
39 Edina's roses: a euphemism for the foul waste daily poured from high Edinburgh windows into the street below, traditionally with the warning 'Gardyloo!' (bad French for 'Mind the water!').
63 Cross: the Mercat Cross in the High Street; it had actually been demolished in 1756 (see 'Mutual Complaint of Plainstanes and Causey', line 107).
191 Sybil, Trojan: the line refers to the visit that the Trojan hero Aeneas, aided by the Cumaean sibyl or prophetess, makes to the underworld in Book 6 of Vergil's *Aeneid*.
219 Gillespie: John and James Gillespie had a tobacco shop in the High Street. James left his fortune to found the school named after him, and immortalised in Muriel Spark's novel *The Prime of Miss Jean Brodie* (1961).
227 Hottentot: a member of a South African race supposed to treat pieces of meat as objects of value, worn like jewellery.

253 Comely Garden, the Park: a public garden to the east of the city, and the King's Park around Arthur's Seat (see line 263), the small mountain behind Holyrood Palace.
255 Newhaven, Leith or Canonmills: respectively a fishing village to the north of Edinburgh, the seaport beside it, and what was then a village also to the north of the city.
273 Holyrood-house: the royal palace a mile east of Edinburgh Castle, begun at the end of the fifteenth century by James IV and much expanded in the reign of Charles II. It was hardly used in Fergusson's time.
277 Hamilton: the Duke of Hamilton, hereditary keeper of Holyrood Palace; see previous note.
285 debtors: they could claim sanctuary from creditors and the law within the precincts of Holyrood Abbey, including the King's Park around Arthur's Seat.
291 St Anthon: St Anthony's Chapel, a ruin on the north side of Arthur's Seat.
300 Simon Fraser: the keeper of the Tolbooth Prison.
303 St Mary: dealers in old clothes occupied St Mary's Wynd.
314 Drummond: George Drummond (1687–1766), six times Lord Provost of Edinburgh, who led the move to build the New Town and established the Edinburgh Royal Infirmary in 1729.
320–21 Forth, Lothian, Fife: the firth or estuary of the river Forth lies between Lothian in the south, where Edinburgh stands, and Fife to the north.
333 brig: the North Bridge in Edinburgh, connecting the Old Town with the ridge upon which the New Town was to be built. Begun in 1765, the bridge collapsed in 1769 and had to be rebuilt.
342 Berwick Law: a prominent hill on the south shore of the Firth of Forth east of Edinburgh.

The Daft-Days (1772)

The Daft Days are the New Year holidays in January.

66 City-Guard: the City Guard was Edinburgh's police force, a semi-military body which as well as controlling street disturbances and petty crime also paraded on ceremonial occasions. As a symbol of authority it was the object of insult from boys and the uproarious. It had a guardhouse in the High Street and included in its ranks many ex-soldiers from Highland regiments (the Gaelic poet Duncan Ban Macintyre served in it from 1766 to 1793), and Fergusson frequently makes fun of their attempts to speak English. See Chapter 3 of Sir Walter Scott, *The Heart of Midlothian* (1818).

Hallow-Fair (1772)
The fair was held at Hallowmas, the beginning of November, at Castlebarns, on Edinburgh's west side, in the area now known as Fountainbridge.

37 Sawney: Sawney (or Sandy) speaks with an Aberdeenshire accent, including the distinctive replacement of 'wh' by 'f' in words like 'wha' (English 'who') and 'oo' by 'ee' in words like 'loom'.

Leith Races (1773)
Leith, on the Firth of Forth, is the port of Edinburgh. The races were held in July.

80 birth-day wars: see Fergusson's poem 'The King's Birth-Day in Edinburgh' (p. 238); in the year 'Leith Races' was published, a baker had died in the fighting with the City Guard on the king's birthday, and the bakers were out for revenge.

91 Bow: the West Bow, which linked the Lawnmarket, at the top of the High Street, with the Grassmarket below, under the south side of the castle rock, was where many tinsmiths traded.

95 Leith Walk: the road from Edinburgh to the port of Leith.

118 Buchan: in north-east Scotland, where the accent is like that of Sawney in 'Hallow-Fair' (line 37; see note above).

145 Lyon: the Lord Lyon, King at Arms, chief Scottish Herald, has power to punish those who display unregistered heraldic devices; at the time there was controversy about this, some claiming that any gentleman should be free to paint a coat of arms on his carriage door. Fergusson calls such progressive people 'Whigs', the name of the liberal faction in British politics.

149 Jamie: a law authorising the Lord Lyon to punish those bearing false coats of arms was passed in 1592, during the reign of James VI.

The Rising of the Session (1773)
The highest civil law court in Scotland, the Court of Session, sat from November to March and from June to August; this poem was published in March.

51 protests: formal declarations about the non-payment of bills of exchange.

56 Robin Gibb: he kept a tavern in the old Parliament Hall, where then, as now, lawyers from the nearby court-rooms gather.

62 Indian Peter: Peter Williamson (1730–99), after an adventurous life, including capture by American Indians, ran a tavern in Parliament Close; he had other interests, including publishing and a penny post.

The King's Birth-Day in Edinburgh (1772)
The annual celebration of George III's birthday on 4 June continues in ceremonies such as Trooping the Colour in London on the British monarch's 'official' birthday. There is an amusing description of events similar to those in Fergusson's poem in John Galt's novel *The Provost* (1822), Chapter 10. The epigraph is from lines 112 and 115 of William Drummond of Hawthornden's macaronic poem 'Polemo-Middiana' ('the fight over a midden', 1645) and may be translated 'Oh, what a hurly-burly there was, if you could have seen it'.
31 Mons Meg: a huge Edinburgh cannon (see note to 'Blythsome Bridal', page 300).
41 Clackmannan: the smallest shire in Scotland, just west of Fife.

Epilogue, spoken by Mr Wilson, at the Theatre Royal, in the Character of an Edinburgh Buck (1773)
A fine satirical monologue in English mock-heroic couplets.
9 sun: paradoxically this must mean the moon, since the events described happened 'last night' (line 5); the buck's valour is not much seen in true daylight.
11 Quixote: Don Quixote (Fergusson gives the name a trisyllabic Spanish pronunciation), in the novel by Miguel Cervantes (1547–1616), is a crazed enthusiast for chivalry who mistakenly acts like a knight errant in a cynical modern world; the buck's misapplied comparison suggests his lack of the Don's idealism.
31 George's Square: George Square, begun in 1766, was one of the first attempts to expand Edinburgh with upper-class residences; it lies to the south of the Old Town (whereas the New Town was built to the north) and is now mainly occupied by the University of Edinburgh.
42 Meadows: a stretch of open grass on the south side of Edinburgh, a public park, with a small golf course; note that to rhyme with 'decreed us' Fergusson uses a Scots pronunciation.
44 Bridge and Cage: the first crossed a small stream in the Meadows; the second was a small circular shelter at the end of the central walk.
52 Troy: the ten-year siege of Troy, the subject of Homer's *Iliad*, began as an attempt by the Greeks to recover the beautiful Helen, who had run off with Paris, a Trojan prince.

Braid Claith (1772)
23 Meadow, Park: for the Meadows, see above; the Park is probably the King's Park (see notes to *Auld Reikie)*.
50 Sir Isaac Newton: (1642–1727), the greatest scientist of the time.

Caller Oysters (1772)
The epigraph consists of the first four lines of *The Splendid Shilling* (1705), a Miltonic burlesque by John Philips (1631–1706).
39 Luckie Middlemist: Lucky Middlemass kept an oyster tavern in the Cowgate.
43 Saunt Giles: St Giles Cathedral, the main Edinburgh church, in the High Street in front of Parliament Hall and the law courts.
61 Musselbrough: Musselburgh, a fishing village east of Edinburgh.

Mutual Complaint of Plainstanes and Causey (1773)
1 Merlin: there was a tradition that a Frenchman called John Marlin first paved the High Street; Fergusson's spelling of his name turns him into the legendary wizard at the court of King Arthur (note the reference to Arthur's Seat, the small mountain in Edinburgh, line 103).
6 Fraser's ulie: the city's oil ('ulie') lamps were supplied by a man called Fraser.
16 Balaam: see Numbers XXII in the Bible.
102 *magnum damnum datum*: great loss given; that is, the case won with expenses, and your opponent fined, too.
108 Guard: though the Mercat Cross had been removed in 1756 (it has since been restored), the City Guard House remained in the middle of the High Street until 1785.
116 Charlie's statue, Exchange: a statue of Charles II stands in front of the law courts behind St Giles Cathedral; the Exchange (now the City Chambers) was a new building across the High Street from the Cathedral.

The Ghaists: A Kirk-yard Eclogue (1773)
A dialogue between the ghosts of George Watson (1654–1723) and George Heriot (1563–1624), who both left part of their fortunes to found charitable schools named after them (these schools still exist, but are much grander today). In 1773 the British government in London proposed the Mortmain Bill which would have allowed the trustees of such schools to put their funds into government securities at a fixed rate of interest. This was opposed in Scotland because the interest rate was low and the money would have gone to England. The bill did not become law.
3 Geordie Girdwood: the sexton of Greyfriars churchyard, which is on the east side of Heriot's school on the south side of Edinburgh; Watson's school stood opposite Heriot's.
32 royal Jamie: James VI, to whom Heriot was goldsmith.
37 Danish Jones: Inigo Jones (1573–1652), wrongly believed to be the architect of Heriot's school; he had worked in Denmark.

40 busk wi' flow'rs: on the first Monday of June each year Heriot's statue in his school is garlanded with flowers in a ceremony of commemoration.
43 Major Weir: Thomas Weir was executed in 1670 having confessed to incest, murder and sorcery; he had been commander of the City Guard.
49 Adam's tomb: the burial place of William Adam (1689–1748), architect and father of the famous architects and interior designers Robert and James Adam.
58 Union: the union of the Scottish and English parliaments in 1707.
66 grassum gift: a fee paid to a landlord by an incoming or renewing tenant.
87 Castlehill to Netherbow: that is, the length of Edinburgh High Street, from the castle down to the gateway to the neighbouring burgh of Canongate.
121 Tweed: the river in south Scotland which partly marks the border with England.
125 Mackenzie: Sir George Mackenzie (1636–91), founder of the Advocates' Library (which became the National Library of Scotland), was notorious as the prosecutor of the religious rebels known as the Covenanters, who called him 'Bluidy Mackenzie'. Small boys used to dare each other to go to his tomb in Greyfriars churchyard after dark and call on him to come out.

Elegy, on the Death of Mr David Gregory

Though first published in 1773, this poem may have been written as early as 1765, when Fergusson was a student at St Andrews. David Gregory, one of a family of famous doctors and mathematicians, succeeded his father as professor of mathematics at the University of St Andrews in 1739, but resigned in 1764, the year before his death, and before Fergusson matriculated, so that it is unlikely that Fergusson ever heard him lecture.

Elegy on John Hogg (1773)

A porter is a university servant who takes care of buildings, handles messages and assists at ceremonies.
3 Alma Mater: a Latin phrase, meaning 'fostering mother', traditionally applied to a university by those taught there.
9 Kate Kennedy: a bell in the college steeple, named after the niece of Bishop Kennedy, the college founder.
13 Pauly Tam: Thomas Tullidelph (died 1777), the Principal, a strict disciplinarian; his nickname means either 'pale and sickly' or 'flat-footed'.
19 regents: university teachers, who took groups of students through the

entire course; by the middle of the eighteenth century regenting was being replaced by the modern system of lectures and special study. 'Common schools' were formal assemblies of all the students.

41 Solomon: the allusion is to Proverbs VI, verses 9 and 10.

55 psalms: Psalm 24, verse 2: 'For he hath founded it upon the seas, and established it upon the floods.'

67 red gowns: undergraduates at St Andrews traditionally wear red gowns.

75 Nazarene: a native of Nazareth and a name given to Christians as followers of Jesus of Nazareth; but Fergusson may mean 'Nazarite', a name given to Hebrews who took vows of abstinence.

86 prodigal: an allusion to the story of the Prodigal Son, Luke XV, 11–32.

An Eclogue, to the Memory of Dr William Wilkie (1772)

For information on Wilkie, see page 315. He died 10 October 1772. Wilkie had taken care of Fergusson when he was a student. His combined reputation as poet and agricultural improver made him a fit subject for a pastoral elegy.

To Dr Samuel Johnson: Food for a New Edition of his Dictionary (1773)

Samuel Johnson (1709–1784) published his dictionary in 1755. His reputation for anti-Scottish wit meant that some of his definitions caused offence north of the Border, but Fergusson also seems to have realised that Johnson's attempt to standardise English spelling and meaning posed a threat to non-standard forms, including Scots. In 1773 Johnson made a tour of Scotland with his friend and future biographer, the Scot James Boswell (1740–95), starting in Edinburgh before crossing to Fife and then travelling north and west to the Highlands and Islands. In his poem Fergusson parodies Johnson's heavy style, with its complex sentence structure and use of words derived from Latin. No attempt has been made to gloss all of these Latinisms, some of which Fergusson has invented for the poem, since they are meant to astound the reader. The epigraph to the poem appears to be Fergusson's invention, but he borrowed the title 'Rodondo' from a poem mocking the oratory of William Pitt the Elder, Earl of Chatham (1708–78).

31 Baillies: town magistrates, next in rank to provosts, the Scottish equivalents of mayors, hence the reference to chains of office in line 33.

39 oats: in his dictionary Johnson defined oats as 'a grain, which in England is generally given to horses, but in Scotland supports the people'.

48 Churchill: Charles Churchill (1731–64), English verse satirist,

especially of the Scots, and associate of the anti-Scottish politician John Wilkes (1727–97), an acquaintance of Johnson's.

60 usquebalian: a word coined from 'usquebae', from the Gaelic 'uisge beatha', literally 'water of life', meaning whisky.

68 plum-puddenian: 'pock-puddings', meaning dumplings or steamed puddings, was the Scots nickname for Englishmen, because of their alleged fondness for such solid fare.

To the Principal and Professors of the University of St Andrews (1773)
Johnson and Boswell (see note to preceding poem) were entertained at St Andrews on 19 August 1773; Fergusson's poem was published a fortnight later.

29 aits: oats (see note to line 39 of preceding poem).

61 Drummond: William Drummond of Hawthornden (1585–1649); his poem 'Polemo-Middiana' (1645) opens with a list of seafood from Fife.

65–66 roast beef, East Nook of Fife: allusions to popular tunes, 'The Roast Beef of Old England' and 'East Neuk of Fife'.

90 Dumfarline: Dunfermline, in west Fife; Fergusson had been challenged to a duel by a man from Dunfermline who objected to the disparaging remarks on Fife in his poems.

Elegy, on the Death of Scots Music (1772)
The epigraph is from *Twelfth Night*, Act II(iv).

37 Macgibbon: William Macgibbon (c. 1695–1756), principal violinist to the Edinburgh Musical Society, published collections of tunes for the Scots fiddle (but was also a composer in the ornamented Italian style which the poem attacks).

59 'Birks of Invermay': a song Fergusson himself was noted for singing; the words by David Mallet are on page 176.

62 Roman: patriotic Scots like Fergusson gloried in the fact that the ancient Romans had failed to subdue the Caledonians.

The Sow of Feeling (1773)
The epigraph, from the play *The Prince of Tunis* (1773) by Henry Mackenzie (1745–1831), confirms this poem is a mock-heroic lampoon of Mackenzie's novel *The Man of Feeling* (1771). This was a contribution to the fashionable craze for sentimental writing begun by Laurence Sterne (1713–68) with his novel *Tristram Shandy* (1760–67). The hero of Mackenzie's book, the 'man of feeling' of its title, moves through a series of scenes of woe and dismay which often reduce him, and others, to sympathetic tears. It is striking that Fergusson makes fun of such tender emotions, whereas Burns claimed the novel was one of his favourite books.

70 Pythagoras: the Greek philosopher of the sixth century BC who believed in the transmigration of souls between humans and animals after death.

Ode to the Gowdspink (1773)

45 Tantalus: a figure in Greek mythology who was condemned to stand in a pool of water which always sank as he bent to drink, so that he could never quench his thirst.

On Seeing a Butterfly in the Street

Published in 1773.

The Farmer's Ingle (1773)

The epigraph is from Virgil's fifth Eclogue, lines 69–70, and may be translated 'and, my first aim, making the feast merry with much wine in front of the fire, when it is cold'. This poem is a version in Scots of the eighteenth-century part-realistic, part-idealised pastoral tradition which includes poems like parts of James Thomson's *The Seasons* (1726–30), William Shenstone's 'The Schoolmistress' (1742), Thomas Gray's 'Elegy in a Country Churchyard' (1750) and, of course, 'The Cotter's Saturday Night' by Burns.

43 Denmark's daring sons: Kenneth III (d. 1005) is supposed to have defeated a Danish army at Luncarty in Perthshire.

ANNE LINDSAY (1750–1825)

Daughter of the fifth earl of Balcarres, Anne Lindsay married Andrew Barnard who became colonial secretary to the governor of South Africa in 1797. Extracts from her journal of life at Capetown can be found in *The Scotswoman at Home and Abroad*, edited by Dorothy McMillan (1999). After her husband's death she returned to London where she moved in the highest circles.

Auld Robin Gray

Anne Lindsay's own account of the writing of this song in 1772 is included in the selection edited by Dorothy McMillan mentioned above.

JOHN TAIT (c. 1750–1817)

No information about this poet has been found.

The Banks of the Dee

4 Dee: the river that flows eastwards through the Grampian Mountains to Aberdeen on the east coast of Scotland.

10 rebels: the only overseas rebellion of the second half of the eighteenth century was that of Britain's American colonies.

ELIZABETH HAMILTON (1758–1816)
She was born in Ireland, brought up in Stirlingshire and lived for a time in London. A friend of Joanna Baillie and Maria Edgeworth, she wrote several novels, the best-known of which is *The Cottagers of Glenburnie* (1808). There is a fragment of autobiography in *The Scotswoman at Home and Abroad*, edited by Dorothy McMillan (1999), pages 83 to 87.

JOANNA BAILLIE (1762–1851)
Born at Bothwell in Lanarkshire, she lived most of her life in London. She published her first book of poems in 1790, but acquired greater fame with her *Plays on the Passions*, the first volume of which appeared in 1798 and included the tragedy *De Monfort*. She was a close friend of Sir Walter Scott. Autobiographical memoirs by her can be found in *The Scotswoman at Home and Abroad*, edited by Dorothy McMillan (1999).

Wooed and Married and A'
Based, like Alexander Ross's 'Married and Wooed an' A' (page 169), on a traditional song.
33 kerchief: a head-covering suitable to a married woman, in contrast with the snood or ribbon (see line 2) with which unmarried girls tied back their hair.

Fy, Let Us A' to the Wedding
Based on 'Blythsome Bridal' (see page 3).
72 Dumbuck: a steep hill east of Dumbarton on the Clyde.

Glossary of Common Scots Words

a'	all
ablins	perhaps
aboon	above
ae	one
aff	off
aften	often
ain	own
alang	along
amaist	almost
amang	among
an'	and
ance	once
ane	one
anes	once
aught	eight
auld	old
awa	away
ay	always
ayont	beyond
bairn	child
baith	both
bane	bone
be	by
bide	stay, remain, endure
birk	birch
blaw	blow
bogle	ghost
bonny	pretty, attractive
bra	fine
brae	hill
braid	broad
braw	fine
brig	bridge
burn	stream
but	without
caller	fresh
canna	cannot
canny	careful
canty	cheerful
cauld	cold
claise	clothes
claith	cloth
cleathing	clothing
de'il	devil
drap	drop
een	eyes
eithly	easily
fa'	fall
fae	foe
fald	fold
fash	trouble
fauld	fold
fause	false
faw	fall
flee	fly
forby	besides
fou	full, drunk
fouk	folk
fow	full, drunk
frae	from
fu'	full, drunk
ga	go
gab	talk
gade, gaed	went
gae[s]	go[es]
gane	gone
gang	go
gar	cause
gate	way
gaun	going
gee	give
geed	went
gie	give
gif	if
gin	if
glen	valley
gowd[en]	gold[en]
grain, grane	groan
greet	weep
gude	good
ha'	hall
had[s]	hold[s]
hae	have
haflins	half

hail, hale	whole
hame	home
het	hot
hie	high
hing	hang
how	hollow
hunder	hundred
i'	in
ilk[a]	each
ingle	fireside
ither	other
kail	cabbage
ken	know
kirk	church
kittle	tickle, ticklish
ky	cattle
laird	lord
lane	loan, lone
lang	long
lave	rest
lear	learn[ing], teach
lee	lie
loo	love
loun	fellow
loup	leap
lown	fellow
lug	ear
main	moan
mair	more
maist	most
mak	make
mane	moan
'mang	among
manna	must not
maun	must
meikle, mickle	great, large
mony	many
mou	mouth
muckle	great, large
naething	nothing
nane	none
na[e]	not
neist	next
ony	any
oot	out
owr	over
pat	put
pauky, pawky	crafty, amusing
reek	smoke
rig	ridge, field-section
rin	run
sae	so
saft	soft
sair	sore
sall	shall
sang	song
saut	salt
sax	six
shak	shake
shaw	show
sic	such
siccan	such a
sicker	sure
siller	silver, money
simmer	summer
skaith	harm
sma	small
speer, speir	ask
stane	stone
stap	stop
strang	strong
syne	since
tak	take
tap	top
tent	care
thae	those
thir	those
thole	endure
tinkler	tinker
toom	empty
trow	believe
twa	two
tyne	lose
unco	strange, extraordinary
wad	would
wae	woe
wale	choice, choose
wark	work
war[se]	worse
waur	worse
wee	little
weel	well
wha	who
whase	whose
whilk	which
wi'	with
winna	will not
yon	yonder